INDIA

Toby Sinclair first arrived in India over 18 years ago to work as an organizer of mountain and wildlife tours. He then worked with Dass Media, a book distribution company based in New Delhi. Sinclair has contributed to many guides on India and acted as consultant editor for The Guidebook Company's Indian series.

Contributing authors: Marie D'Souza, Royina Grewal, Rudrankshu Mukerjee, Sumita Paul, Shobita Punja, Pramesh Ratnarkar and Pepita Seth.

INDIA

Toby Sinclair

ODYSSEY GUIDES
Hong Kong

Grateful acknowledgement is made to the following authors and publishers for permissions granted:

John Murray (Publishers) Ltd. for *An Experience of India* by Ruth Prawer Jhabvala

Harper Collins Publishers for
Jesting Pilate © Harper & Row 1924, renewed 1954 by Aldous Huxley

William Heinemann Ltd. and A M Heath & Co. Ltd. for *Rich Like Us* © Nayantara Sahgal 1985

Victor Gollancz Ltd. and Murray Pollinger for *The Wedding of Jayanthi Mandel*
© Sara Banerji 1987 published by Victor Gollancz Ltd. and Arrow Books

Anthony Sheil Associates Ltd. for *My Days* © R K Narayan 1973/4,
first published in the United Kingdom by Chatto & Windus

William Morrow & Company Inc. for *India: Labyrinths in the Lotus Land* © Sasthi Brata 1985

Penguin Books Ltd. for *"Love's Question"* by Rabindranath Tagore, from his
Selected Poems translated by William Radyce

Memoirs of a Bengal Civilian by John Beames, drafted in 1875-80, completed in 1896,
and first published by Chatto & Windus in 1961 is now in print in paperback edition
published by Eland Books

Distribution in the UK, Ireland, Europe and certain Commonwealth countries by
Hodder & Stoughton, Mill Road, Dunton Green, Sevenoaks, Kent, TN13 2YA

Editor: Don J Cohn
Series Editors: Rose Borton and Claire Banham
Picture Editor: Caroline Robertson
Map Design: Bai Yiliang
Design: John Ng
Cover Concept: Raquel Jaramillo and Aubrey Tse
Artwork: Au Yeung Chui Kwai
Photography: Front cover by Alain Evrard; back cover by Sarah Lock; Helka Ahokas 193 (bottom),
198, 209, 270 (top left), 288; Anthony Cassidy 5, 16, 27, 86-87, 119, 122, 126, 127, 129, 152-153;
David Chappell 9, 19, 40 (middle, bottom), 41 (top left and right), 177, 193 (top), 194-195, 271
(bottom); Nigel Hicks 8, 40 (top), 55, 59, 95, 217; Earl Kowall 72, 77, 162-163, 291; Nazima
Kowall 170, 171, 175, 280; Paul Lewis 41 (bottom), 100, 101 (bottom), 270 (bottom left); Sarah
Lock 101 (top), 270 (top right, middle and bottom), 271 (top right); Toby Sinclair 6, 7, 80, 82, 108,
109, 112, 115, 140 (top), 271 (top left), 285; Luca Tettoni 18, 23, 30-31, 36, 48, 68, 140 (bottom),
141, 149, 160, 180, 185, 213, 221, 244, 252, 259, 267; Wattis Art Gallery 137, 277.

Produced by Twin Age Ltd
Printed in Hong Kong

ISBN: 962-217-157-5

British Library Cataloguing in Publication Data has been applied for.

Cover: Jami Masjid, Ahmedabad

Contents

Market trader, Ernakulam, (above); Colourful silks for sale
(bottom left); Variegated leaves (bottom right)

Excerpts

Introduction

For thousands of years the countries of South Asia—pre-Independence India and her neighbours—have occupied a special place in the European consciousness. This guide highlights some of the many areas of interest that a visitor to modern India can enjoy. The rich cultural mass populated by a fifth of the world's people is a vital and exciting country. To many, and this includes her own citizens, India is a mass of contradictions. The visual clash of natural and cultural riches contrasted with the sad plight of urban poverty cannot be explained away or hidden. The glamour of Bombay's film and industrial worlds contrasts with the squalor of those who flock to India's commercial capital. The ninth city of Delhi, New Delhi, has grown from less than half a million when the British quit in 1947 to a stretched sprawl of over eight million in 1990. But New Delhi is surely one of the greenest and most attractive capitals of the 20th century. Many observers are hard on India: V S Naipaul titled one of his books *A Wounded Civilization*.

The civilizations that spanned South Asia are now divided between Afghanistan and Pakistan to the west, Bangladesh and Burma to the east, Sri Lanka to the south and Nepal, Tibet and Bhutan to the north. India is therefore only one of nine modern nations that are home to thousands of years of history. But India's historical sites and places of natural beauty are linked and supported by a network of accommodation (ranging from the spartan to the magnificent) and an acceptable transport system.

You can travel in India by executive jet or at the more exciting and often extremely comfortable pace of Indian Railways. However you travel, within a group or independently, a certain amount of planning is needed. This book is a general introduction. Other titles in the series deal with the magnificence of *The Museums of India*, the great cities of *Delhi, Agra & Jaipur,* the *Hill Stations of India*, the remote beauty of *Kashmir & Ladakh* and the contrast of a great city and wonderful beaches in *Bombay & Goa*. All these Illustrated Guides cover in depth some of the areas introduced in this guide.

History

The earliest remains of Indian civilization are in what is today Pakistan. The history of the Indus Valley civilization, despite the archaeological discoveries of Harappa, Mohenjodaro, Lothal and other sites, is still obscure. We do not know, for example, who lived in these cities and what language they spoke. Most of our knowledge of this culture is based on archaeology, which reveals that the inhabitants of these cities lived in spacious houses connected by wide roads and served by a sophisticated drainage system. The Great Bath unearthed in Mohenjodaro suggests a high level of hygiene, while a massive granary discovered in the prehistoric port of Lothal (Gujarat) indicates trade and accumulated wealth.

While iron and its technology was unknown, literacy is attested to by the discovery of seals with as yet undeciphered inscriptions on them. This civilization seems to have come to an abrupt end. We do not know how, but it is possible that the cities could not cope with the regular flooding of the Indus, or that they were ravaged by conquerors.

The next known phase of Indian history, the period from 1300 to 700 BC, has been reconstructed largely from the sacred *Vedas* and the two great ancient Indian epics, the *Ramayana* and the *Mahabharata*. During this period, the Indo-Aryans transformed themselves from a pastoral people to settled agriculturalists, cultivating land seized from subjugated indigenous peoples. The growth of agriculture and control over the land led to the emergence of states. North India was dotted with small kingdoms and principalities, often vying with one another for supremacy. Control over the land was facilitated by the use of iron, the earliest traces of which (*c*. 800 BC) were found in Atranji-Khera near Aligarh.

The age of the great empires began with the Mauryas (fourth century BC) and lasted until the early medieval period was ushered in by the Muslim invasions of the 13th century. The Mauryas succeeded in establishing a bureaucratic administration and it was their rule that saw the major expansion of Buddhism. This was due mainly to the patronage of the great emperor Ashoka, who after a bloody war turned his back on violence and adopted Buddhism and the concept of moral conquest through the peaceful propagation of that faith. Stone inscriptions from Ashoka's time are scattered throughout India. The spread of Buddhism continued under the Kushans who probably came to India from Central Asia. Under the Kushans, Indo-Roman trade flourished. The Kushans were in turn overtaken by the Sakas, while in south and central India the post-Mauryan years were dominated by the great empire of the Satavahanas.

The Gupta empire was the last great empire of ancient India. The Guptas displayed tremendous political and military ability, as epitomized in the conquests of Samudragupta, but also made their mark as patrons of the arts and science. The disintegration of the Gupta empire under a succession of weak monarchs led to the emergence of regional monarchies.

The coming of the Muslim rulers (1206) marked a new era in Indian history. The first Muslim rulers were Turko-Afghans. It would be erroneous, however, to think of this as the beginning of the Muslim period. In fact only the kings were Muslims; the ruling class was a mixture of Hindus and Muslims. The Muslim kings established their supremacy by force of arms through prolonged campaigns, especially against the Rajputs and in the Deccan. Some of the major Turko-Afghan leaders were Iltutmish, his daughter Raziya, Alauddin Khalji, Mohammad bin Tughlaq and Firoz Shah Tughlaq. The basis of the Turko-Afghan empire, or the Delhi sultanate as it is known (Delhi was its capital), was land. The emperors developed an elaborate land-revenue system whereby they paid bureaucrats through assignments of land revenue known as *iqta*, the system Akbar later modified into the *mansabdari* system. At the height of its power, the

Delhi sultanate was strong enough to repulse the Mongols who threatened the area northwest of Delhi throughout the 13th century. But in the 14th and 15th centuries, the sultanate was unable to withstand peasant and *zamindar* (large landholders) protests in northern India, as well as external invasion in the person of Timur and his horsemen.

The political vacuum that the decline of the Delhi sultanate left was filled by the Mughals, who were the descendants of both Timur and Genghis Khan. The first Mughals—Babar, Humayan, Akbar, Jehangir, Shah Jahan and Aurangzeb—are most often remembered for their magnificent buildings, which often overshadow the fact that they were perhaps the first Indian rulers to establish a uniform political and administrative system. The frontiers of the Mughal empire extended from Multan in the northwest to Bengal in the east, and from the foothills of the Himalayas to Konkan in the south. In these far-flung areas they set up an administrative system that governed even the remotest localities. The bureaucracy consisted of nobles of two specific ranks, or *mansabs*. A *mansab* had two components: *zat* (the holder's position in the court hierarchy) and *sawar* (the number of troops the holder had to maintain and supply when the emperor ordered him to do so). The *mansabdars* were paid through revenue-collecting assignments known as *jagirs*.

Under Mughal rule, trade and production flourished. Each region had its own specialized products which were bartered for the products of other regions. Agriculture remained the basis of the empire which flourished on surplus production. It was this drain on the peasantry, as much as 50 percent of the total produce, that led to widespread anti-imperial protests in the late 17th and early 18th centuries. The breakdown of the central empire led to the emergence of regional powers in Bengal, Awadh (near Lucknow), Maharashtra, Hyderabad and the Punjab.

The British, who originally came to India as traders like the Portuguese, Dutch and French, conquered these regional powers and eliminated their European rivals, both by clever deployment of their forces and by intrigue. A major landmark in the rise of the British was the Battle of Plassey in Bengal (1757), which gave them access to unlimited political and economic power in a rich province. Using Bengal as a base, the British expanded into the rest of India.

The expansion of British rule was not unresisted. In every region, dethroned rulers, dispossessed landholders, unemployed artisans and exploited peasants opposed the British incursion. The introduction of British administration, British law and order, English education and Western medicine, and the activities of the Christian missionaries were all perceived as efforts to overturn the traditional Indian world. Throughout the 19th century there were sporadic regional outbursts which achieved a united expression, at least in North India, in the Great Mutiny of 1857, which is known as the First War of Independence. Beginning as a mutiny in the ranks of the sepoys (Indian soldiers serving the British), it soon turned into a general conflagration which wiped out British rule in North India for nearly six months. It took the British well over a year to reconquer the area and re-establish their authority. The Mutiny also sparked certain changes in British rule in India. In the century from Plassey to the revolt, India had been governed nominally by the British East India Company over whose operations in India the British government in London had statutory supervision and control. After the revolt, the British government ruled India directly.

The second half of the 19th century also saw other significant developments. Before then the Western-educated intelligentsia, especially in Calcutta, had supported British rule and believed that the British were preparing them for self-rule. The post-1857 years saw British rule growing confident and therefore more racist. This shocked the native Western-educated literati: they became aware of their subordinate status and of the oppressive and exploitative aspects of this rule. They began to articulate their interests and grievances in a number of associations and on platforms which converged in the Indian National Congress, founded in 1885.

Initially the Congress tried to stop the British from acting in an 'un-British' manner. Their economic critique of British rule was trenchant, but politically they remained loyalist. They took special care to distance themselves from any kind of violent opposition to British rule. But events soon overtook the Congress. In 1905 the Swadeshi Movement broke out in Bengal against Lord Curzon's decision to partition Bengal on the grounds of administrative expediency. Thousands of people took to the streets in the Congress's first experience of mass boycott. Even the national poet, Rabindranath Tagore, participated in the demonstrations. However, India had to wait for Gandhi's debut in Indian politics over a decade later for the Indian national movement to reach maturity. Gandhi succeeded in establishing a Congress network over the whole of India. He spoke simply and kept the mass movements (1921–3, 1929–33 and 1942) non-violent, the key idea of his world view. Gandhi succeeded in drawing the propertied and business classes into the Congress-led national movement. By the same token, however, the Congress often failed to articulate the aspirations of the masses who, especially in the 1940s, expressed their grievances in a variety of protest movements, all outside Congress control.

Despite widespread awareness and several warning signals, the Congress was unsuccessful in dealing with the religious divisions within the country. Communalism, boosted by Jinnah's Muslim League and the British policy of divide and rule, gained in force and broke out in Hindu–Muslim rioting in the Punjab and Bengal. This made it possible for the British to transfer power to two nation states, India and Pakistan, in August 1947. Indian nationalism thus succeeded in winning freedom for India at the cost of national unity. The leadership could only come to power on the basis of a major compromise. A very old civilization thus received the political garb of a new nation state.

Religion

The religion most closely associated with India, Hinduism, probably originated around 1500 BC when the Aryans first arrived on the subcontinent. Hinduism is more than just a set of religious beliefs and customs; it is the way of life of the majority of Indian people. High philosophy and folk culture, spiritualism and mundane customs, literary and artistic notions are all interwoven to form a whole.

Hinduism has no one founder and no single sacred text. The Hindu pantheon—populated with thousands of major and minor gods and goddesses—centres on the trinity of Brahma (the Creator), Vishnu (the Preserver) and Shiva (the Destroyer). In the Hindu view the purpose of life is to attain *moksha*: to free the soul from its worldly existence. There is an inherent fatalism in Hinduism which marks many aspects of Indian life and civilization.

Buddhism also originated in India, some 500 years before the birth of Christ. Gautama Buddha was born a prince, but constant exposure to death, illness and old age led him to renounce his family and kingdom and seek the path to salvation or *nirvana*. The Buddha, the Enlightened One, did not preach in metaphysical terms, but rather propounded the gospel of the Middle Path—a life that avoided extremes and therefore spoke, heard, thought and did no evil. The pursuit of goodness liberated the individual from worldly suffering and enabled him to attain *nirvana*. Buddhism, with its simplicity and non-ritualistic approach to life, appealed to large numbers of people, especially merchants and traders. But though it spread widely to East and Southeast Asia, its popularity declined in India. Today it is still practised in pockets, particularly in the remoter regions of the Himalayas.

Mahavira, the founder of Jainism, was a contemporary of the Buddha. Mahavira was also of royal descent and, like the Buddha, chose to renounce worldly life and undergo austere discipline. Central to Jainism is the idea of the ascetic life: only through self-conquest can man attain perfection. Like Buddhism, Jainism emphasizes right conduct and rejects the caste system which orthodox Hinduism imposed on society. Unlike Buddhism, Jainism still commands a large following in India, especially in Rajasthan and Gujarat.

Arab traders brought Islam to India around the eighth century. The basic tenets and practices of Islam include a belief that 'there is no God but Allah and Muhammad is his Prophet'; the saying of *namaz* five times a day; the injunction to be charitable; the annual fast during the month of Ramadan; and the pilgrimage to Mecca once in one's lifetime. The *Koran*, the revelations made by Gabriel to Muhammad, is the sacred text of the Muslims. In India, Islam was the religion of the major ruling dynasties from the 13th to the 18th centuries. When people from Persia and Transoxiana settled in India, there were conversions but there is no evidence that they were achieved at the cost of communal violence. On the contrary, a fusion of Islam and the indigenous Indian culture gave birth to magnificent architectural forms, as well as to developments in music, dress and cuisine which in places like Delhi and Lucknow resulted in new lifestyles.

One product of the Indo-Islamic encounter was Sikhism, founded by Guru Nanak (1469–1539) who tried to combine the best of Islam and Hinduism in one faith. Like Islam, Sikhism is monotheistic and pays homage to a single sacred text, the *Granth Sahib*. Sikh men can be recognized by five symbols, three of them highly visible: their uncut hair, tied in a top-knot and hidden under a turban; the steel bangle *(kara)* worn on the wrist; and the sword *(kirpan)* worn at the waist. The two other symbols are the shorts *(kaccha)* and the comb *(kangha)*. The early history of the Sikhs is one of torment, as they were persecuted by Mughal state power. Their rejection of the caste system and the simplicity of Sikh devotion have made Sikhism a popular religion in the Punjab, and has moulded the Sikhs into a tight-knit community.

The Parsis fled to the west coast of India when the Arabs conquered Persia in the eighth century. Parsis follow the religion founded by Zoroaster in the sixth century BC. Their sacred text is the *Zen Avesta* and at the core of their beliefs is the worship of fire as a symbol of God. There is a large and influential Parsi community in Bombay.

India also has a thriving and substantial Christian and a minuscule Jewish community, both ancient in origin. Christianity is said to have come to India with St Thomas in AD 54, but it spread only after the European trading companies began to operate in India in the 17th century. Today, many Christian denominations are represented in India.

India's Artistic Heritage

Indian culture has intrigued and sometimes awed visitors through the ages, from Megasthenes, a Greek traveller of the third century BC, Hsüan Tsang, the Chinese pilgrim of the seventh century, Arab travellers of the 13th century like Ibn Batutah, and the British and other Europeans, down to our own day. For Indians, too, Indian civilization remains elusive, too vast and varied to comprehend in its entirety.

Art historians characterize Indian art as the handmaiden of religion. But it is perhaps more appropriate to credit geography with being the dominant influence in the development of Indian culture. The high mountain ranges in the north have inspired poets and philosophers and, in mythology, the Himalayas are the abode of the gods. The forests and river valleys, the deserts and coastal plains, have been home to people for thousands of years. The elephant, lion and bull, as well as numerous flowers and plants, became motifs in sculpture, painting and poetry. In India's monochrome deserts, the inhabitants of Rajasthan and Gujarat adorn themselves in a rainbow of colours; in the tropical forests, people wear white, perhaps reluctant to compete with the exuberant colours of nature.

One feature of Indian civilization is its antiquity and the continuity of its age-old traditions and aesthetic principles, which even today influence artistic activity. In Madhya Pradesh, at Bhimbetka, near Bhopal, are some natural caves, their walls and ceilings covered with paintings of running deer, stags with magnificent antlers and delightful drawings of hunting, dancing and merry-making, dating back to the Stone Age, some 8,000 years ago. The dancers in the pictures are often shown wearing ritual masks and there are depictions of flutes, cymbals and drums. The jasper and agate stone tools, flints and blades found in these caves represent the beginnings of India's rich and diverse material culture.

Ancient City Cultures

In the early 20th century, archaeologists unearthed ruined cities over 5,000 years old: Harappa and Mohenjodaro (now in Pakistan), Kalibangan and Lothal. This urban culture is known as the Harappan or Indus Civilization, as the cities were concentrated on the banks of the Indus River. Lothal (Gujarat) is a well-preserved site with brick buildings laid out along broad streets. Each house has a 'living room', kitchen, well and bathing area. This civilization produced elegantly shaped wheel-thrown pottery with painted designs, which still serve as models for pottery produced in India today. Clay toys in the form of animals, birds and bullock-carts found at the sites display a sense of artistry and humour. Tiny seals bearing an undeciphered pictographic script and emblems, possibly used by traders and merchants, have long fascinated historians. Tools and bronze images, such as the celebrated dancing girl and the bullock cart and bulls, testify to the Harappans' skill in metallurgy. The National Museum in New Delhi and the Indian Museum in Calcutta have sizeable collections of artifacts from this period, contemporary with the ancient cultures of Mesopotamia and Egypt.

Prosperous villages along the Ganges and Indus rivers supported these large cities and supplied them with food. It was in these villages that artifacts in clay, wood and other perishable materials were produced. As new techniques developed, it became possible for artists to produce buildings and sculpture in stone. This happened most dramatically around the second century BC and accompanied the spread of Buddhism.

Buddhist Architecture

At Sanchi in Madhya Pradesh, near Bhopal, the emperor Ashoka (ruled third century BC) built a number of Buddhist stupas, or funerary mounds. These solid stone structures, elaborated upon in later centuries, rise out of the hill like hemispherical bubbles, each crowned with a stone umbrella. The great Sanchi stupa, said to contain relics of the Buddha and of saints, has a stone railing around it with four large stone gateways *(toranas)* nine metres (30 feet) high. The railing and *toranas* are some of the finest examples of early Buddhist sculpture. Similar stupas have been found in various stages of ruin at Sarnath in Uttar Pradesh. The remains of the railing that stood at Bharut are in the Indian Museum, Calcutta, and those from Amaravati in Andhra Pradesh are at the State Museum in Madras and elsewhere.

These early Buddhist sculptures derive from the Hinayana (Lesser Vehicle) phase of Buddhism, when it was improper to portray the Buddha in human form. For the education of the pilgrim the sculpted panels and medallions depict the Jataka tales, detailing previous incarnations of the Buddha. The tales are like parables, with a moral or lesson woven into the narrative. The artists used pictorial shorthand to depict the various events on a single panel. The low-relief modelling of the figures, with fine details of jewellery, costumes and even tattoos, was executed with great care. The composition of each panel, with the figures in various postures suggesting movement, gives the illusion that the space within the frame is limitless. There is a sensuousness in the portrayal of figures not usually associated with the Buddhist religion. The artists revelled in nature, crowding compositions with trees, birds, lotuses, fish and snakes, sometimes glorifying the beauty of the human form, at other times ridiculing human foibles. The sculptures are a delight to study for they bubble with vitality and humour.

Buddha Images

The Hinayana phase of Buddhism was followed by the Mahayana (Great
Vehicle) period when images of the Buddha began to appear in the Gandhara
region (now spread over Pakistan, Afghanistan and northwest India), Mathura
(Uttar Pradesh) and in the rock-cut prayer halls of Ajanta. Various episodes in
the life of the Buddha are portrayed: his miraculous birth, his mother's dream of
a white elephant that augered his birth, his departure from his palatial home to
lead a simple life, his attainment of nirvana, and his preaching of the 'middle
path'.

Ajanta has superb examples of Indian mural painting depicting scenes from
the life of the Buddha and his incarnations. The early images are quite small,
often less than one metre (three feet) high. He is often shown standing with his
right hand raised in the *mudra* (hand position) of blessing and offering protection. When shown seated in the yogic posture of meditation, the Buddha's face
is always beautifully proportioned in a graphic manifestation of his inner
equilibrium. In the Gandharan sculptures there is a marked Greek and Roman
influence in the treatment of the wavy hair and the fall of the toga-like robe.
This Greco-Roman influence followed upon Alexander the Great's invasion of
northwest India and the subsequent development of trade and other forms of
contact with the West.

As Buddhism spread to Ceylon, Nepal, Tibet, Burma, Siam and China,
stupas became taller and more elongated until they assumed the shape of
Japanese pagodas with their sloping roofs. Buddha images also became larger,
often three to five metres (10–15 feet) tall, and their expression grew more
controlled and meditative, almost stern, replacing the laughter and sensuousness
of the early sculptures.

One interesting feature of the art of the early centuries of the Christian era,
later to become the hallmark of Buddhist and Hindu art, is the philosophical
symbolism of even the smallest detail. One example is the lotus, which thrives
in stagnant water and became a symbol of purity. In numerous examples,
Buddhas and Hindu deities are shown seated or standing on lotuses to symbolize
their purity in contrast to the dark, murky waters of the rest of humanity.

Hindu Temple Art

Hinduism as a philosophy of life inspired the notion of wholeness and oneness
with nature and the universe. The all-encompassing philosophy analysed and
explained every aspect of life, both trivial and significant, from birth, growth,
maturity and procreation through death and rebirth. Many forms of worship and
thinking were tolerated, from religious asceticism to atheism. The best evidence
of this outlook is seen in the Hindu temple. The economics of the temple made
it the centre of village and town life, where pilgrims and devotees thronged for
festivals and where merchants and craftsmen conducted their business. Unlike

the secluded beauty and contemplative ambience of a church, Hindu temples are all bustle and noise. Temples patronized sculpture, painting and flower-garland making, as well as story-telling, music, dance and theatre. Schools and universities grew up beside Hindu temples and even today, Kanchipuram (Tamil Nadu) and Varanasi (Uttar Pradesh) are seats of learning and religious education.

Classical temple design was inspired by numerous factors. Throughout India, you will notice small shrines built under a tree, by the rockface of a hill or perched on hilltops. Such shrines commemorate a visit by, or an incident in the life of one of the innumerable Hindu deities. Myths and legends describe the travels of Hindu gods to almost every corner of the country. The idol in a shrine may be of clay, wood, stone or metal, or may even be—as at Amarnath in Kashmir—an icy stalagmite in a Himalayan cave. The earliest temples were simple mud and brick or bamboo shelters built to mark a holy spot and protect an auspicious idol. A single cubicle, often too small to enter, is the seed from which the great temples of India grew. Some, as in Chidambaram and Kanchipuram (Tamil Nadu), became so large that they encompassed an entire city within their walls.

Mud, brick and wooden shrines were soon replaced by stone, as the fifth-century AD single-chamber temple (No. 17) at Sanchi in Madhya Pradesh

The Hindu Temple

The Hindu temple, where the deity is always accessible to the devotee, is conceived as a sacred microcosm, an analogy for the entire universe. In the past, in India, it was also the focus of the religious, social and economic life of the community. The temple and its immediate surroundings served some of the vital needs of the people, whose lives revolved around its multi-functional activities. It was the creation of the architect of genius, of many sculptors and thousands of skilled and unskilled labourers, organized into a highly efficient work force. The priests who represented the deity and took charge of the ritual joined forces with the ruler and the trading and professional guilds. All gained prestige and power, and in the case of the king, the continuity of his dynasty.

The earliest extant stone temples date back to the sixth and seventh centuries AD, of which those at Deogarh, Nachna and Bhumara in the north and the Malegittin Shivalaya Temple at Badami in Karnataka are the best known. Temple groups are generally known by the name of the dynasty in power when they were constructed. Chronologically they fall into broad categories, beginning with the Gupta-Vakatak dynasty of the fifth and sixth centuries. Many great temples were constructed during the famous Chalukya, Pallava, Chola and Kalachwu reigns of the seventh to tenth centuries. The 11th and 12th centuries under the Hoysalas, Chandelas and minor rulers witnessed a magnificent proliferation of sacred stone edifices, which had evolved into complex aggregrates of diverse, separate, often exquisitely wrought single elements integrated into a coherent whole.

The finest period examples are at Halebid and Khajuraho. The contemporaneous temples at Bhijolia, Rajasthan, Konarak and Orissa, to name only the most famous, are examples of variations of style, but there are numerous other, lesser-known sites on the beaten tourist paths and even more at remote sites available to the intrepid researcher. A decline in aesthetics, though not in size, due partially to Islamic intrusions, can be detected in the Vijayanagar temples of the 15th and 16th centuries.

Approach the evolved Hindu temple as you would a symphonic performance. The interior and the exterior function in a mutual relationship which depends entirely on an interlocking, rhythmic system of calculated, perfectly proportioned measurements. As you circumambulate the temple—always in a clockwise direction—and as you observe the ever-changing views, think of yourself as a single element in the grand conglomeration of stone, rhythms, line, light and shadow, space, order, mobility and, most of all, living energy. Observe how horizontal sections are superimposed upon one another to create the architectonic verticality that stretches towards the sky. Variations in the form, dimensions and relationships among the parts define the chronological sequences and categories of style, broadly divided into northern (*nagara*) and southern (*dravida*) types.

Starting at the bottom of the temple exterior, the plinth *(adistana)* is composed of distinct moulded, horizontal tiers of various shapes and sizes. In the earlier Gupta and Chalukya periods, they are few and ample in width. The later plinths grow higher and have many more levels. In the highly evolved temples of the Hoysala dynasty in Karnataka, the plinth is extended laterally to create a large platform. Sharp triangular extensions, forming a star-shaped platform, give this style its distinctive form. At Halebid, Belur and Somnathpur, themes based on the *Mahabharata* and *Ramayana* epics are depicted on friezes in profuse and intricate detail. Other temples carry friezes, but none are as magnificent as those of the finest Hoysala temples. The wall *(bhitti)* encloses the hall *(mandapa)* and the shrine. The Chalukya temples display alternating pilaster/niche arrangements, with a statue in the niche and plenty of blank wall space. Two hundred years later, the walls are clustered with magnificent arrays of hundreds of individually carved figures of deities.

This is a good opportunity to become familiar with the myths and the names and forms of the deities. Myriads of gods, goddesses and celestial beings are wrought in a tremendous display of projected emotional states, ranging from the horrific to the erotic to the sublime. Kali, Chamunda, Narasimha, Andhakasura—these are some of the aspects of the goddess or god in terrifying form. At Khajuraho and Konarak, eroticism merges with playfulness, charm and linear rhythms and as in all the temples, the deity is characterized as protective and beautiful, but detached. Episodes in the life of the gods are shown; often they dance, get married, play games on their mountain retreats or battle ferociously. In repose, they meditate.

But the temple is also a veritable encyclopaedia of human psychology. Here the devotee identifies unconsciously with all aspects of his or her inner life. While these supremely complex carved works of art may fascinate, we must not forget that we are in a sacred environment, meant to elevate the devotee out of his or her mundane situation. The proliferation of forms and aspects of the gods are mere manifestations of a single, unnameable, ineffable Supreme Absolute known as Brahman. This is the essence of Hinduism which ultimately unites the All in the One. Once this is understood, a fresh beginning can be made in the attempt to understand Indian religion.

The northern style can be immediately identified by the shape of the superstructure *(sikhara)*. It is situated directly above the sanctum, which is always the central nucleus of the temple. At its simplest, the *sikhara* has a square base. The narrow horizontal tiers, composed of brick-shaped, perforated, closely-packed stones, diminish in width as they taper towards the top. A finial shaped like a round and flattened fruit *(amalaka)* rests on the second square, the top of the curvilinear structure. In the later styles, the forms of this basic order multiply and expand into organic elaborations. Smaller replicas of the *sikhara* hug the main tower, now greatly increased in height, and are superimposed on *mandapa* and porch, as at Khajuraho.

The southern superstructure is entirely different and easily recognizable. It is characterized by miniature temple elements, large and bold, arranged horizontally. Together they form tiers *(tala)* which gradually diminish in size as they rise, culminating at the top in a domed or four-sided element with a single finial.

Temple entrances are often guarded by large figures *(dvarapalas)*. The door frames are carved in profusion, often with couples in love poses and with floral decorations, suggesting ancient fertility associations. The internal space follows the basic sequence of porch, columned hall and narrow vestibule, constructed along an east–west axis which leads into the sanctum, but there are many variations. A pathway for circumambulating the shrine *(pradakshinapatha)*, recessed parts of the walls, columns and windows, and carved ceiling designs based on squares and circles are some of the features of interiors which vary from temple to temple.

The central focus of every Hindu temple is the sanctum and the deity who resides within. It is called the *garbha griha*, literally 'womb house'. Having come into contact with the god or goddess there, the devotee departs, symbolically reborn. There are many surprises to be found within the sacred shrine as the icon representing the particular deity may be an important ancient work of art. More likely it will be a cylindrically shaped stone *(lingam)* symbolizing Shiva as Absolute.

If you arrive in Bombay, you might begin your exploration of Hindu temples by visiting Ambernath, only an hour's journey by train. There you will find a medieval temple, built in AD 1040. In terms of proportion, order and rhythmic unity, it is one of the most perfect, if somewhat decayed, examples of the evolved style.

Even though modernization has invaded village life, the people of India are still gripped by a traditional fervour for the worship of their gods and goddesses. Therefore, it is also important to visit contemporary places of worship. Some hours spent at a living, working temple will help to connect the historical experience with contemporary realities. While most modern Hindu temples are constructed with only vestigial reference to the great architectural past (although some try unsuccessfully to recreate them), what is lost in aesthetics is made up for with traditional rituals which have been handed down with few changes by generations of priests. While some new temples are large and may be constructed, for example, of marble, many are much simpler, with a large, brightly painted hall built of cement and the ubiquitous shrine housing a recently carved or cast icon. But by far the most numerous temples are those that are merely a single shrine where local gods are worshipped. The icon may be of Hanuman, the monkey god; Lakshmi, the goddess of wealth; Shiva/Parvati or their local doubles; quite often a *lingam*; and most frequently a stone or a group of stones. Trees are also worshipped all over India, and at festivals you often see a group of women circumambulating and dabbing a tree with red powder. For the village people, who are the vast majority, god is in everything, everywhere.

Non-Hindus may enter and worship in most temples. Or you may be happy to observe the priests chanting and the devotees with their offerings of flowers and metal dishes full of fruits and vegetables. There are prayers, prostrations, circumambulations, bells ringing, the aroma of burning incense, much chatter and the vibrations of the comings and goings. Sacred space in India requires neither silence nor proper decorum. It is the place for the free expression of inner feelings which include everything from fear, awe and submission to joy in god and hope as well.

All this is best observed at the great festivals where thousands and sometimes millions gather to pay homage to a particular god or goddess on an astrologically determined date. In Calcutta, the whole city celebrates the annual autumn festival of Dussehra in honour of the goddess. At the Kumbha Mela in Allahabad, the confluence of three sacred rivers, millions gather for absolution, prayer and, not least of all, communal participation. To know India's religious life is to know India.

Carmel Berkson

shows. Further south, in Mahabalipuram on the coast near Madras, the artists of the Pallava period launched a new experiment. For centuries, Buddhists had carved out prayer halls and monastic dormitories from the natural rock of the hillsides. The best-known sites are at Ajanta, Ellora and Udaigiri (Orissa). In Mahabalipuram, massive temples were carved out of solid rock detached from the hillside.

The designers of rock temples, the Palavas who ruled Southeast India and the Rashtrakutas who ruled over large areas of the Deccan and west coast from about 642 to 973, were faced with the problem of building stone roofs on their temples. Should they resemble the thatch of a village hut or, tall and inspiring, a mountain of hundreds of roofs? Soon temple design became standardized, with a plan of one room, the dark and silent *garba griha* housing the main idol, and a *mandapa,* or hall, in front for the faithful to gather in for worship. The exterior walls of the temples were adorned with sculptures of gods and goddesses, positioned according to their importance.

The Chola period (ninth and tenth centuries) saw the development of temples with magnificent towering roofs, or *sikharas* up to 55 metres (180 feet) high. A superb example is the Brihadeswara Temple in Tanjore. The proportions of the temple were perfected at this time, and additional shrines for the consort and children of the main deity were accommodated in the temple complex.

The incessant redefining of the boundaries of kingdoms as a result of unending warfare helped to disseminate a common set of basic principles of temple design throughout the subcontinent that also influenced the temples of Ankor Wat in Cambodia. Inspired by the temples of Kanchipuram, conquering kings sought to replicate this design in Karnataka and Maharashtra, where the great rock-cut temple of Kailasha at Ellora is a superb example.

The code of temple building also governed the construction of prestigious buildings in the west, north and east. The seventh to 14th centuries saw the flowering of the Orissan style of temple architecture at Bhubaneshwar, in particular the Lingaraja and Mukateswara temples. In Orissa the particular native stone and regional influence resulted in the towering *sikharas* of the temples being conical, unlike the southern pyramidal structures, and the sculpture attained its own distinctive style and sensuous elegance.

At Konarak the Ganga rulers built a monumental temple dedicated to the sun god. Conceived as a chariot of the sun, it has huge stone wheels and sculpted horses. Unfortunately, the entire central shrine and its *sikhara* have collapsed, but from the proportions of the *mandapa*, the magnificence of the temple can be imagined. The dancing figures and musicians in pale pinkish-yellow sandstone are exquisite, and the whole temple reflects the ever-changing mood of the sun, a radiant offering to its presiding deity.

In central India at Khajuraho, the Chandella dynasty patronized the building of temples. Here the temple stands on a high platform and the *sikhara* is built up of rising layers of smaller replicas of its conical roof, giving the impression of a mountain range. Following this pattern, the walls of the temples at Khajuraho are alive with sculptures of gods and goddesses, celestial female figures and mythical animals in every conceivable gesture of movement and action, including explicitly erotic ones.

In the 11th century, Muslim armies invaded India from the northwest. The invasions coincided with a period of great temple building. The majestic sun temples of Modhera, the Khajuraho group, and the temples of Karnataka all date from this period. Related arts such as sculpture, literature, painting, music and dance also flourished; the magnificent Chola bronzes of South India are also a product of this period.

The Age of Islam

The Islamic rulers of India set about constructing forts and palaces, mosques for worship, and tombs for their saints and royalty. Their mode of congregational worship demanded that the mosque, or *masjid,* follow a certain plan, with a large open courtyard for the congregation to gather in to pray and a *mirhab,* or west-facing façade, to mark the direction of Mecca. The Muslims brought with them the concept of the arch as an element of architectural construction, which immediately made Islamic buildings distinctive. Hindu temples have pillars and beams, narrow doorways and pyramidal roofs, while Islamic buildings are characterized by tall, wide archways, pointed onion domes and spacious, well-lit rooms. However, the new rulers had to make use of Indian artisans, with their own traditional skills and building materials. The process of 'Indianization' is discernible in the earliest Islamic buildings, such as the Qutb Minar complex in New Delhi, which includes one of the first mosques to be built in India. The coloured tiles favoured by the Persians, whose influence predominated, were replaced by calligraphy and wall decorations in sandstone and marble, with intricate inlaid stone designs known as *pietra dura.* The Indian fondness for floral motifs found expression in the wall decoration of mosques, as did the geometric designs and calligraphy so characteristic of Islamic monuments in Western and Central Asia.

The area around the ancient city of Delhi became the centre of Islamic power and each new dynasty commemorated its advent by building a new city. The Slave Kings, the Khaljis, the Tuglaks and finally the Mughals built a total of seven cities here. Forts with impressive bastions and massive walls protected the royal quarters. The Mughals built their palaces in marble and pink sandstone, hence the red forts in Delhi and Agra. The Muslim invaders and the later Mughals retained the traditions of their nomadic past. In their palaces, they supplemented the few stone buildings by erecting elaborate decorative tents and cloth canopies, set in tastefully laid-out formal gardens with ponds, fountains and elevated watercourses.

The Muslims gave a new impetus to the art of the manuscript in India. Previously, superbly handwritten and illustrated books were prepared on dried palm

leaf, and Hindu, Jain and Buddhist sacred texts were passed down for generations in this form. Arab traders brought paper and the technique for making it from China. Books of the Mughal period were profusely illustrated with paintings, often executed with a single-haired brush. The exquisitely handwritten texts were illuminated with mineral pigments, including crushed precious stones, that lent them a glow and radiance unmatched by any other school of illumination.

Throughout the 14th and 15th centuries, the love themes of Indian music blended with the romance of Persian poetry. Indo-Islamic architecture flourished. Dance enjoyed wide patronage. A new and lyrical language, Urdu, closely related to Hindi, was developed. Even today, in the *kurta* and *pyjama,* in foods like *nan* and *kebabs*, in the music of the Hindustani tradition and Kathak dance, this historical synthesis is apparent. With the emergence of the Mughal empire in the 16th century, a new era opened in the subcontinent, a large portion of the country falling under either direct Mughal sovereignty or suzerainty.

Babar, the first of the line, laid the first Mughal garden in Jhor, south of Agra, with its geometric layout and almost rigid symmetry, its watercourses and fountains, its orchards and flowering plants. Humayun, Babar's son, exiled briefly from India, went to the Persian court for assistance. Returning to India, he brought with him artists and plans which inspired the building of his own tomb in Delhi and eventually the Taj Mahal, built by his great-grandson, Shah Jahan. Humayun's son Akbar moved his capital to Agra and then to Fatehpur Sikri, where he built a fortified palace. Akbar followed the political dictum of alliance through matrimony and had several Hindu wives. Even in the artistic ventures of this period the Hindu influence is prominent. Fatehpur Sikri, built in the pink sandstone of the region, has very few domes; the hundreds of pillars and the terraced pavilions point to Akbar's interest in blending Hindu and Islamic elements.

Shah Jahan, Akbar's grandson, moved his capital back to Delhi and built the Red Fort and Jami Masjid (Friday mosque) there. His reign is referred to as the Age of Marble because of his great wealth. The Taj Mahal, dedicated to his wife Mumtaz Mahal, who is buried there, is a pure white, marble-faced mausoleum decorated with delicate inlay and surrounded by a Mughal garden. The building is exquisitely proportioned, the result of years of experimentation by earlier generations of architects throughout India.

European Influence in India

During the Mughal period, European traders began to gain supremacy over the trade routes that linked Europe, Africa and Asia. By the 19th century they were able to establish administrative and political control of the Indian subcontinent. During the 17th and 18th centuries the British created the trading centres of Madras, Calcutta and Bombay; the French had links with Pondicherry and Mysore; and the Portuguese had established themselves in Goa. Modest buildings for trade, warehouses and small churches met the needs of the early traders. But as their power grew, the colonizers began to erect imposing railway stations, administrative buildings, grand bungalows and clubs. In Bombay, Madras and Calcutta, the law courts, post offices, secretariats and public works offices were all built by the British. Victoria Terminus, in Bombay, is one of the most impressive Victorian legacies. Gothic arches, stained glass and sculpted images of Justice and Peace adorned massive colonial structures which, by their very size and scale, impressed upon the natives of these cities what their colonial rulers were about.

Queen Victoria was crowned Empress of India in 1858 and many buildings were named in her honour. Lord Curzon planned the Victoria Memorial in Calcutta as a monument to the history of the British presence in India. For this, he said, 'Some variety of the classical or renaissance style is essential, and a European architect must be employed.' This summed up the approach taken to town planning and building in India during this phase of British rule.

Foreign rule in India expressed itself in subtler ways. It was not unusual to see the aspiring 'Brown Sahib' wearing a jacket and tie along with the traditional dhoti, and Indian women wearing blouses with puffed sleeves done up with ribbons and bows after the fashion of the white memsahibs. Homesick British wives brought with them flowers quite foreign to India—such as hollyhocks and dahlias—to plant in their Indian gardens.

At the turn of the century the mood began to change; Delhi replaced Calcutta as the new capital and a new city was laid out. The Viceregal Lodge, now Rashtrapati Bhavan, the home of the Indian president, was built by Sir Edwin Lutyens in an attempt to develop an Anglo-Indian architectural style, with Doric pillars, a dome resembling a Buddhist stupa, sculptures of elephants and other Indian motifs.

During the period of British rule, artists from Europe, commissioned to paint and engrave prints, produced landscapes and portraits of British administrators. The British had established many schools and colleges where the artistic traditions of the West were taught. The small yet significant coterie of artists, painters and poets who emerged from these schools sought new forms of Indian expression once the country attained independence. Amongst them are Jamini Roy, Nandal Bose, and the Tagores. Rabindranath Tagore, India's poet laureate, Vallathol of Kerala, and Subramania Bharati of Tamil Nadu through their writings, inspired the Indian people in their struggle for freedom.

Today, painters like M F Hussain, Bendre, Biren De, Bhupan Khakar and Gulam Sheikh exhibit at major art galleries throughout India and a good collection of contemporary Indian art is on display at the National Gallery of Modern Art in New Delhi. Literature thrives as well, with excellent writings in numerous Indian languages. Apart from the Indian writers who have been competently translated, there are also some who write in English: Anita Desai, Nayantara Seghal, R K Narayan, Salmon Rushdie and Vikram Seth, to name but a few.

India has a long and rich tradition of handicrafts characterized by great diversity. Many contemporary crafts are available today at government cottage emporia. Stonework, from temple carvings to the finest jewellery, has always been the pride of India. The handloom textile industry, famous for its production of dreamlike fabrics and muslin, has evolved a variety of weaves, prints and embroideries. In every village in India, artists continue to work and create, contributing to the country's cultural identity.

Some Festivals

With at least seven major faiths and a large agricultural population, India seems to celebrate one festival or another every day in the year. In addition, each seasonal change—such as the coming of spring, the monsoon and the harvests— is celebrated. Yet another factor here is the strength of the bonds of familial affection and concern. Festivals further strengthen these ties across the extended family system which embraces in-laws, distant relatives and friends.

Indian festivals can be specific to a region, or the same festival will be celebrated in different places in a slightly different form. In fact, every community has its own special emphasis and unique form of expression in the celebration of a festival.

Officially, India follows the Gregorian calendar. However, the older lunar and solar calendars determine the dates of festivals and thus they vary each year. Three secular national holidays are fixed: 26 January is Republic Day, 15 August is Independence Day and 2 October is the birthday of Mahatma Gandhi.

The January sugarcane harvest in North India is celebrated in the **Lohri festival**, an occasion for joy and thanksgiving for the bounty of nature. There is music, song and the sharing of sweets made out of the new sugar and sesame seeds. In South India, where rice is the staple food, the harvest festival is called **Pongal**; it is **Bihu** in Assam and **Makara Sankranti** in other parts of the country. A delightful occasion in South India is **Mattu Pongal**, also in January, when cattle (and cars, tractors and buses) are washed and decorated with garlands and honoured for their hard work in bringing in a good harvest.

Republic Day is celebrated with massive parades on 26 January to mark the day in 1950 when India was declared a republic and the Constitution of India came into effect. In New Delhi, the army, navy and air force parade is followed by a display of floats with dancers from different parts of India. The government hands out awards to eminent people in the fields of science, the arts and social work, and there is a special Bravery Award for children. The event, which takes place in New Delhi and in every state capital, is televised. Tickets and passes are available for those who want to watch it live. The curtain rings down two days later with a **Beating of the Retreat**, an impressive hour-long performance of music and marching by the combined bands of the armed forces.

Basanta Panchami and **Holi** are the major spring festivals, held in February and March. They are best experienced in North India, where the changing seasons are more noticeable. Homes are cleaned, and on the eve of Holi, huge bonfires burn away the old year and usher in the new. Children play with coloured powders and water, visit the homes of relatives and romp in the streets splashing colours on everyone. This ancient ritual has inspired some lovely— and often bawdy—songs which can be heard in the villages. By noon an exhausted silence reigns and the festivities are over.

Soon after Holi, on 13 April, there is a festival of music and dance especially important to Sikhs and Punjabis. By April and May, the gulmohar, laburnum and cassia trees are in flower and it is time for **Pooram**, celebrated at Trichur (Kerala) with processions of temple elephants carrying ceremonial umbrellas to the accompaniment of music. Soon the summer heat becomes unbearable even for the gods, and in the **Rath festival** at Puri (Orissa), the presiding deities— Jaganath, Balaram and Subhadra—are taken from the temple to their summer abode in huge wooden chariots pulled by thousands of people.

Before the monsoon there are occasions when it is auspicious to bathe in the Ganges and other rivers. Once the rains come, there are further celebrations. Nowhere in the world does rain inspire so much spontaneous music and poetry as in India. During **Teej**, celebrated in honour of Parvati (the wife of Shiva), it was customary for women and young brides to return to their parents' home. Swings were hung on trees and in the houses, and the girls would get together with their old friends. Far from the watchful eye of their in-laws and husbands, the women abandoned themselves with their companions as in former days.

In North India during July and August, **Raksha Bandhan** is an occasion for brothers to reiterate their affection for and their pledge to protect their sisters, who tie a delicate *rakhi* thread (now made with gold and tassels) to their brothers' wrists as a symbol of affection. They, in turn, present their sisters with a gift or money, symbolizing their protection.

Janmashtami is a nationwide festival in honour of the god Krishna, represented as a naughty child, cowherd, divine lover and destroyer of evil. You can observe Janmashtami at Mathura, Krishna's birthplace, or at any Vishnu temple. Like at Christmas, houses are cleaned and devotees decorate Krishna's image with dolls and toys for his enjoyment. Other festivals for the gods include **Sivaratri** (for Shiva) in February–March, an occasion for fasting and prayers; **Ramanavami** (for Rama, the hero of the *Ramayana*) in March–April; and **Buddha Jayanti** and **Mahavir Jayanti** from March to May.

India's **Independence Day** is 15 August. The prime minister addresses the nation from the ramparts of the Red Fort in Delhi and there are celebrations throughout the country.

Onam is an important festival in Kerala which marks the end of the monsoon (August–September). It features boat races in which elegant snake-boats decorated with flowers and flags and manned with 30 to 40 rowers compete, while crowds line the banks of the river and cheer them on.

The secret of fine Indian cooking is the inspired use of spices. Far from always being chilli-hot, Indian sauces are blended to complement the main ingredient.

Rotis and Pilaus

Cereals are the staple of every Indian meal. Here again the variety is staggering. Among the many different **rotis** (unleavened breads), **chapattis** are the most common. Like their cousins the handkerchief-thin **rumali roti**, they are cooked on a griddle. Others are oven-baked, like the fluffy rectangular **nan** and the simpler **tandoori roti**. Then there is the array of fried **parathas**, **puris** and **baturas,** some of them stuffed with vegetables or meat. Most rotis are made of various combinations of refined and wholemeal wheatflour, although ground **gram** (chickpeas) is used for the delicious **puranpoli** of Maharashtra and Gujarat, maize for the **makai ki roti** popular in rural Punjab, millet for the hearty **bajara ki roti** found in most villages, and ground rice for the other varieties, especially on the west coast.

Rice is cooked in many different ways. Simple steamed rice usually accompanies spiced, soupy main dishes. More elaborate variations include coconut, lemon and tamarind rice, frequently served in the south. Then there are the **pilaus** (pilaff), rice cooked in a rich, spiced chicken or meat broth, considered in North India to be the test of a fine chef. The king of rice dishes, however, is **biriyani**, a fragrant, layered rice and meat extravaganza characteristic of the Mughlai cuisine of North India and of Hyderabad in southern India, once a Mughal province.

A common accompaniment to most Indian meals is **dal,** or lentils, valuable for their high protein content. Dozens of different kinds, innumerable methods of preparation and a wide range of accompanying ingredients create a bewildering variety. There is the thick tamarind-flavoured **sambhar** from the south, the slightly sweet dals of Gujarat and the thick **dal makhani** of the north.

Among the daily products used in Indian cuisine, **ghee**, clarified butter, is a traditional cooking medium with a unique full flavour. Rising prices have now restricted its use to special occasions. Yoghurt, known as **dahi** or **curd**, integral to Indian meals, is used as a marinade, as a tangy base for rich sauces, and is also served to counter rich or spicy food. It is sometimes lightly spiced and mixed with vegetables or fruit to create the soothing **raitas** of the north and the **pachadis** of the south. Churned and salted or sweetened dahi also makes a refreshing summer drink called **lassi**. **Paneer**, similar to cottage cheese, is a favourite source of protein among vegetarians in the north.

A selection of pickles and chutneys—sour, hot and sweet—accompanies every meal. Chosen to complement the main course, they stimulate the appetite and aid digestion. Mango and lime are common pickle bases, while fresh mint, coriander, ginger and coconut are also used. Sweet chutneys of mango and tomato are often served. **Papads**, roasted or deep-fried savoury crisps, accompany meals in all parts of the country. Usually made of rolled and dried rice or lentil dough, they have a delightful crunchiness.

Vegetarian Delights

India's large vegetarian community has inspired its chefs to develop a highly sophisticated vegetarian cuisine. 'Pure' vegetarian food is usually cooked without the otherwise ubiquitous garlic, ginger and onions. 'Heating' or stimulating spices like cloves, cardamom and cinnamon are also excluded. Gujarati vegetarian food, served in many restaurants, is presented in the form of a **thali**, a circular metal tray holding numerous small bowls (**katoris)** filled with a delectable variety of vegetables, dal and **kadi**, a mixture of curd and chickpeas. The use of **gur** or jaggery (brown sugar) in Gujarati cooking adds an interesting hint of sweetness and distinguishes it from food in other parts of the country. **Aam rasa**, pureed mango, appears on menus in summer and is eaten with the **puris** (deep-fried puffed bread) that are always placed in the middle of the thali next to a small mound of rice. **Papads** (or pappadums, lentil flour crisps) round off the meal.

South Indian food, also predominantly vegetarian, is popular throughout India for its zesty flavours and generally low cost. The crisp, paper-thin, pancake-like **dosa**, served plain or stuffed with lightly spiced potatoes, steamed **idli** and deep-fried doughnut-shaped **vadas** are served together piping hot with a mustardy **sambhar** and a more bland but equally delicious coconut chutney. Dosa, idli and vadas, a popular breakfast combination, are all made of a slightly fermented rice and lentil batter. **Upma**, crumbly semolina cooked with curry leaves and garnished with nuts, is another southern favourite. Less well known but equally delicious are dishes like the thick **avial** stew of Kerala, cooked in coconut oil; **kaottu**, in a coconut and chickpea sauce; and **rasam**, a thin peppery soup, all served with mounds of rice saturated with ghee.

The vegetarian food of North India derives from the lightly spiced dishes of Varanasi. Many specialities are based on **paneer** (cottage cheese), which may be cooked with spinach (**palak paneer**), in a gravy with peas (**mattar paneer**) or with lotus seeds (**paneer phoolmakhana**). A typical farmer's meal in the north would consist of parathas stuffed with potatoes, cauliflower or horseradish eaten with dahi (curd) or mustard greens (**sarson ka saag**) and cornmeal bread.

Mughlai Magic

Several of India's famous meat dishes come from the north where Muslim influence introduced considerable sophistication. The superb Mughlai cuisine with its luscious sauces of milk, dahi, cream and crushed nuts is available in major restaurants in the big cities. There are rich, creamy **kormas**; tender, steak-like **pasindas** in an almond sauce; **nargisi kofta**, mince (usually mutton)

moulded around a hard-boiled egg and simmered in a piquant sauce; the famous **do pyaza**, cooked with onions; and the succulent **raan**, a whole leg of mutton marinated overnight and gently roasted until it is butter-soft.

Contributions from Kashmir are culinary triumphs: **gaustaba**, pounded meat shaped into meatballs and simmered in a yoghurt sauce; **haleem**, mutton cooked with wheat, milk and curds; deep-fried **tabak maas** (a Kashmiri meat dish); and the fragrant **roghan josh** (mutton). Perhaps the most significant innovation, however, is the tandoor, a charcoal-heated clay oven, which produces the magnificent **tandoori** food now available everywhere: tandoori chicken and fish, **boti kababs** (chunks of marinated grilled meat), chop-like **barra kababs**, **seekh kababs** (spiced mince grilled on a skewer), and its exotic variation, the **kakori kabab**, which melts in your mouth. With the increased interest in regional food, a huge number of traditional recipes have been revived, many from the kitchens of the former maharajas.

Meat dishes in southern and western India offer a different range of flavours. Coconut-based sauces are common in Kerala and other parts of South India. Vinegar and a liberal use of cinnamon distinguish the food of Goa. Pork **sorpotel** (cooked with vinegar), spicy **vindaloo**, chorizo sausages and chicken **shakuti** or **cafreal** are wonderful, but often very pungent. Portuguese dishes transformed by local adaptations can be unusual but delicious.

Goa is also famed for its seafood, cooked in creamy but slightly sour coconut sauces, or stuffed with a delicious combination of spices. Elsewhere, seafood recipes vary tremendously. There are the mustard-flavoured **macher jhol** and **jhonga malai** (cream prawns) of Bengal, the chilli-hot curries of Andhra Pradesh and the coconut and curry-leaf-flavoured specialities of the south and west coast. Dried fish and shrimp, cooked with vegetables and dal, add interest to the simple fare of the coastal villages. The Parsis, eighth-century migrants from Persia, created **patrani machi**, lightly spiced fish steamed in banana leaves, and **saas ni machi**, fish cooked in a delicate sauce. **Dhansak**, meat cooked in a gravy of mixed dals, is another delightful Parsi dish.

Delectable Desserts

Indian desserts are often too sweet for the Western palate. Most are flavoured with cardamom, saffron, essence of rose or **kewda** flower extract and have a garnish of nuts and a thin layer of edible silver foil. Bengal is particularly famous for its milk-based confections: juicy **rasgulla** (cream cheese balls); **sandesh** (Bengali milk sweet); steaming hot **gulab jamun** (fried cream cheese); **rasmalai** (cream cheese balls in double cream); and **mishti dohi**, the delicious caramel-flavoured curd. **Kheer**, a richer version of rice pudding; **shahi tukra**, an exotic counterpart of bread pudding; **phirni** (**firnee**) made of powdered rice and milk; and **kulfi**, a delicious nutty ice-cream, are favourite northern sweets. **Barfi**, milk fudge, plain or enriched with coconut or crushed nuts, is common on festive occasions. Sweets from the south include **Mysore pak** (sweet-meat with raisins and ghee) and creamy **payasum** pudding, while both Maharashtrans and Gujaratis are partial to **shrikhand**, made of drained, sweetened and spiced curd. Crisp golden **jelabi**, dripping with syrup, available in even the tiniest bazaars, are served piping hot at breakfast and tea time.

A **paan** is often served at the end of a traditional Indian meal. Paan consists of a betel leaf smeared with **catechu** (a tannin-rich powder), lime paste (not the fruit) and fragrant essences, wrapped around shredded betel nut, cardamom, aniseed and other ingredients, all secured by a clove pierced through the folds of the leaf. Given the acclaimed digestive properties of the package, it is a perfect and sometimes necessary finale to a rich Indian meal—and definitely an acquired taste.

National Parks and Sanctuaries

Many of India's 443 protected areas are obscure and rarely visited, and some are only protected on paper. However, there are many parks and sanctuaries of outstanding natural beauty, with a healthy population of wild animals. Unlike Africa, where despite the pressures of war and population increases game is generally more abundant, wildlife watching in India can be an adventure.

For almost a hundred years, naturalists have been concerned about the threats to India's natural wealth. Organizations such as the Bombay Natural History Society (Hornbill House, Saheed Bagat Singh Road, Bombay; next to the Prince of Wales Museum), founded in 1883, combine scientific research with campaigns for habitat and species protection. As late as the 1940s large herds of blackbuck grazed on large open areas throughout northern India. Now the herds are greatly reduced and confined to sanctuaries such as **Tal Chappar**, near Bikaner (Rajasthan), and **Velavadar**, near Bhavnagar (Gujarat). Herds of swamp deer thrived in the Terai (riverine grasslands and forests) region until the malaria eradication programmes of the 1950s allowed the area to be farmed. The northern race is now restricted to Kaziranga and Dudhwa national parks and a few areas in southwest Nepal.

The tiger population reached a low of about 1,830 in 1972. A few years later the Indian government launched Project Tiger with substantial support from the World-Wide Fund for Nature (WWF). In 1989 the tiger population had officially reached 4,334. But while the tiger population has increased in the 18 reserves that now come under Project Tiger management, the total forest area of India has continued to shrink. Officially 13 percent of the country is forested but the actual figure is 8 percent, including marginal lands. The increase in India's human population is both directly and indirectly responsible for the decline in wildlife. The need of villagers for grazing land and fuel has put enormous pressure on the country's forests and today threatens the protected areas. The axe and the chainsaw have accelerated the destruction of wilderness areas and

Arts and Sciences

*T*he following are to be studied, together with the **Kama Sutra**:

1. Singing.
2. Playing on musical instruments.
3. Dancing.
4. Union of dancing, singing, and playing instrumental music.
5. Writing and drawing.
6. Tattooing.
7. Arraying and adorning an idol with rice and flowers.
8. Spreading and arranging beds or couches of flowers.
9. Coloring the teeth, garments, hair, nails and bodies.
10. Fixing stained glass into a floor.
11. The art of making beds, and spreading out carpets and cushions for reclining.
12. Playing on musical glasses filled with water.
13. Storing and accumulating water in aqueducts, cisterns, and reservoirs.
14. Picture making, trimming and decorating.
15. Stringing of rosaries, necklaces, garlands, and wreaths.
16. Binding of turbans and chaplets, and making crests and topknots of flowers.
17. Scenic representations. Stage playing.
18. Art of making ear ornaments.
19. Art of preparing perfumes and odors.
20. Proper disposition of jewels and decorations, and adornment in dress.
21. Magic or sorcery.
22. Quickness and dexterity in manual skill.
23. Culinary art, that is, cooking and cookery.
24. Making lemonades, sherbets, acidulated drinks, and spirituous extracts with proper flavor and color.
25. Tailor's work and sewing.
26. Making parrots, flowers, tufts, tassels, bunches, bosses, knobs, and so on, out of yarn or thread.
27. Solution of riddles, enigmas, covert speeches, verbal puzzles, and enigmatical questions.
28. A game, which consists in repeating verses, and as one person finishes, another person has to commence at once, repeating another verse, beginning with the same letter with which the last speaker's verse ended.
29. The art of mimicry or imitation.
30. Reading, including chanting and intoning.
31. Study of sentences difficult to pronounce. It is played as a game, chiefly by women and children.

32. Practice with sword, single-stick, quaterstaff, and bow and arrow.
33. Drawing inferences, reasoning or inferring.
34. Carpentry, or the work of a carpenter.
35. Architecture, or the art of building.
36. Chemistry and mineralogy.
38. Coloring jewels, gems, and beads.
39. Knowledge of mines and quarries.
40. Gardening; knowledge of treating the diseases of trees and plants, of nourishing them, and determining their ages.
41. Arts of cockfighting, quail fighting, and ram fighting.
42. Art of teaching parrots and starlings to speak.
43. Art of applying perfumed ointments to the body, and of dressing the hair with unguents and perfumes, and braiding it.
44. The art of understanding writing in cipher.
45. The art of speaking by changing the forms of words. It is of various kinds. Some speak by changing the beginning and end of words, others by adding unnecessary letters between every syllable of a word, and so on.
46. Knowledge of languages and of the vernacular dialects.
47. Art of making flower carriages.
48. Art of framing mystical diagrams, of addressing spells and charms, and binding armlets.
49. Mental exercises, such as completing stanzas or verses on receiving a part of them or arranging the words of a verse written irregularly by separating the vowels from the consonants, or leaving them out altogether; or putting into verse or prose sentences represented by signs or symbols.
50. Composing poems.
51. Knowledge of dictionaries and vocabularies.
52 Knowledge of ways of changing and disguising the appearance of persons.
53. Knowledge of the art of changing the appearance of things, such as making cotton to appear as silk, coarse and common things to appear as fine and good.
54. Various ways of gambling.
55. Art of obtaining possession of the property of others by means of mantras or incantations.
56. Skill in youthful sports.
57. Knowledge of the rules of society, and of how to pay respects and compliments to others.
58. Knowledge of the art of war, of arms, armies, and so on.
59. Knowledge of gymnastics.
60. Art of knowing the character of a man from his features.
61. Knowledge of scanning or constructing verses.
62. Arithmetical recreations.
63. Making artificial flowers.
64. Making figures and images in clay.

The Kama Sutra, *translated by Sir Richard Burton*

what is not already protected is considered by pessimists to be doomed. But as Project Tiger has shown, well-managed conservation plans can, and occasionally do, work.

Throughout the country, small forest rest houses built and run by the Forest Department provide basic accommodation for visitors: beds but rarely board. Some offer commanding views of forested hills and valleys which more than compensate for the lack of facilities. Very few wildlife lodges or camps in India are run along the lines of those in Africa.

In the Kashmir Valley, **Dachigam National Park** is only 23 kilometres (14 miles) from Srinagar and can be easily visited with permission from the Chief Wildlife Warden in Srinagar. The last refuge of the Kashmir stag, Dachigam also protects the catchment area of much of Srinagar's water supply.

In Rajasthan and Uttar Pradesh the habitat varies from the lush mixed deciduous forest and riverine grasslands of the Terai region to desert and scrubland. In Rajasthan the tiger reserves of **Sariska**, near Alwar, and **Ranthambore National Park**, 132 kilometres (82 miles) southeast of Jaipur, are both within easy distance of Delhi and have a range of accommodation. At Sariska the old hunting lodge has become Sariska Palace, which organizes jeep trips into the park. Thirteen kilometres (eight miles) from the entrance to Ranthambore is Sawai Madhopur Lodge, and there is other accommodation near the camp. Near Jaisalmer, the Desert National Park covers over 3,000 square kilometres (1,175 square miles) of scrub and dune. Permission to visit must be sought from the Forest Department and District Magistrate's office in Jaisalmer.

Rajasthan is also home to one of the world's most important wetland sanctuaries. The **Keoladeo Ghana National Park** at Bharatpur, 53 kilometres (33 miles) west of Agra, covers only 29 square kilometres (11 square miles) but is host to numerous nesting species of storks, herons, spoonbills, cormorants and ibises. By November, thousands of migratory waterfowl, waders and birds of prey arrive from Siberia, the Russian steppes, Central Asia and Tibet to winter in the sanctuary. By far the rarest visitor is the Siberian crane whose western population now numbers less than 30. (There are approximately 1,500 in the eastern population which nests in China.)

In Uttar Pradesh, along the Himalayan foothills, are two important Project Tiger reserves. The earliest of these, **Corbett National Park**, is a seven-hour drive northeast of Delhi. The park includes the ridges of the Bivalik Hills of the Himalayan foothills, through which the Ramganga River flows. Apart from the occasional glimpse of a tiger or the more elusive leopard, the park has resident herds of elephants and numerous prey species. Because of its varied topography and habitat and the large intrusion of Ranganga Reservoir, the park has a wide range of bird species. There are forest rest houses and a small 'tourist complex' in the park which can be booked through Uttar Pradesh Tourism in Lucknow or New Delhi (Chandralok Building, Janpath). Outside the park, overlooking the

Kosi River, is the Quality Inn–Corbett Jungle Resort (book through Quality Inn, 51 Vasant Marg, Vasant Vihar, New Delhi 110057, tel. 675347). The other tiger reserve in Uttar Pradesh is located on the southwest border of Nepal, 260 kilometres (162 miles) northwest of Lucknow. The park owes its creation to one of India's foremost conservationists, Billy Arjan Singh. Arjan Singh's farm, **Tiger Haven**, on the edge of the park, can accommodate small groups or individuals subject to prior booking (write to Tiger Haven, PO Pallia, Dist. Kheri, Uttar Pradesh, tel. 262902).

In Gujarat there is a lodge at the **Gir National Park** which is now the last refuge of the Asiatic lion. At the edge of the little Rann of Kutch is **Dhrangadhra Sanctuary** and nearby **Camp Zainabad** which organizes visits across the flat saline wilderness of the Rann to see blackbuck, chinkara and the Indian wild ass (book through Desert Coursers, Camp Zainabad, Nr Dasad, Gujarat, tel. 3827511).

In Madhya Pradesh there are two excellent parks, both with good private facilities and game viewing from elephant back and jeep. The 1,945-square-kilometre (750-square-mile) **Kanha National Park**, 160 kilometres (100 miles) south of Jabalpur, was one of the first areas to come under Project Tiger. On the western edge of the park is Kipling Camp, with excellent food and well-organised game viewing (book through the Tollygunge Club, 120 D P Sasmal Road, Calcutta, tel. 700003). Further north the smaller **Bandhavgarh National Park,** 210 kilometres (131 miles) from Khajuraho airport and 35 kilometres (22 miles) from Umaria railway station, has a reputation for good tiger viewing and varied birdlife. Near the small village of Tala at the entrance to the park is Bandhavgarh Jungle Camp, which has excellent naturalists on its staff (book through Tiger Tops India, 1/1 Rani Jhansi Road, New Delhi 110055, tel. 523057).

In Karnataka beside Kabini Lake on the edge of the **Nagarhole National Park**, 75 kilometres (47 miles) southwest of Mysore, is the attractive Kabini River Lodge (book through Jungle Lodges & Resorts, Shrungar Shopping Centre, M G Road, Bangalore 560001, tel. 575195). Nagarhole is adjacent to three other protected areas. **Bandipur Tiger Reserve** is bisected by the Mysore–Ooty national highway but it, together with **Mudumalai Sanctuary** in Tamil Nadu to the south, has a large number of locally migrant elephants. There are two private farms at Masinagudi, 18 kilometres (11 miles) from Mujumulai: Bamboo Banks and Jungle Hut provide good accommodation, food and access to the sanctuary (book through Jungle Hut, PO Masinagudi, tel. 643223). West of Bandipur and also merging with Nagarhole is **Wynad Sanctuary** in Kerala. These four areas in three states form a Biosphere Reserve which will hopefully soon have joint management.

Along the Western Ghats, stretching from southern Maharastra to Kerala, are many small and little-known areas. In Kerala two areas stand out: **Eravikulam National Park,** 16 kilometres (ten miles) from Munnar, has the largest population of Nilgiri tahr grazing on the rolling hills that lead up to South India's highest peak, Anaimudi, at 2,695 metres (8,853 feet). Still further south is **Periyar Tiger Reserve**, which includes the hundred-year-old reservoir near Thekkady, 190 kilometres (118 miles) east of Cochin. Although a tiger reserve, Periyar is better known for its elephants. One of the most attractive and popular parks in the country, Periyar has a range of accommodation at Thekkady, run and booked through the Kerala Tourism Department (PB 46, Behind Secretariat, Trivandrum 695001, tel. 64705, 642612).

In Assam only **Kaziranga National Park** offers good accommodation. A lodge established by ITDC on the edge of the park will, in early 1991, be supplemented by the privately run Wild Grass near the southern boundary (book through WG Resorts Pvt Ltd, Uzanbazar, Guwahati, tel. 781001). Although one of the most interesting and important parks, **Manas Tiger Reserve** has only Forest Department accommodation. The park protects at least 20 of India's most endangered mammal species and a spectacular range of birds. Situated on the southern border of Bhutan, the park is a six-hour drive north of Guwahati.

Most travel agents organize trips to India's parks. Only a few of the parks are located near major railway stations or airports and thus involve hiring a car. Visitors should be aware that some parks are closed during and after the monsoon—usually July to October.

Facts for the Traveller

When to Go

India is at its most pleasant between October and March when much of the country enjoys balmy blue skies and fresh clean air. In the north from December to late February the nights turn chilly and a sweater or jacket is required. By mid-March the days start getting warmer and from late April the temperature in central India becomes too hot for comfortable travel. In May the dust and thunderstorms with occasional showers precede the monsoon. This is when the British Raj used to move to the hills, as many Indians still do.

Most of India, with the exception of the Trans-Himalayan area of Ladakh, is in some way affected by the southwest monsoon. In Kerala the rains arrive by the first week of June. They then make their way northward, reaching Bombay in the middle of the month and Delhi by early July. The rains last for almost three months and after the initial chaos of flooded roads, the people take the downpours and regular drenching in their stride. By the end of September the humidity decreases and in October temperatures begin to drop.

In Kashmir, Himachal Pradesh and Uttar Pradesh, the winter months are often extremely cold. These areas are best visited from April to July or after the monsoon. Sikkim and Arunachal Pradesh, while part of the Himalayan chain, are more affected by monsoons and have rain from May.

Southern India has a more regular climate that is also controlled by the monsoon. The southeast coast gets rain from October to late December as the northeast monsoon moves across the Bay of Bengal.

Getting There

Travel in India is in itself an adventure, sometimes pleasant, sometimes not. International flights often arrive at unsociably early hours and hotel touts and persistent taxi drivers wait outside the arrival buildings, ready to pounce on the vulnerable and ill-prepared traveller. Travelling within the country also has its drawbacks when the demand for seats on a train, plane or bus exceeds availability. Any trip to India therefore involves a certain amount of preparation and forethought. Even the most basic information on what to expect will help to make your stay more enjoyable.

By Air

Bombay and New Delhi are well connected with most cities in the Far East, the subcontinent, the Middle East, Europe and East Africa. The majority of long-haul flights still arrive between midnight and 6 am but an increasing number of airlines are introducing evening departures from Europe, allowing for morning arrivals. Many of the major international airlines (Aeroflot, Air India, Air

Climate Chart

Temperatures and average rainfall in New Delhi, 2181 m (714 ft)

	Jan	Feb	Mar	Apr	May	Jun	Jul	Aug	Sept	Oct	Nov	Dec
Max °C	21	24	30	36	43	44	35	34	37	35	29	23
Min °C	4	10	15	21	27	29	27	26	25	19	12	7
Max °F	70	75	86	97	110	112	95	93	98	95	84	73
Min °F	39	50	59	70	81	84	81	79	77	66	54	45
mm	25	22	17	7	8	65	211	173	150	31	1	5
in	1	0.9	0.7	0.3	0.3	2.6	8.3	6.8	5.9	1.2	0	0.2

Temperatures and average rainfall in Bombay, 10 m (37 ft)

	Jan	Feb	Mar	Apr	May	Jun	Jul	Aug	Sept	Oct	Nov	Dec
Max °C	31	32	33	33	33	32	30	29	30	32	33	32
Min °C	16	17	20	24	26	26	25	24	24	23	20	18
Max °F	88	90	91	91	91	90	86	84	86	90	91	90
Min °F	61	63	68	75	79	79	77	75	75	73	68	64
mm	0	1	0	0	20	647	945	660	309	117	7	1
in	0	0	0	0	0.8	25.5	37.2	26	12.2	4.6	0.3	0

Temperatures and average rainfall in Calcutta, 6 m (21 ft)

	Jan	Feb	Mar	Apr	May	Jun	Jul	Aug	Sept	Oct	Nov	Dec
Max °C	26	29	34	36	36	34	32	32	32	31	29	27
Min °C	12	15	20	24	26	26	26	26	26	24	18	13
Max °F	79	84	93	97	97	93	90	90	90	88	84	81
Min °F	54	59	68	75	79	79	79	79	79	75	64	55
mm	13	22	30	50	135	263	320	318	253	134	29	4
in	0.5	0.9	1.2	2	5.3	10.3	12.6	12.5	10	5.3	1.1	0.2

France, Alitalia, British Airways, Emirates, Gulf Air, Iraqi, Kuwait, Lufthansa, Pan Am, PIA, Saudi, Singapore and Turkish) fly to both cities. JAL, KLM, MAS and Thai fly only to New Delhi, while Air Canada, Cathay, Iberia, Qantas, Swissair and TWA fly only to Bombay. Air India, Thai, Aeroflot, Yugoslav, Royal Jordanian and Singapore have flights to Calcutta. British Airways, MAS, Air India and Lufthansa service Madras. Other international airports are Amritsar (with connections to Kabul), Varanasi and Patna (with flights to Kath-mandu), Dabolim–Goa (receives charters from Europe), Hyderabad and Trivandrum (flights to and from the Middle East), Bangalore (flights via Madras to Singapore) and Trichy (flights to Colombo).

Air India has the greatest number of flights into India, with frequent evening departures from London, Amsterdam, Paris, Frankfurt and Rome in addition to daily morning departures from London (linked to flights that originate in New York the previous evening). British Airways offers the most frequent service of any European carrier, with flights to Bombay, Madras and New Delhi, and connections to Beijing and Hong Kong.

The Middle Eastern and Gulf carriers (Emirates, Gulf Air, Iraqi, Kuwait and Saudi) fly into both Bombay and New Delhi, all with connections to and from major European cities. The South Asian carriers Air Lanka and Biman Bangladesh fly into Bombay, as do Air Mauritius, Air Tanzania, Egypt Air, Ethiopian, Kenya Airways and Zambia Airways from Africa. PIA has flights connecting Karachi and Lahore with both Bombay and New Delhi. RNAC connects Kathmandu with Calcutta, New Delhi and Patna.

On Arrival

On arrival in India the first delay travellers will experience is the immigration queue (see Visas below). You may have to wait up to an hour for your checked luggage while it undergoes X-ray scrutiny. However, customs inspections are usually quick and painless.

There are bank counters inside the arrival terminals and money can be changed at the prevailing bank rate while you wait for your baggage to appear.

Outside the arrival halls there are various counters offering car rental, transfer buses and prepaid taxis. If travelling on a budget the EALTS (Ex-Servicemens Air Link Transport Service) bus service costing only a few rupees connects the airports at Bombay, Calcutta and New Delhi with most of the nearby and downtown hotels. The local police operate a system of prepaid taxis at most airports which eliminates the possibility of an unscrupulous driver taking an exhausted visitor on an involuntary ride through the back streets to inflate the meter charge. Taxi rates are fixed and a receipt is issued detailing the destination zone and any baggage. Give the driver the receipt when you reach your destination.

Visas

All foreign visitors to India require a valid visa. A tourist visa, valid for 90 days from the date of entry, can be obtained from any Indian embassy, high commission or consulate abroad. If you intend to leave India and return within the 90-day period (on a trip to Nepal, Sri Lanka or Pakistan), apply for a double- or triple-entry visa. An extension of 90 days can be obtained at Foreigners Regional Registration Offices in Bombay: Annexe 2, Office of the Commissioner of Police, Dadabhoy Naroji Road, tel. 268111, open 10 am–5 pm; Calcutta: 237

Acharya Jagdish Bose Road, tel. 443301; Madras: 13 Victoria Crescent Road, Egmore, tel. 88864; and New Delhi: Hans Bhawan, 1st floor, Indraprastha Estate, tel. 3319489, 3318179. Extensions can also be issued by the Superintendent of Police at District Headquarters. The visa fee varies by nationality, with British passport holders paying the highest (post-colonial revenge)! In mid-1990 there was talk of relaxing some visa requirements but this has not happened. One plan is to issue five-year multiple-entry visas for regular business travellers, valid for a stay(s) totalling six months.

If you stay in India longer than 90 days, you are required to hand in an Income Tax Clearance Certificate at the time of departure. This is available from the main tax offices in Bombay, Calcutta, Madras and New Delhi.

Customs

Visitors are usually asked if they have anything to declare on arrival. You should not bring in more than US$1,000 in cash without declaring it. Likewise, video and camera equipment and other expensive, easily sold items should be declared on arrival. If the customs officer issues you a Tourist Baggage Re-export Form (TBRE) detailing the items declared and their value, these items must be shown when leaving the country. If currency was declared and noted when entering the country, exchange receipts must be shown on departure if you take less than the declared amount out.

India allows one bottle of spirits, 200 cigarettes and a reasonable amount of gifts to be imported free of duty. Indian customs officers are thorough and professional. Usually on the lookout for smugglers, they rarely trouble tourists.

Souvenirs can be exported from India without restriction. Only Rs2,000 worth of gold and up to Rs10,000 worth of manufactured jewellery or precious stones can be exported without a permit. Any object over 100 years old needs an export certificate from the Director of Antiquities, Archaeological Survey of India, Janpath, New Delhi (for other cities, see Useful Addresses, page 241). India is a signatory to CITES and the export of ivory, animal and snake skins and products made from them is forbidden. CITES certificates can be issued by the Deputy Director of Wildlife Preservation in the major cities.

Getting Around

Apart from the extensive domestic air and railway networks, India has a vast but overworked road network. Cars with drivers can be hired quite easily through travel agents and hotels. Self-drive cars have only recently become available for hire in India. Due to insurance problems and the fact that a chauffeur is an affordable luxury in India, self-drive car hire is rather limited. However, a valid international or Indian driving licence is required along with a photocopy of your passport (for identification) and a passport-size photograph. As elsewhere, rates vary with the type of car and the number of days it is rented, so it is worth getting more than one quotation. Hiring a car for an eight-hour day to visit the suburbs of a particular city will often work out cheaper than a taxi. A good driver should be tipped at the end of your stay.

Some cities have well-developed public transport networks. The BEST bus service in Bombay, run by the Bombay Electrical Supply and Transport Company, has good service to most areas. In Delhi the quality of the public service varies from area to area and is supplemented by private buses operating numbered routes. In all cities it is advisable to avoid the rush hours. Calcutta has an excellent underground railway service linking Tollygunge in the south with the city centre. This will soon be extended to the airport at Dum Dum.

Bombay, Delhi and a few other cities have metered taxis and auto-rickshaws. In many towns the taxis, when you can get one, are unmetered, so negotiate the rate before the journey. In some towns bicycles can be hired. They are an ideal way of exploring such places as Srinagar, Mysore and Khajuraho.

Each state has its own road transport system but the service varies widely. Buses in South India tend to be of a better standard, but Rajasthan, Haryana and Jammu and Kashmir all operate 'deluxe' services in the north. The overnight bus service on many routes is a convenient and cost-effective alternative to trains. Unfortunately the craze for video coaches on the trunk routes requires the ability to sleep through anything or a passion for Hindi films.

Domestic Flights

In both Bombay and New Delhi the domestic and international terminals are located at opposite ends of the same runway system and the international airports are further from the city centre than the domestic terminals. Most of the other airports which handle international flights have dual terminals. There are two domestic airlines operating a variety of routes within the country, Indian Airlines and Vayudoot. Indian Airlines operates Airbus A300s and A320s on major trunk routes linking Bangalore, Bombay, Calcutta, Dabolim (Goa), Guwahati, Hyderabad, Madras, New Delhi, Srinagar and Trivandrum. On other routes Indian Airlines operates Boeing 737s and links 57 towns in India and ten in neighbouring countries.

Vayudoot Airlines, established in the 1980s, flies small passenger planes on feeder routes connecting the major cities with many of the smaller towns not served by Indian Airlines. Vayudoot is also beginning to operate flights from New Delhi to Bangalore, Bombay and Guwahati.

Both domestic carriers have a mixed reputation for reliability. Many flights have long waiting lists and the shortage of aircraft is only exacerbated when more than the routine number are taken out for their regular servicing. Indian Airlines has a dual fare structure, with foreign nationals being charged a higher dollar tariff even if the ticket is purchased in India. Reconfirmation of internal sectors is vital. Being waitlisted is unsatisfactory regardless of the promises made by the reservations staff.

In 1990 a new 'open skies' policy came into effect and now anyone with a plane is allowed to fly! In fact a small regional airline, UB Air, operates from Bangalore with scheduled flights to Madras, Hyderabad and Mangalore.

In Delhi, India International Airways Pvt Ltd charters an executive jet, whilst in Bangalore, you should contact UB Air.

If you are connecting from an international arrival at Bombay or New Delhi airports to a domestic flight, take one of the airport transfer buses or a prepaid taxi (see page 51). If you have more than a few hours between flights and do not want to go into the city, the four major cities have a number of airport hotels. The best and most expensive is the Leela Kempinski near Sahar at Bombay. At both Bombay and New Delhi airports there is a Centaur Hotel nearby. These hotels operate courtesy coaches from all terminals at both airports. At Calcutta there is the Airport Ashoka Hotel and at Madras the Trident Hotel. Most of the other airport hotels in India are unprepossessing and although cheaper cannot be recommended.

Indian Airlines offers a number of promotional fares which are a cost-effective way of seeing a large part of the country in a short period of time. The **Discover India** fare costs US$400 and permits unlimited travel within India for 21 days but with some restrictions on routing. A US$300 **Tour India** fare gives you up to six flight coupons and is valid for up to 14 days. There is also a **25 percent youth discount** on the dollar fare for passengers aged between 12 and 30, valid on both domestic flights and those between India and Nepal.

Indian Railways
Travelling by train in India is more than a nostalgic return to the great days of steam. Indian Railways is an important system linking the entire country. There are 62,000 kilometres (38,750 miles) of track and 7,000 trains carrying over 11 million passengers daily.

There are three gauges: broad, metre and narrow. Most of the major trunk routes are broad-gauge and the trains are generally fast and comfortable. The metre-gauge lines are found in Gujarat, Rajasthan, northern Uttar Pradesh and Bihar. There are also branch lines in Assam and the south. The four narrow-gauge lines are the hill railways linking Kalka with Shimla, New Jalpaiguri with Darjeeling, Mettupalagam (near Coimbatore) with Coonoor and Ooty, and the line to Matheran in the Western Ghats near Bombay.

Indian trains have their own complex 'caste' system. Airconditioned first class on the major routes costs about the same as air travel. Airconditioned second class (AC-2 tier) carriages are becoming more common but still operate mostly on the major routes. Another option is 1st class, which like 1st AC has four-berth compartments. If travelling in a small group this is perhaps the best way to go, although from April to June the heat and dust may drive you to AC-2. Finally, the most common and thus often overcrowded service is 2nd class with its wooden seats. On a few trains such as the new rapid Shatabdi services

linking New Delhi with Agra, Gwalior and Bhopal, as well as Kanpur; and Chandigarh and the Rajdhani from New Delhi to Bombay and Calcutta, there are airconditioned 'chair car' carriages.

Fares are computed according to distance and class. Mail and express trains are faster and tend to be punctual. Passenger trains travel at their own slow pace and are generally 2nd class. If you stay in India for a period of between one week and three months, an **Indrail Pass** offers unlimited travel and much convenience. While they do not represent much of a saving, an Indrail Pass enables you to avoid queues at train station ticket booths and to take advantage of the tourist and VIP (government) quota for seats.

A quarterly publication, *Trains at a Glance*, published by Indian Railways and available at most major station bookstalls, is invaluable for planning journeys. A more comprehensive series of timetables for each of the seven rail zones are the monthly *Bradshaws*. There are special tourist booking offices at New Delhi, Bombay and Madras.

In the early 1980s the railways teamed up with Rajasthan Tourism and started a 'Palace on Wheels' service using coaches inherited from the maharajas which were adapted for modern use. The train leaves New Delhi Cantonment Station once a week and makes a circular route to Udaipur, Jodhpur, Jaipur, Bharatpur, Fatehpur Sikri and Agra before returning to Delhi. The trip includes side trips, and all accommodation is on the train. Another special train is the Maharaja of Jodhpur's private car. Book through Umaid Bhawan Palace.

Immunization and Health

Yellow fever certificates must be shown by travellers arriving from Africa, Latin America and Papua New Guinea. Other shots, although not officially required, are advisable. Typhoid, polio and tetanus are important. A gamma globulin injection for hepatitis immediately before departure is also advisable. Many countries require arrivals from India to have an up-to-date cholera vaccination. A jab against rabies is now available but you must visit the nearest hospital immediately following any bite from a dog or monkey for a further course of shots.

Malaria is still widespread in many parts of India. Advice as to which pills to take is constantly being revised but at present one suggested regime is Nivaquine (or Avloclor) twice a week and one or two Paludrine daily. Both courses must be continued for four to six weeks after leaving an affected area.

Most modern medicines are available over the counter in India but it is wise to have your own small reserve stock. If prescription drugs are required, bring enough for the duration of your visit. It is advisable to keep a second stock of these packed in a separate bag in case you lose your baggage. A small kit should include a remedy for 'Delhi-belly' (upset stomach), some antiseptic cream, lip salve, mosquito cream, suntan lotion for long days on Goa's beaches, water purifying tablets if bottled water is not available, elastoplast, etc. Many tourists develop problems on their second or third day because of 'climate shock' (heat exhaustion rather than contaminated food and water), but if an upset stomach persists seek medical advice (big hotels have a doctor on call). Many people in India advise drinking lots of fluids (boiled and filtered water with a little salt and sugar) and keeping to a diet of rice and yoghurt for a couple of days.

There are a few things to be careful about in India health-wise. Drink plenty of fluids but *never* drink tap water. The flask in hotel rooms contains filtered water and bottled water is now available almost everywhere. Avoid fresh salads, even in hotels, and do not eat street food until you know how much you can abuse your body for the sake of your palate.

Time Zones

Despite its breadth, India has a single time zone. It is two and a half hours behind Hong Kong and Singapore, five and a half hours ahead of London (GMT; four and a half hours ahead of British Summer Time), ten and a half hours ahead of New York and thirteen and a half hours ahead of San Francisco.

Photography

The light in India, especially during the summer months, can be harsh so the best times for photography are the 'magic hours' immediately after dawn and before sunset. Taking pictures of airports, railway stations, bridges, military installations and from the air is prohibited. Most people do not mind having their photograph taken, but take care in some Muslim areas and at bathing ghats.

Permission is also required to take snapshots in museums and, occasionally, to use a flash or tripod both inside and outside monuments. The Archaeological Survey of India office, behind the National Museum, Janpath, New Delhi, gives written permission to photograph any site under its care. You also need written permission to shoot videos at many sites, including the Taj Mahal. If in doubt, ask.

Colour print film is now readily available in India but the price and vintage varies. Only a limited range of slide film is generally available and no Kodachrome has been imported since the Kodak laboratory in Bombay closed. Bring a good supply of film with you—some people suggest at least twice what you expect to use. Film left over at the end of your trip makes a good and welcome present for someone who has been of help.

Things Electrical

Bombay is the only city with a reliable electricity supply, thanks in part to the nuclear power station at Thrombay. The voltage is theoretically 220 volts, although outside Bombay it tends to fluctuate, usually downwards. Sensitive equipment such as portable computers should be hooked up to a voltage stabilizer (readily available but bulky). Computer users should also have a 'spike strip' as a secondary defence against power fluctuations and surges. Hotels can loan or arrange the hire of a stabilizer.

Penlight cells and other batteries are available but not AAA size (unless on the black market).

A warning: Some security checks at domestic airports not only take away pen knives but also batteries. It is best to put them in your checked baggage.

Money

The currency of India is the rupee (Rs), divided into 100 paise (p). There are coins of Rs1 and 50p, 25p, 20p, 10p and 5p. The banknotes are in denominations of Rs100, Rs50, Rs20, Rs10, Rs5, Rs2 and Rs1. Try to avoid accepting notes that are torn as they are very hard to get rid of. Carry as much small change as possible as no one selling anything seems to have any change.

Approximate exchange rates in 1990:

US$1 = Rs16.15–20
UK£1 = Rs27.5–39.

Foreigners must pay all hotel, air and rail bills with foreign currency, travellers' cheques or international credit cards. Rupees can only be used if you can present an 'encashment certificate' to prove you bought them from a bank or authorized foreign exchange dealer. The amounts of your purchases are noted on the back of the certificate and deducted from the face value. There is a small and not particularly risky black market giving a premium of about 15 percent. Large denomination notes, especially US dollars and British pounds, are the most welcome.

Departure

For most international flights you are asked to check in two or three hours in advance. For domestic flights, reporting time is 90 to 60 minutes before takeoff except for flights to and from Srinagar when security concerns dictate a reporting time two hours prior to the flight.

An airport tax of Rs300 is charged at the check-in counter for all foreign travel except to the neighbouring countries of Afghanistan, Bangladesh, Bhutan, Burma, the Maldives, Nepal and Sri Lanka, when the tax is Rs150.

Communications

Most hotels in the main cities have in-room direct-dial facilities for both local and international calls. In smaller hotels and towns it is easier to have the hotel operator connect both local and long-distance calls. Most large hotels have telex facilities and many now have fax lines. Hotels mark up calls by anything between 100 and 250 percent so check the rates before calling home. The postal service varies but is generally secure and reliable. While a letter takes only three days to arrive from London, it can take up to ten days to get there. Postcards often take longer and parcels take their own time. It is advisable to watch your letter or parcel being postmarked.

Sending registered parcels can be a lengthy procedure. Most parcels have to be stitched into cotton cloth and then sealed (there are usually people outside major post offices offering this service). Two customs forms also need to be completed. Once the parcel has been weighed and the stamps affixed, make sure they are franked in front of you and that you get a receipt of registration.

Most major international courier companies operate in India, offering both domestic and international services.

Beggars

Begging is a fact of life in India. In many towns, and especially near tourist areas, begging is an organized profession. Each gang works an area and the child receiving the alms may not keep more than a small percentage while the organizer takes a large cut. If you decide to give to a beggar, one rupee or less is enough. Fruit, biscuits, small coins from home or pens are also appropriate gifts for a child beggar but be discreet, otherwise a crowd will form.

There are numerous good charities working throughout India and hotel staff will be able to advise if you wish to give to a reputable charity.

Women Travellers

The frequency with which women travellers are hassled by Indian men seems to vary with the amount of flesh exposed. Wearing conservative Indian clothing is perhaps the best way to disappear in the crowd, but otherwise avoid exposed shoulders, very short skirts and pants, sleeveless blouses, and generally letting it all hang out.

Northern India

Many of the physical contrasts that are part of India's fascination are found in the north. The trans-Himalayan area of Ladakh, in Jammu and Kashmir, and Spiti, in Himachal Pradesh, includes part of the Tibetan plateau and then merges into the northern face of the great Himalayan range. This is an area of harsh winters and low rainfall, sparsely populated but claimed by China to the east and Pakistan to the west. The Himalayas stretch from the great knot in Central Asia where the Hindu Kush, the Pamirs, the Karakoram and the Himalayas meet, southeast through the states of Jammu and Kashmir and Himachal Pradesh and then east to form the border between Uttar Pradesh and Tibet. The sweep of the Himalayas continues eastward through Nepal with the important geographical divide of the Kali Gandarki and the great peaks of the Everest region before reaching Sikkim, Bhutan and the remote Indian state of Arunachal Pradesh. Over 1,280 kilometres (800 miles) of the Himalayas fall within India.

The lower ranges of the Himalayas protect the valley of Kashmir and form the fertile upper reaches of great rivers. The five rivers of the Punjab (literally 'five rivers', the Jhelum, Ravi, Chenab, Sutlej and Beas) flow west to join the Indus in Pakistan. The Yumana and the holy Ganges rise in Garhwal and flow east, irrigating the large states of Uttar Pradesh, Bihar and Bengal before emptying into the Bay of Bengal. The great trekking areas of Himachal Pradesh, Uttar Pradesh and Kashmir are in the middle ranges. Several of the hill stations of the British Raj, which in the last few decades have become popular with the Indian middle classes, were built on ridges of the lower Himalayas or in valleys. Kasauli at 1,927 metres (6,325 feet) looks down on the modern city of Chandigarh in the plains a few kilometres to the south. Shimla and Mussoorie are on ridges, while Nainital surrounds a lake; all are reasonably close to the large towns of the northern states.

North of Delhi are the great farming states of Punjab and Haryana. Although both states have become increasingly industrialized since Independence, the hardworking farmers produce a disproportionate percentage of the country's grain and their income is 50 percent higher than the national average. In 1947 the Punjab was divided between Pakistan and India, and in 1966 the Indian portion split again when Haryana was created and the new Punjab became predominantly Punjabi-speaking. Both states share the modern city of **Chandigarh** as their capital. For hundreds of years the farmland north of Delhi was the route taken by invaders from the northwest. Great battles were fought at **Panipat**, 92 kilometres (57 miles) north of Delhi, in 1526, 1556 and 1761 and at **Karnal,** 25 kilometres (15 miles) further north, in 1739. The epic battle described in the *Mahabharata* was fought at **Kurukshetra**.

The state of Uttar Pradesh stretches east from Delhi. Its population of almost 140 million makes it the largest state in the country. The sacred River Ganges rises at Gaumukh in the Garhwal and flows through the state. The Hindu shrines at Gangotri, Badrinath and Kedarnath in Garhwal have been visited by pilgrims every summer for hundreds of years. The great pilgrimage towns of Hardwar, Allahabad and Varanasi (Benares) lie along the Ganges' banks. The Yumana also has its source in the Garhwal region of the state and flows south to Delhi and Agra before joining the Ganges at **Allahabad**, 135 kilometres (85 miles) west of Varanasi. The vast, overpopulated and flat Ganges plain suffers from floods after every monsoon and droughts if the rains fail. Along the foothills of the Himalayas the once great forests have been reduced to small pockets. These are now the great parks of Corbett, Dudhwa and Rajaji.

Delhi and New Delhi

As the most popular entry point into India, New Delhi, the capital of India, has much to offer the visitor. Successive dynasties have left their imprint in monuments all over the city. Delhi is also a modern city, with hotels to suit every budget, shops to satisfy every whim and transport connections to every point in North India.

You will encounter many of India's paradoxes in Delhi. The ramparts of the 15th-century **Purana Quila** (Old Fort) overlook a sprawling exhibition complex with state-of-the-art engineering products on display. In the heart of New Delhi an 11th-century astrolabe, the **Jantar Mantar**, is hemmed in by chrome and glass high-rises. Outside each outlet of Nirula's fast-food restaurants, with their trendy Western decor and piped-in rock music, you will find *paanwallahs* selling the traditional digestive that Indians take at the end of their meal. Wide, tree-lined boulevards minutes away from narrow, congested alleyways may seem irreconcilable to the first-time visitor, but they are simply two sides of the same coin.

Delhi is too big and too sprawling to be seen in one day. A sensible plan is to tour one area at a time over the course of three to five days.

Imperial Circuit

At the centre of New Delhi are the buildings erected by the British when, early this century, the imperial capital was moved from Calcutta. The brief to the architect, Sir Edwin Lutyens, was 'neither British, nor Indian, but Imperial', and the massive outlines of sandstone buildings on the finest site in the city are nothing if not regal. Facing west from **India Gate**, a war memorial arch, the lawns lead the eye along **Rajpath**, the *camino real*, for over a kilometre to the impressive Secretariat buildings, **North** and **South block**, with their images reflected in cleverly placed pools of water below. Beyond the Secretariat is **Rashtrapati Bhavan**, now the residence of the president of India and once the British viceroy's palace. Nearby are **Parliament House** and the **Cathedral Church of the Redemption**. With its sprawling lawns and wide roads, the area is seldom busy by Delhi's formidable standards, and it makes a pleasant walk during the day. After dark, the lawns are a favourite picnic spot for local

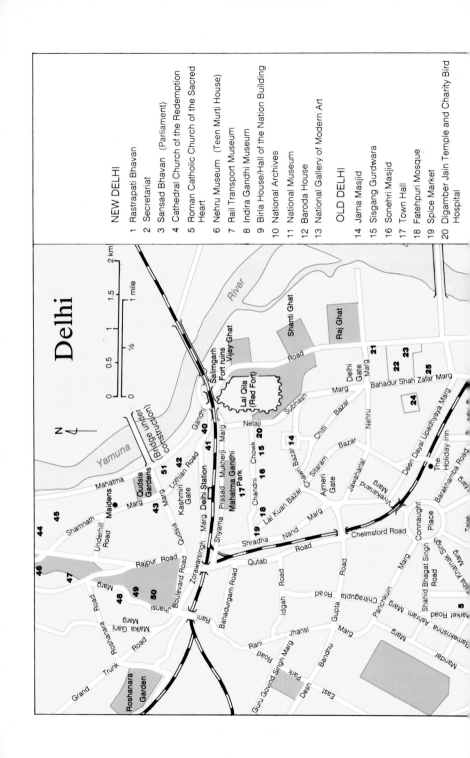

Delhi

0 0.5 1 1.5 2 km
0 ½ 1 mile

NEW DELHI

1 Rastrapati Bhavan
2 Secretariat
3 Sansad Bhavan (Parliament)
4 Cathedral Church of the Redemption
5 Roman Catholic Church of the Sacred Heart
6 Nehru Museum (Teen Murti House)
7 Rail Transport Museum
8 Indira Gandhi Museum
9 Birla House/Hall of the Nation Building
10 National Archives
11 National Museum
12 Baroda House
13 National Gallery of Modern Art

OLD DELHI

14 Jama Masjid
15 Sisgang Gurdwara
16 Sonehri Masjid
17 Town Hall
18 Fatehpuri Mosque
19 Spice Market
20 Digamber Jain Temple and Charity Bird Hospital

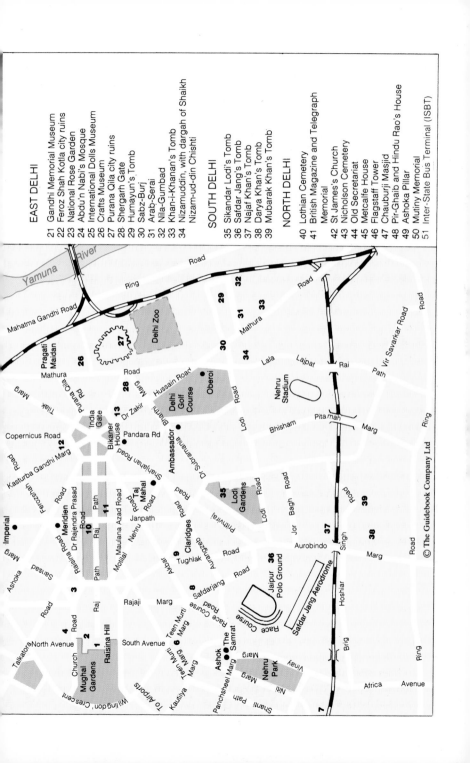

EAST DELHI

21 Gandhi Memorial Museum
22 Feroz Shah Kotla city ruins
23 National Rose Garden
24 Abdu'n Nabi's Mosque
25 International Dolls Museum
26 Crafts Museum
27 Purana Qila city ruins
28 Shergarh Gate
29 Humayun's Tomb
30 Sabz-Burj
31 Arab-Serai
32 Nila-Gumbad
33 Khan-i-Khanan's Tomb
34 Nizamuddin, with dargah of Shaikh
    Nizam-ud-din Chishti

SOUTH DELHI

35 Sikandar Lodi's Tomb
36 Safdar Jang's Tomb
37 Najaf Khan's Tomb
38 Darya Khan's Tomb
39 Mubarak Khan's Tomb

NORTH DELHI

40 Lothian Cemetery
41 British Magazine and Telegraph
    Memorial
42 St James's Church
43 Nicholson Cemetery
44 Old Secretariat
45 Metcalfe House
46 Flagstaff Tower
47 Chauburji Masjid
48 Pir-Ghaib and Hindu Rao's House
49 Ashoka Pillar
50 Mutiny Memorial
51 Inter-State Bus Terminal (ISBT)

© The Guidebook Company Ltd

families, especially in the summer months when finding a parking space becomes something of a feat, and the dozens of ice-cream vendors who converge there nightly do a roaring trade.

Just south of the Rajpath and Janpath crossing is the recently expanded **National Museum** (open 10 am–5 pm, closed Mondays). Although a young museum, it has an excellent collection. The bronze gallery is especially fine, as are the Central Asian and tribal galleries. There are comprehensive sections on sculpture, Rajput and Mughal painting, calligraphy and the Indus civilization. Near India Gate is the equally impressive **National Gallery of Modern Art** (open 10 am–5 pm, closed Mondays) in Jaipur House, with its comprehensive collection of 20th-century Indian art and earlier work by European artists in India.

From here **Connaught Place** is a short drive away. Laid out during the period of British rule, it is fast turning into a veritable forest of high-rise buildings. Originally planned as three concentric rings of two-storey buildings around a central park, Connaught Place is a favourite shopping centre for locals and tourists alike. Two decades ago, the whitewashed colonnaded arches still retained the aura of the days of the Raj. Not anymore, however, as sky-rocketing real estate prices have forced out many of the old shops, which are gradually being replaced by modern stores, airline offices and restaurants.

Eight radial roads fan out from Connaught Place. **Janpath** is lined with a profusion of tiny well-stocked shops and pavement stalls selling everything from junk jewellery, shoes and handbags to folk embroidery, brassware and ready-to-wear garments. Many of the clothes are the overflow of India's large garment export trade to Western countries, which Janpath dealers sell at astonishingly low prices. Here also is the **Central Cottage Industries Emporium** which sells representative handicrafts from all over India. Two radial roads west of Janpath is **Baba Kharak Singh Marg,** where each state and union territory has its own emporium selling handicrafts, fabrics and a variety of other goods. **Gurjari**, the Gujarat emporium, maintains a particularly high standard.

In recent years contemporary Indian art has become an important dimension of the cultural scene. The **Centre for Contemporary Arts** in Connaught Place and **Triveni Kala Sangram** and **Lalit Kala Academy,** both off Barakhamba Road, periodically hold exhibitions by Indian painters and sculptors. Triveni also has a small auditorium for regular dance performances.

While art has only just begun to make its way into upper-class homes in Delhi, Indian corporations have been patronizing the arts for years. One of the most accessible collections is in the Welcomgroup Maurya Sheraton Hotel on Sadar Patel Marg. Another gallery is run by CMC Ltd at their corporate office on the Ring Road, opposite Maharani Bagh.

Other museums include the small and well-designed **Natural History Museum** (open 10 am–5 pm, closed Mondays) at the corner of Barakhamba Road and Tansen Marg. The excellent **Crafts Museum** (open 9.30 am– 4.30

pm, closed Sundays) is at the corner of Pragati Maidan (the Exhibition Grounds) opposite the Purana Qila. Every month a different group of artists and craftsmen from various parts of the country come to the museum to demonstrate, display and sell their work.

Lodi and Mughal Delhi

South of the imperial capital are the remains of cities dating back a thousand years. Most of the monuments are located within a short distance of one another.

The largest is the **Purana Qila,** or Old Fort, a remnant of the first Mughal capital to be built in Delhi. The fort is imposing in terms of bulk as well as its slight elevation over the surrounding area. Although the fort dates back a mere 460 years to the reign of Humayun, the second Mughal emperor, the site itself goes back several millenia, when it was referred to as Indraprastha in the Hindu epic the *Mahabharata*.

Humayun's father, Babur, the first Mughal emperor, was more preoccupied with military matters than with building, and although he laid out the first two Mughal gardens in India, it was Humayun who was responsible for the earliest Mughal monuments. Sher Shah Sur, a ruler of Afghan descent, ousted Humayun for a brief period from 1540 and continued, with surprising altruism, to work on the Old Fort.

The fine old mosque and the octagonal **Sher Mandal** are at once the earliest examples of Mughal architecture in India and yet not Mughal at all, because Sher Shah Sur was of a rival dynasty! Both monuments mark the transition from Lodi to Mughal architecture and the mosque bears distinct Hindu influences, a tradition that was to continue as a hallmark of the Muslim emperors of the Mughal dynasty. Across the road from the Old Fort are two other surviving examples of Sher Shah's rule—a gateway of a wall built to enclose his city, and a mosque and religious school. The recently renovated **National Zoological Park** (open 8 am–6 pm in summer, 9 am–5 pm in winter, closed Fridays) is just south of the Purana Qila.

Humayun's Tomb, off the Mathura Road and dating back to the 1560s, is an important landmark in the history of Mughal architecture, for it marks the advent of grand tombs set in gardens designed in the Persian manner. (Paradise is referred to repeatedly in the Koran as a garden with running streams and shade-giving trees.) The massiveness of the structure, the octagonal plan (achieved by chamfering the corners), the dome within a dome, the bold decorative inlay on the external walls, the massive plinth and the cupolas surrounding the central dome were all used 70 years later in the Taj Mahal, for which Humayun's tomb was undoubtedly the prototype.

Further up the road is the sadly dilapidated **tomb of Khan-i-Khanan**, one of the nine 'jewels' of Akbar's court. The mausoleum was stripped of its cladding for use in other buildings and, as a result, suffers by comparison with other better-maintained structures of the same period. It also takes its inspiration from the tomb of Humayun and marks a further step on the way to the Taj Mahal.

The **shrine of St Nizamuddin** is of atmospheric rather than architectural interest. The *dargah*, or shrine, and the crowded village that surrounds it have been in existence since the 14th century. Life in the area continues mostly undisturbed by the modern world.

The shrine to the saint has been rebuilt so often that nothing remains of the original plan. However, the throng of pilgrims who seek favours, the priests and the vendors of everything from religious souvenirs to rose petals are an interesting aspect of Delhi life. The *urs* (death anniversary) celebrations take place in November. Around the shrine is a mosque containing the graves of the poet Amir Khushro and Princess Jahanara, daughter of Shah Jahan. A short detour through winding lanes and covered passages takes you into the tiny mausoleum of Agya Khan, the husband of Emperor Akbar's wet-nurse. Noted for the profusion of low-relief calligraphy and geometric mosaics that cover its surface rather than for the state of its preservation, the tiny tomb is but one of hundreds of fine old monuments in Delhi that suffer from neglect.

Two kilometres (just over a mile) away are the **Lodi Tombs**, preserved in what is now known as **Lodi Gardens**, a complex that dates to the Lodi dynasty (1451–1526) immediately preceding the Mughals. Six structures—five tombs and a mosque—were enclosed in a landscaped garden in 1930 and, like the complex surrounding Humayun's tomb, Lodi Gardens is as much a fine place for an evening stroll as a tourist attraction. The **tomb of Sikandar Lodi** marks the advent of the double dome—an ingenious device whereby the outer dome maintains the proportions of the external façade while the inner one conceals the unnatural proportions of the void inside. The idea was repeated at Humayun's tomb and later at the Taj Mahal.

Opposite the end of Lodi Road is **Safdarjung's tomb,** built in 1753 during the Mughal decline. Just as Humayun's tomb heralds the beginning of a tradition, Safdarjung's tomb marks the end—note its confusing details and lack of vigour. The shape of the dome too, inherited from the Lodi dynasty and perfected during Mughal rule, is too bulbous for the monument beneath it.

Sultanate Delhi

Qutb Minar, near the village of **Mehrauli**, 15 kilometres (nine miles) south of Connaught Place, was built by the first Muslim dynasty to rule India. Consequently, the Qutb Minar complex set the tone for Islamic architecture in Delhi during the next 500 years. The Qutb Minar is something of a landmark in Delhi, being 90 metres (278 feet) high. Made of sandstone, its fluted form narrows at the top, producing the illusion of even greater height. Nearby are the **Quwwat ul Islam (Might of Islam) Mosque** and the entrance gate, the **Alai Darwaza**. The mosque was built on the site of more than 20 Hindu and Jain temples, columns from which were used in the construction of the mosque. This mélange of Islamic spatial relationships and heavily carved Hindu pillars makes its appearance in later years throughout India, notably in Gujarat where it is a chief characteristic of mosque architecture. Calligraphic inscriptions and decorative carving cover the surface of the mosque and the entrance gate.

A later sultan of the same dynasty, Alauddin Khalji (1296–1316), planned to build another tower higher than the Qutb Minar. However, it never came to be and its unfinished base still stands a few metres away. In fine weather, the complex and the surrounding tombs and mosques make a splendid place for a morning's exploring. Eight kilometres (five miles) east of the Qutb Minar is the 14th-century city of **Tughlaqabad,** now colonized by troops of monkeys.

Hauz Khas, nine kilometres (five miles) south of Connaught Place, is an upmarket residential community with a wealth of Sultanate monuments. The most imposing of these is the **Madrassa**, or religious school, an L-shaped building dating from 1352. On the same grounds is the **tomb of Feroz Shah**, a sultan of the Tughluq dynasty.

Just outside the walls is an old village, complete with cow sheds and ruminating buffaloes. **Hauz Khas Village** has become Delhi's most fashionable shopping centre. A few years ago the village was a bucolic little enclave, surrounded by a lush green deer park. A few enterprising businesswomen opened up boutiques here, and before long, more than 50 shops and restaurants had jumped on the bandwagon. Most of the shops are owned by young women from the upper strata of Delhi society. What gives the market its piquancy is the way classy shops are juxtaposed with village dwellings, narrow lanes and covered alleys. It is all available here: designer labels, pink ginger ale, chocolate brownies, courses in aerobics. Closed on Sundays, Hauz Khas Village Market is open from 10 am to 7 pm.

Old Delhi

From the year 1526, which marked the downfall of the Sultanate dynasties and the advent of the first Mughal, Babur, Agra rather than Delhi served as the capital city. But in 1638 Shah Jahan moved the capital back to Delhi, probably to enjoy the distinction of building a city quite separate from his forebears.

Jami Masjid and Red Fort are the most important buildings of the original **Shajahanabad**, now simply called Old Delhi. Jami Masjid, the Friday mosque, is the largest in the city. Located on a high outcrop of rock, its domes and minarets are easily visible above the surrounding cluster of rooftops for many kilometres around.

The **Jami Masjid** can be visited at any time of the day except during prayer sessions. Quite apart from the architecture, the Friday Mosque is interesting for the life within and around it. The labyrinthian paths through the crowded bazaars are more a place for the sightseer than the would-be shopper. Prize pigeons, aluminium trays, religious souvenirs, live poultry—Shajahanabad may not be what it was 350 years ago, but in its congested lanes life goes on supremely unaware of the rest of Delhi.

Across the road are the solid ramparts of the **Red Fort**, named after the red sandstone of which it is built. Within the walls are the halls of public audience and private audience, a mosque, royal apartments and women's quarters, all indispensable to a Mughal monarch as buildings with similar functions are found in the earlier Agra Fort. Compared to the latter, Delhi's Red Fort has a more unified style—most of the buildings were built during Shah Jahan's reign except for the attractive mosque, Moti Masjid, which was the contribution of his son, Aurangzeb. Every evening after dark there is a sound and light show in the fort gardens.

With the decline of the Mughal empire after Aurangzeb and its final downfall in 1857, an unparalleled era came to an end. At midnight on 14 August 1947, the Union Jack was moved from above the Fort's Lahore Gate, and the flag of independent India was raised for the first time. For some families in the walled city around Jami Masjid, the Mughal empire hasn't quite ended—they trace their descent back to Bahadur Shah Zafar, the last Mughal, and whereas they are now no more than private citizens, a sense of 'it might have been' lives on.

Nearby **Chandni Chowk** leads away from the Red Fort. A fashionable promenade and shopping centre in Shah Jahan's time, Chandni Chowk is now the busiest area of Delhi, thronging with people and traffic. You can ride through it by cycle rickshaw, a less daunting prospect than walking. Its side streets each specialize in a particular commodity—textbooks in Nai Sarak, silver and gold jewellery in Dariba Kalan, beads and ribbons in Kinari Bazaar. Most of the residences and offices above the shops that line Chandni Chowk date from the early years of this century. When the crumbling moulding and pierced stonework falls to ruins, they will doubtless be replaced by concrete boxes.

Jammu and the Road to Kashmir

Most people rush through Jammu on the way to Srinagar. This is a pity, as the city is worth a visit. Situated on the southern slopes of the Siwaliks, Jammu consists of two towns on opposite banks of the Tawi River. As the winter capital for the state of Jammu and Kashmir and as the state's second-largest town and the gateway to Kashmir, Jammu has grown into a prosperous trading centre.

According to legend, the city was founded by Raja Jambulochan, from whom its name was derived in the ninth century. In 1730 the old city came under the rule of the Dogra chiefs and in the 1830s Zorowar Singh marched from Jammu through Kistwar and Zanskar and then annexed Ladakh. Following the collapse of the Sikh empire, Jammu merged with Kashmir, and in 1846 the Treaty of Amritsar resulted in the Dogra ruler becoming the Maharaja of Kashmir.

Because of recent problems in the Punjab, most tourists get to Jammu by air or overnight train from Delhi (twelve and a half hours) via Pathankot. Buses for Srinagar connect with the train, but it is worth breaking your journey and spending a day in and around Jammu. Although not at a high altitude (300 metres, or 1,127 feet) the old town and the surrounding countryside are hilly. As in most of northern India, the summers are hot and dusty, with temperatures reaching 43°C (110°F) in June.

The station and most of the new government buildings are in the new town south of the river. The old city, with its small bazaars, alleys, remote courtyards and temples, is set above the river. There are three major temple complexes, of which two are worth visiting. The **Raghunath Temple**, built in 1835, stands at the centre of a larger group a few minutes walk from the **Tourist Reception Centre** and the bus-stand. The temple is dedicated to Lord Rama and much of the interior is covered in gold leaf. The nearby **Rambireswar Temple**, built in 1883, is possibly the largest Shiva temple in northern India. Famous for its large crystal *lingams*, the temple also has a tower 76 metres (246 feet) high.

Every Tuesday and Sunday, people flock to the **Kali Temple** in the **Bahu Fort** above the town (five kilometres, or three miles, by road). Below the fort, the terraced **Bagh-i-Bagh Gardens** offer a fine view of the Tawi River.

Two collections in Jammu are also worth visiting. The **Amar Mahal Palace** was built in 1907 on a small hill overlooking the river. The **museum** (open 8 am–12 noon Sundays, 5–7 pm Tuesday–Saturday) has some excellent examples of Pahari and Kangra painting, together with family memorabilia. In the town, the **Dogra Art Gallery** was established in 1954 in **Gandhi Bhawan** opposite the new Secretariat. The excellent miniature paintings are, unfortunately, poorly presented but worth seeing. Ask to see the reserve collection. The gallery is open 11 am–5 pm in winter, 8 am–1.30 pm in summer. It is closed on Mondays.

Just under two hours away by bus, 48 kilometres (30 miles) north of Jammu, the small village of **Katra** is the start of a 13-kilometre (eight-mile) walk, with tremendous views, to the holy **shrine** of **Vaishno Devi**, dedicated to the Mother

Goddess. The shrine is set deep in a cave. Katra is off the main highway to Srinagar which then passes through the cantonment town of **Udampur** and the small hill stations of **Kud** and **Batote**. After **Ramban** the scenery becomes bleaker until, 200 kilometres (125 miles) from Jammu, the road passes under the **Banihal Pass** (2,975 metres, or 9,763 feet) through the long **Jawahar Tunnel** and emerges dramatically into the lush Vale of Kashmir. Srinagar lies 93 kilometres (57 miles) further on.

Kashmir

The Kashmir region starts near **Banihal**, 17 kilometres (11 miles) before the Jawarhar Tunnel, where the dominant language changes from Dogri to Kashmiri and more of the houses and costumes are in the Kashmiri style. The landscape blossoms north of the pass where the lush fields of the Vale of Kashmir stretch away to the north.

This is certainly one of the most beautiful regions in India, and since the time of the Mughal emperors it has provided a popular escape from the summers of the North Indian plains. The image of houseboats reflected in the waters of Dal Lake against a backdrop of snowcapped mountains is a reality, but this is only part of what Kashmir has to offer. The valley, or vale, is a large oval plain 136 kilometres (85 miles) long and up to 40 kilometres (25 miles) wide, with Srinagar, at 1,593 metres (5,225 feet), at the approximate centre. Although Srinagar is the focal point of any visit to the area, the nearby villages of Gulmarg and Pahalgam have developed into major destinations in their own right. The area has become a national centre for a range of sports of which walking, trekking or climbing, golf and fishing are only a few.

Recent events have given prominence to the aspirations of a minority who seek to reunify the two halves of the old state and be independent of both India and Pakistan. With over 50 percent of the population dependent on the tourism and handicraft industries, one hopes that normalcy will soon return.

Summer is no longer the only season to visit Kashmir. The autumn colours and the saffron harvest near **Pampore** are a wonderful backdrop to a low-altitude trek; from mid-December to early March there is some excellent skiing; in the early summer the trout begin to bite and the snow-fed streams come to life. From June onwards the oppressive heat of the plains makes the cooler days in and around Srinagar even more attractive.

Since the partition of India divided the state and cut the old road via Rawalpindi and Baramulla, the longer route via Jammu is the only practicable land link with the rest of India. (There is also a road linking Himachal Pradesh with Ladakh.) An ever-increasing number of visitors now arrive by air, but for those with time, the longer route by rail and road is certainly more exhilarating.

Originally a vast lake enclosed by the Pir Panjal range of the Himalaya, the valley is now drained by the Jhelum River, which flows northwest out of the valley and then south into the Indus. The fertile soil produces a rich variety of produce, from rice and wheat to saffron, apples and, more recently, hops. Some 2,000 years ago King Ashoka supposedly visited the valley on a pilgrimage. In the 16th century the great Mughal Akbar came and was followed by Jehangir and Shah Jahan, all of whom left their mark in the form of buildings and gardens. In the late 19th century the area assumed its present appearance. Since then tourism has had a major, but not always positive, influence. What Jawaharlal Nehru, whose family was from Kashmir, recalled in 1940 is still true: 'Sometimes the sheer loveliness of it all was overpowering. How can those who have fallen under its spell release themselves from its enchantment?'

Srinagar

Srinagar grew up on the Jhelum River which loops around the town and along the banks of Dal Lake. It is a colourful, crowded city, the hub of which is a fascinating jumble of bazaars selling everything needed for a trek or a stay in the valley. Along the **Bund** are a number of old shops, many with a pre-Independence flavour, as well as the Post Office and some of the major banks. The **Tourist Reception Centre** and **Government Arts Emporium**, in the old British Residency, are at the eastern end of the Bund. The Reception Centre is a useful contact point with an information centre, Indian Airlines and Road Transport offices along with those of the wildlife and fishing departments.

Within the old city are some impressive and distinctive buildings. The wooden **Shah Hamdan Mosque**, with its tall spire, is unfortunately closed to non-Muslims but a good view of it can be had from behind the **Pather Mosque** on the opposite bank of the Jhelum. The large **Jami Masjid,** also wooden, with over 370 pillars each made from a single deodar trunk, is open to all.

On the riverbank opposite the Bund, the **Sri Pratap Singh Museum** (open 10.30 am–4.30 pm, closed Wednesdays) has some interesting sculpture from Martand and the ninth-century Avantisvamin Temple at Avantipur, tiles from the fourth-century Buddhist site at Harwan, and third-century terracotta heads from Ushkur. There are also exhibits from outside the valley: some early bronze Buddhas from what is now northwest Pakistan and Gandhara.

The focal point of most holidays in the valley are the **houseboats** on **Dal** and **Nagin lakes**. Introduced in the last century when non-Kashmiris were forbidden to buy land, the houseboat has become a popular base for long holidays away from the heat of India's plains. The quality varies from the mediocre to the extremely luxurious. Avoid the touts who will offer you a range of prices for accommodation of similar quality. Prices are fixed in five broad categories and the Tourist Reception Centre maintains a list of recognized boats. But you would do well to bargain on your own.

Above Dal Lake rises **Shankaracharya Hill** which offers a commanding view of the city from near the temple on its summit. Beyond the lake, on the other side of the city, is the massive **Hari Parbat Fort**. Built mostly in the 18th century, it is often mistakenly attributed to Akbar's reign. The **Boulevard** skirts

the southern shore of Dal Lake and passes the Oberoi Palace Hotel and the new
Centaur Conference Centre, with its golf course carved out of what was to be a
'City National Park'. Above the road, the **Chashma Shahi Gardens** and the old
Sufi college at **Pari Mahal** have fine views looking west across the lake. The
greatest legacy of the Mughals' fascination with Kashmir is their gardens. Apart
from Chashma Shahi, gardens were built at **Nishat Bagh,** 11 kilometres (seven
miles) from Srinagar, and at **Shalimar Bagh,** four kilometres (two miles) beyond. Both date from the early 17th century and are well maintained. During the
summer there is a *son et lumière* programme at Shalimar Bagh at 9 pm.

A road heading north from Dal Gate passes through the city and leads to
quiet Nagin Lake. Beyond Nagin, overlooking the northern part of the much
larger Dal Lake, is the great **Hazratbal Mosque** which houses a precious relic,
a hair of Muhammad. A little further on are the Clairmont Houseboats, next to a
private garden, and then the oldest Mughal garden at **Nasim Bagh** laid out for
Akbar in 1586. Nasim Bagh is now part of the Engineering College grounds,
eight kilometres (five miles) from Dal Gate.

Out of Srinagar

The hill stations of Pahalgam and Gulmarg make excellent side-trips from Srinagar. **Pahalgam** is 95 kilometres (60 miles) from Srinagar and at 2,130 metres (6,988 feet) in the beautiful **Lidder Valley**. It has well-forested hillsides and snow on the peaks for much of the year. The river that flows through the small town offers good trout fishing. (While tackle is available locally, fishing permits must be obtained from the Fisheries Department at the Tourist Reception Centre in Srinagar.) Pahalgam is a convenient base for treks to the **Kolahoi Glacier**, the **Suru Valley** and **Upper Dachigam**. There are also numerous shorter walks which can serve as 'warm ups' for longer treks. Following the Lidder up-stream towards **Aru** takes a full day, but shorter walks up to the **Baisaram Meadow** give a good view of the valley. Ponies can also be hired locally, although the saddles are not always the most comfortable.

Gulmarg is both higher than Pahalgam and closer to Srinagar. The 52-kilometre (33-mile) journey from Srinagar is an easy one by bus or car. Buses only go as far as **Tangmarg** from where the last seven kilometres (four miles) can be done on foot or by pony. Gulmarg, the 'meadow of flowers', at 2,730 metres (8,956 feet), is a popular ski resort from late December to March. A second ski-lift has recently been installed and with the introduction of helicopters some superb areas have opened up. Gulmarg was originally a summer resort and the walks to **Khilanmarg**, **Alpather** and the **Ferozpore Nullah** are relatively easy. From the northern side of the meadow there are good views of **Nanga Parbat** in Pakistan-occupied Kashmir.

Only 23 kilometres (15 miles) from Srinagar is the entrance to **Dachigam National Park** and the **trout hatchery** at **Harwan**. The park is 140 square kilometres (55 square miles) of grassland, forest and alpine pasture. Originally a small hunting reserve, the park includes the catchment area for Srinagar's water supply. Among the many animals and birds in the park is the only viable population of the Kashmir stag, or hangul. Permits to visit the park must be obtained from the Chief Wildlife Warden in Srinagar.

Prior to the introduction of Islam the valley was, at various times, Hindu and Buddhist. Most of the remains of these eras are now unrecognizable, but the eighth-century **Surya Temple** suggests the scale and former grandeur of these sites. Although the temple is badly damaged it is worth stopping to see it on the way to Pahalgam. Climb up to the plateau where the temple commands a superb view of the valley. The small 12th-century **Shiva temple** at **Pandrethan** just off the Jammu road, five kilometres (three miles) south of Srinagar, has a good example of the Kashmiri style of temple roof.

The Road to Leh and Ladakh

The 434-kilometre (270-mile) drive from Srinagar to Leh takes two days, although the often spectacular flight takes less than 40 minutes. The road journey is preferable for many reasons. The drive passes through an extraordinary range of scenery and crosses three major passes: **Zoji La** at 3,529 metres, **Namika La** at 3,718 metres and **Fatu La** at 4,092 metres (11,578, 12,198 and 13,425 feet respectively). The landscape changes from the fertile green valleys and forested hillsides of Kashmir to the bare hillsides of Central Asia. The two-day drive also allows the body to acclimatize to the change in altitude. This is especially important if you plan to trek from Leh, itself at 3,505 metres (11,500 feet).

The high passes, especially the Zoji La on the Great Himalayan Range, are effective barriers against rain-clouds, and the monsoons fail to penetrate. This is borne out by the closure of the Zoji La between late October and June each year due to snowfall while many of the higher passes east of Kargil remain open.

For those with the time and energy, there are three interesting routes of varying length between Kashmir and Ladakh which can be trekked in 10 to 16 days. Most visitors, however, rely on the regular bus services during the summer with an overnight halt in Kargil. Six-seater jeeps can also be hired in Srinagar.

The road climbs over Zoji La, 110 kilometres (68 miles) from Srinagar, leaving the last of the green valleys behind. The first village, **Dras**, with its distinct population of Shia Muslim Baltis, is in winter one of the coldest inhabited places on earth. The road then drops slightly to the district headquarters of Kargil at 2,650 metres (8,700 feet). Once a trading town on the ancient caravan route, it is a night halt on the road to Ladakh. The cease-fire line with Pakistan is only a couple of kilometres to the north. There are numerous mediocre hotels, but only one good one, Highlands, ten kilometres (six miles) east of the town.

Another jeepable road goes south from Kargil, around the **Nun Kun** massif (7,100 metres, or 23,300 feet), over **Pensi La** (4,400 metres, or 14,520 feet) and enters the Buddhist area of **Zanskar**.

After Kargil there is an invisible divide between the predominantly Muslim and Buddhist areas. The village of **Shargol** has a small **gompa** (monastery) but the town of **Mulbekh** is more often thought of as the gateway to Ladakh. A little beyond Mulbekh a huge **rock carving** of Maitreya, the Buddha of the future, towers over the road. After crossing Namika La and Fatu La the road looks down on the incredible **Lamayuru Gompa** perched on the opposite hillside, with a village at its base. The first monastery was built on this site in the tenth century and part of the central building serves as home to about 30 lamas. After Lamayuru the road joins the Indus Valley at **Khalsi** and follows the river upstream to **Leh**. There are numerous places of interest en route but the 11th-century **Alchi Gompa,** a few kilometres south of **Saspol** (70 kilometres, or 45 miles, west of Leh), is among the most important. The temple wall paintings and frescos are among the most beautiful and best-preserved examples of

Ladakhi Buddhist art. Most of the paintings show stages of the Buddha's life, royal personages, figures of various Bodhisattvas and tantric deities.

The drive to Leh is an exhilarating experience and there is plenty to discover along the way.

Ladakh was an independent western Tibetan kingdom until 1834 when it was taken over by the rulers of Kashmir. It is also one of the few areas where the Tibetan way of life and religion continue to thrive. After Indian independence Ladakh remained closed to visitors until 1974. **Nubra,** to the north of the Karakoram, and the large area east of the Leh–Manali road south of **Upshi** remain closed.

Leh was long an important stopover on the ancient trade routes between Kashgar, Tibet, Kashmir and the Indian plains. Now close to the sensitive borders with China and Pakistan, the caravans have been replaced by military convoys supplying forward units. Leh has one main street with a few stores and numerous alleys running off it. The 16th-century deserted and damaged **palace** on the slopes of **Tesemo Hill** rises above the town. The view south from the roof across the Indus Valley and towards the Zanskar mountains is worth the climb. Some of the palace rooms are open in the early morning. Above the palace an older **gompa** houses a fine image of a seated Buddha (open 7–9 am, 5–7 pm).

There are numerous seasonal hotels and guesthouses in Leh of variable standards (not always linked to price!). It is best to arrive with a confirmed booking and to spend the first day acclimatizing. Ultraviolet rays at high altitudes are deceptively strong and it is advisable to wear a hat in addition to using some form of cream. The Tourist Office (open 8 am–8 pm in summer) will help you find accommodation.

Leh is the most convenient place from which to explore the many interesting gompas along the Upper Indus Valley. Most of the monasteries are linked by bus, and jeeps can be hired. Many gompas now charge an entrance fee and the lama guides also expect a tip, which supposedly goes towards the upkeep of the gompa.

The gompa closest to Leh is a pleasant walk from the town centre. The **Sankar Gompa** with its multi-armed **Buddha of Compassion** is only open in the early morning and evening. Near the end of the Leh airport runway and on a small hill is the **Spitok Gompa** (eight kilometres, or five miles, from the town). There are excellent views along the Indus from the hillock on which a thousand-year-old **Gonkhang Temple** and other buildings are located. The main hall is richly decorated with hanging *tankas* (Tibetan religious paintings on cloth) and statues.

Following the Indus upstream from Leh, the road passes the **Tibetan refugee centr**e at **Choglamsar** (eight kilometres, or five miles, from Leh). The camp has developed into a major centre for the study of Tibetan literature, history and philosophy. In addition to the schools, the camp runs a handicraft

quicker and there are also flights from Delhi, Chandigarh and Shimla to **Bhuntar,** ten kilometres (six miles) south of Kulu. One of the interesting stops en route is the old hill-state capital of **Mandi.** In February and March the whole town is decked out for the **Shivaratri festival** (the wedding of Shiva and Parvati). Passing Mandi, the road winds through the Mandi–Largi gorge to the beginning of the **Beas Valley.** Never more than several kilometres wide, the valley stretches north for about 80 kilometres (50 miles). The industrious people who work the fertile terraced land are devout and friendly and, undoubtedly, one reason why the area is so attractive. The men wear the distinctive Himachal cap, while the often beautiful women wrap themselves in layers of homespun wool, secured with silver pins and jewellery. Kulu, at 1,200 metres (3,900 feet) is one of the most enjoyable Himalayan towns; Manali is even more attractive!

Perched above the Beas, Kulu gets crowded during the **Dussehra festival** in October. The statue of the presiding deity, Raghunathji, is brought down into the valley from the **Raghunathpura Temple** above **Dhalpur** and joins a procession with almost 200 other deities. Carried in palanquins and accompanied by drums and trumpets, the gods are escorted by the villagers to the grassy *maidan* (open grounds) beside the river south of the town. The Raghunathpura Temple is a five-minute walk from the town. The path there continues up the hill past some small family workshops where the embroidered Kulu shawls are produced on wooden hand-looms. About 40 minutes away from the temple, the trail reaches a ridge. The views are worth the climb, and another 45 minutes of climbing leads to the small **Vaishno Devi Temple.**

Each village in the valley worships its own deity. These are taken out and carried about during festivals other than Dussehra, and village families can even take them to their homes on special occasions. The dominating influence of the deities on the villagers' lives has given the area the name 'valley of gods'.

A road leads to the hot springs of **Manikaran**, 45 kilometres (28 miles) into the Parvati Valley to the northeast of Bhuntar. As with most of the Kulu area the **Parvati Valley** is full of bountiful orchards producing many varieties of apples and pears.

The 42-kilometre (26-mile) drive from Kulu to Manali passes lush fields, productive orchards and villages, each with an interesting wooden or stone temple. The main road follows the west bank of the Beas, while a rougher road runs along the opposite bank. Halfway along the main road at **Katrain**, the valley widens slightly. There is a **trout hatchery** nearby for restocking the river. (Fishing permits are obtainable from the Tourist Offices in Kulu and Manali.) On the eastern bank, high above the river, is the attractive village of **Naggar**, at one time the capital of the valley kingdom before Sultanpur, as Kulu was then known, became the raja's capital. The misnamed **Naggar Castle** is now a well-run Himachal Tourism guesthouse and has a commanding view of the valley. The Russian *émigré* artist Nicholas Roerich, who died in 1947, made

Naggar his home for many years, and his house above the 'castle' is now a private museum. Near the fort are some interesting stone **temples**.

Twelve kilometres (eight miles) north of Naggar, the village of **Jagatsukh** was an even earlier capital for the Kulu rajas.

Beautifully situated at 1,800 metres (5,900 feet), near the head of the valley and surrounded by mountains, the small town and older village of **Manali** is the focal point for most visitors to the valley. The houses of **Old Manali** are mostly made of timber, stone and mud. The new town has grown up downstream from the old village, where most of the activity takes place and where the **Tourist Office** and the bus station are located.

The year starts with the skiing season in January and February. The facilities in nearby **Solang Nulah**, 13 kilometres (eight miles), are limited, but a chair-lift gives access to some higher slopes. Cross-country routes are being developed, and skiing above the **Rohtang Pass** is possible as late as May. In spring the snows begin to melt, turning the streams into small torrents, and the area is at its most colourful. The summer months of May and June are the most popular, but July to September are best for high-altitude treks over the Rohtang Pass and on to Lahaul, Zanskar and Ladakh. The post-monsoon days of October and November are clear and allow wonderful views from the higher ridges.

Whether staying at Kulu or Manali, the area is best explored on foot. The immediate surroundings of Manali offer many short walks. The wooden **Dhoongri Temple** with its four-tiered pagoda roof is concealed in the deodar wood a couple of kilometres away. The temple's goddess, Hadimba Devi, plays an important part in the Kulu Dussehra festival. A local festival takes place each May. A three-kilometre (two-mile) walk north from the village on the opposite bank leads to the hot sulphur springs at the picturesque village of **Vashisht**.

Beyond Manali the road crosses the Rohtang Pass (51 kilometres, or 32 miles) at 3,915 metres (12,845 feet) into the barren region of **Lahaul.** The pass acts as a barrier to the monsoon and the area is similar to the Ladakh region further north. The main town is **Keylong,** 117 kilometres (73 miles) from Manali. It is now possible to travel all the way to Leh by bus, a further 360 kilometres (225 miles) away, with permission obtained locally.

Kalka, Shimla (Simla) and Chail

The small town of Kalka nestling at the foot of the Shivaliks, 14 kilometres (nine miles) from Chandigarh, is the gateway to the eastern part of Himachal Pradesh. A narrow-gauge railway was completed in 1904 between Kalka and Shimla. Although the railway takes four and a half hours compared with two and a half hours by road, the railway trip has a relaxed charm all its own. The track follows the old *tonga* (horse-drawn cart) road for 96 kilometres (60 miles) and passes through 103 tunnels. There are three daily trains each way between Kalka and Shimla, two of which connect with trains from Delhi. Flights are available from Delhi and Chandigarh.

The road criss-crosses the railway track for much of the way. At **Dharmpur** (33 kilometres, or 21 miles, from Kalka) there is a turning to the small hill station and cantonment of **Kasauli,** 15 kilometres (nine miles) away at an altitude of 2,000 metres (6,400 feet). On a neighbouring ridge, a few kilometres to the north, is one of India's foremost schools, the **Lawrence School** at **Sanawar** where Kipling sent his hero, Kim, to be educated.

Stretching 12 kilometres (seven miles) along a ridge at 2,213 metres (7,260 feet), Shimla has grown into a large, prosperous town from its earlier beginnings as Simla, the summer capital of the British Raj. It is now the capital of Himachal Pradesh, the hill state created in 1966. Although it was the temporary capital of the Punjab while Chandigarh was being built, Shimla declined during the 1950s but bounced back as a state capital and major holiday destination in the 1970s.

In 1819, a small village was 'discovered' during the Gurkha Wars and in 1822 Major Kennedy built the first permanent house there. In 1832, the governor-general, Lord William Bentinck, spent the summer in Simla. The town quickly developed as a retreat, becoming in 1864 the summer headquarters of the government of India. The summer arrival of officials has ended, but Shimla remains one of India's most popular summer resorts. While much has undoubtedly changed and the town is far more crowded, much of the old charm remains.

Like most hill stations, the town sprawls along ridges at many levels, connected by steep lanes and steps. The **Mall** is now swamped by advertisements for every conceivable consumer item and the shops that stock them, but **Christ Church** still dominates. Shimla is still a mix of late Victorian Gothic

architecture and later mock-Tudor. Cottages with 'English' gardens and some splendid houses set in the deodar and pine forests can still be seen. During the summer, the bazaar thrives with both old and new stores vying for business.

The social focal point remains the Mall, where vehicles are prohibited. The post office, banks, shops and Gaiety Theatre are all here. Numerous side paths lead down to the colourful local **bazaar** on the southern slopes. The ridge leading down from Christ Church joins the Mall at **Scandal Point.** The Mall leads west past the old **Secretariat**, the turning down to the railway station, the Cecil Hotel, and the **State Museum** (open 10 am–5 pm, closed Mondays) with its small collection of Pahari miniatures and Himachal sculpture. It ends at Observatory Hill, with the old Viceregal Lodge. This huge Victorian pile, built by Lord Dufferin in 1888, is now the Indian Institute of Advanced Study. East from Scandal Point, the Mall passes Hotel Oberoi Clarkes, the best in town, and leads towards Chota Shimla. In this quieter part of town are the present state government secretariat and the governor's residence, formerly known as Barnes Court. A road from the ridge heads north below **Jakhu Hill**, through **Lakkhar Bazaar** and winds around **Elysium Hill** where **Chapslee**, one of Shimla's oldest-surviving houses, is now a family hotel. Part of the road passes through the short **Sanjauli Tunnel** and leads out of the town and up to **Wildflower Hall** (13 kilometres, or eight miles) at 2,593 metres (8,507 feet), once the summer home of Lord Kitchener and now a resort run by Himachal Tourism.

During the crowded 'season', walks out of town are an important recreation. **Jakhu Hill** above Christ Church at 2,445 metres (8,021 feet) gives the best view of the town and suggests which direction to follow. Other walks, to the **Glen Forest** (four kilometres, or 2.5 miles) beyond **Annandale**, reached by a path from near the Cecil Hotel, and to **Prospect Hill** and **Summer Hill** (five kilometres, or three miles) are easy distances away. Shimla is best from April to October although the 'crush' takes place during May and June.

The small village of **Chail**, 45 kilometres (28 miles) from Shimla, became the summer residence of Patiala state when the maharaja had a row with British officialdom. The village is still quiet and what it lacks in amenities is made up for by the idyllic surroundings. The old Rajgarh is now the **Chail Palace Hotel** run by Himachal Tourism. In the deodar and pine woods around the hotel are a variety of walks. Permission is needed from the local range officer to walk through the silver oak forest of the newly created **Chail Sanctuary**. Apart from the abundant birdlife, Chail's great pride is the highest **cricket pitch** in the world.

Chail is also accessible from the Kalka–Shimla road. Beyond **Solan**, at the small village of **Khandaghat**, a side road dips and then climbs to Chail, 84 kilometres (52 miles) from Kalka.

Chandigarh

At the time of partition, Punjab lost its great capital, Lahore, to Pakistan. Amritsar was considered too close to the new border with Pakistan so the old summer capital of the Raj at Shimla (Simla) became the temporary seat of the Punjab government. After a few makeshift years in Shimla, a new site was chosen between two small rivers that flow out of the Siwalik Hills.

Chandigarh, 240 kilometres (150 miles) east of Amritsar and 48 kilometres (30 miles) north of Ambala, is modern India's great experiment in town planning, but it is in many ways an artificial city. Designed in the early 1950s by the Swiss architect Le Corbusier, assisted by Max Fry, it lacks the smells and the hustle and bustle of other Indian towns. While the buildings and city centre seem oddly un-Indian, the well laid-out residential areas make the city extremely pleasant to live in.

The city is divided into 47 (to commemorate 1947) numbered but unequal sectors bisected by broad roads. The **Tourist Office**, Indian Airlines and the bus station are all in the central Sector 17. Although the railway station is some way from the town, Chandigarh is now connected to New Delhi by the super-fast *Shatabdi Express*, which completes the 245-kilometre (153-mile) journey in about four hours.

The main government buildings are in Sector 1. Nearby is a large park with its centrepiece **Sukkna Lake,** which attracts a large number of migratory birds in winter. South of the park is the bizarre fantasy of which Chandigarh residents are so proud, the **Rock Garden**. The **Museum and Art Gallery** (open 10 am– 4 pm, closed Mondays), in Sector 10, has a small but good collection of Gandhara sculpture and a representative collection of Pahari miniatures, many from the schools of the Kangra Valley and Chamba area to the northwest. There is also a small **Museum of Fine Arts** (open 10 am–1 pm, closed Mondays) at Punjab University.

Pinjore

Twenty kilometres (13 miles) north of Chandigarh, on the road to Kalka, are the late-Mughal **gardens** at Pinjore. The gardens are a popular spot but can be crowded at weekends.

Amritsar

Punjab, the land of five rivers, is a largely flat, prosperous agricultural area subject to the extremes of scorching summers and near-freezing winters. Now a land divided by partition, its spiritual centre is only minutes away from the Pakistan border. The Punjabis are a hard-working people who, during the 'green revolution' of the 1960s, turned their state into the granary of India. The rural areas are by far the most prosperous in the country. The Punjabi Hindus, many of whom crossed the new border from West Punjab at the time of partition, together with the Sikhs have made a contribution to the economic development of the country far in excess of their numbers.

Amritsar was founded by Guru Ram Das, the fourth of the ten Sikh gurus, in 1577. Now a prosperous city that has thrived on wealth generated by the 'green revolution', the old city is bounded along the north by the main railway line, while to the south a circular road follows the old city walls. Of the 18 **gates,** only the one opposite the **Ram Bagh Gardens** in the north is original. A small palace built by Maharaja Ranjit Singh in the gardens is now a **museum** (closed Wednesdays) with weapons from the 16th to the 19th century and portraits from the former Sikh princely states.

The focal point of the old city is the **Golden Temple**, first built by the fifth guru, Arjan, to house the *Granth Sahib* (the holy book of the Sikhs). The temple stands in the centre of a large man-made tank, the 'pool of nectar' from which the city takes its name, and is reached by a causeway. In 1802, Ranjit Singh rebuilt the temple, using a reputed 400 kilograms of gold to gild the dome of the **Harimandir Sahib**, hence the name 'Golden Temple'. The **Akal Takht** and some of the surrounding buildings were damaged in 1984 during the eviction of terrorists by the army, but much has now been rebuilt. At present, the area around the temple complex is extremely congested but there are plans to clear it and create a perimeter garden.

The Golden Temple is one of the most impressive and, despite the recent political problems, most tranquil places in India. A visit to the temple with one's head covered, walking barefoot around the outer courtyard with Sikh and Hindu pilgrims from all over India, then along the causeway to the temple itself, is a memorable experience.

Other places of interest are within easy walking distance of the Golden Temple. A 15-minute walk to the northwest is the 16th-century Hindu **Dur-giana Temple**. Five minutes' walk to the east of the Golden Temple is **Jalli-anwala Bagh** where, on 13 April 1919, the British General R Dyer ordered his troops to fire on an unarmed crowd, resulting in 300 dead and 2,000 wounded. This incident was a turning point in India's struggle for independence and the area is now a memorial.

To the west of the old city, the **Govindgarh Fort** was built by Ranjit Singh in 1805–9 incorporating designs by French officers in his army.

To the north of the railway line is modern Amritsar with the cantonment, well laid-out residential areas and government buildings. The **Tourist Office** is opposite the railway station and the main bus station is one and a half kilometres (one mile) to the east along the Delhi road. In recent years Amritsar and parts of the Punjab have been closed to foreign visitors without permits. The nearest Indian mission can provide up-to-date information on which areas are open.

Dehra Dun and Mussoorie

Garhwal

A five-hour drive north of Delhi, or a comfortable but circuitous overnight train journey, Dehra Dun is the gateway to the pilgrimage sites in the Garhwal Himalayas and the hill station of Mussoorie.

The northern part of Uttar Pradesh is distinct from the rest of the state. It is an area of forests, hill stations, important pilgrimage centres and some of the world's highest peaks. Along the foothills of the Himalayas, and stretching east along the Nepal border, are the great tiger reserves of **Corbett** and **Dudhwa national parks** and other lesser-known sanctuaries. The hill stations of **Naini-tal, Mussoorie, Ranikhet** and **Almora** are only a few of the resort towns the fortunate escape to during the hot summer months. The important temples at **Badrinath** and **Joshimath** are now linked by road with the plains, but there are still numerous little-known treks to be explored which follow pilgrimage routes or animal trails. Towards the Chinese border are the great peaks of **Nanda Devi, Karmet, Trisul** and Dehra Dun and Mussoorie.

Situated in a large valley, or *doon*, between the Siwaliks to the south and the higher ranges of the Himalayas to the north, **Dehra Dun** has grown from a sleepy cantonment town to a thriving district centre. Although the town is home to the **Forest Research Institute**, the **Wildlife Institute of India**, the **Indian Military Academy**, the **Survey of India Office** and numerous prestigious schools, Dehra Dun is in itself of little interest. It is, however, an important railhead with direct connections with Delhi, Lucknow and Calcutta. The bus-stand is nearby, with direct connections to Mussoorie, Hardwar and Rishikesh.

The valley is steeped in legend and much of it remains very attractive. Local interest groups have successfully prevented limestone quarrying and the opening of cement factories in the area. Mussoorie is only 35 kilometres (19 miles) north of Dehra Dun. Winding past a series of **ashrams** (religious retreats) and bypassing the village of Rajpur, the road climbs over 1,300 metres (4,300 feet). It takes a car almost an hour to negotiate it.

Situated on a horseshoe-shaped ridge of the outer range of the Himalayas, Mussoorie is the closest hill station to Delhi and, as such, is subject to a huge influx of visitors in May, June and July. It is best visited in the off season when the **Mall** between the **Library** and the **Picture Palace** is relatively uncongested. East of the Picture Palace, the road winds up a further 300 metres (1,000 feet) through **Landour Bazaar**, perched on a narrow ridge, to the quietest part of town. Originally established in the 1830s as a military convalescent area, there are many attractive houses and cottages, some of which accept paying guests. West of the Library end of the mall, a road winds around **Vincent Hill** while another goes northwest towards **Kempty Falls** (15 kilometres, or nine miles) and on to Chakrata. The forested hillsides between Kempty Falls and the gorge

where the Jamuna cuts through the Himalayas have recently been declared a **wildlife sanctuary**. The area around Mussoorie is rich in birdlife, but few animals are seen.

Hardwar and Rishikesh

A few kilometres east of Mussoorie and Dehra Dun, the Ganges emerges from the Himalayas and begins her slow progress to the Bay of Bengal. Hardwar, where the river enters the plains, is an important pilgrimage place (222 kilometres, or 140 miles, from Delhi and 52 kilometres, or 32 miles, from Dehra Dun). Every 12th year the annual **Kumbh Mela** takes place here and millions of pilgrims come to bathe in the river. (The next Mela takes place in 1998.) The winding streets through the **bazaars** crowded with stalls selling every conceivable item connected with Hindu worship lead down to the bathing **ghats**. The **Har Ki Pairi Ghat** marks the point where the river leaves the Himalayas. Every evening at sunset the *arti* ritual is performed by priests and the river is blessed. Small *divas*, or lamps, are floated on the water and glide down the river.

Rishikesh, only 24 kilometres (15 miles) up the river, is a more peaceful and in some ways more pleasant town than Hardwar. On the east bank are numerous temples, interesting ashrams and ghats. A ferry operates and a suspension footbridge crosses the river at **Lakshman Jhoola.** Many of the ashrams run residential courses in Hinduism.

Agra

Agra is so conveniently linked to Delhi by road, rail and air that it is common for visitors to set out from Delhi early in the morning, rush around Agra for the day, and return to Delhi the same evening. Unfortunately, such a whistle-stop tour leaves little time to see India's most famous monument, the **Taj Mahal,** in all its glory as the beauty of the Taj changes with the play of sunlight on its surfaces throughout the day.

Built by the fifth emperor of the Mughal dynasty which ruled India from 1526 to 1857, the Taj Mahal is the crystallization of Emperor Shah Jahan's love for his queen, Mumtaz Mahal. Over the centuries, the Taj has attracted more visitors than perhaps any other monument in the country, and it is all too easy to resort to conventional superlatives when describing it. What makes the Taj unique is its perfect proportions, distinct femininity, medium of construction and ornamentation.

Its marble exterior reflects rose and golden tints at sunrise and sunset, while it is dazzling white during the day and glows pearl-like in the moonlight and during the monsoon. Standing on a high plinth, the Taj Mahal is visible for miles around and forms a backdrop to mustard fields and mud-walled villages. It can be seen from guestrooms at some of Agra's hotels, as well as from the land-scaped gardens to the west of the complex.

It is common today to view the pristine white marble structure in isolation, but this is to do an injustice to the vision of the anonymous builder. The north, east and west entrance gates, the main gateway, surrounding walls, mosque, rest house and gardens comprise an integral architectural plan, of which the mauso-leum is the climax.

Mughal architecture relied heavily on red sandstone, as can be seen in the surrounding structures. Their outlines suggest imperial grandeur and contrast with the feminine contours of the Taj Mahal itself. What links them together is the marble inlay, found on the spandrels of all the arches in the complex. Inside the mausoleum, Mumtaz Mahal's grave at the centre of the chamber and Shah Jahan's grave to the west are profusely decorated with inlaid flowers composed of an astonishing variety of semi-precious stones. If the unspoken theme of the Taj Mahal is an earthly paradise, these *pietra dura* flowers serve to heighten the illusion. Every flower has been executed with as many as 60 precisely cut stones. Running along the outline of the major arches on the exterior of the Taj Mahal and the entrance are verses from the Koran in highly stylized calligraphy. In these inscriptions, designed by the Persian Amanat Khan, all the characters have been rendered to appear identical in size by gradually increasing their size from bottom to top.

It is impossible to visualize the Taj Mahal in any surroundings other than its paradisical garden. Paradise, in Islam, is visualized as a lush garden where running streams flow. When the Mughals brought this concept to India, they elevated it to heights of incomparable artistry.

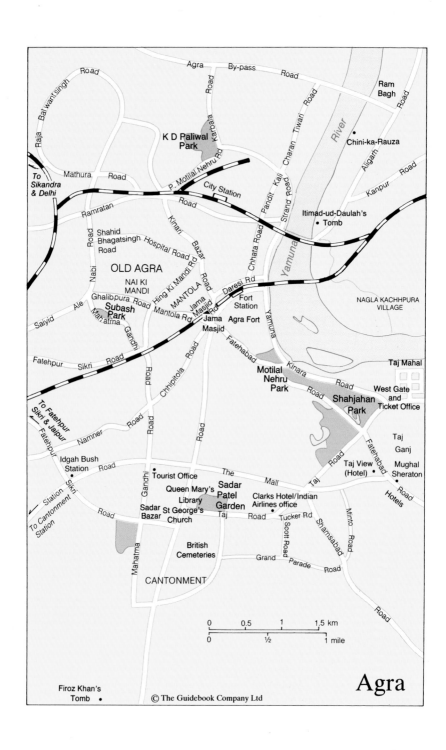

Agra's Other Attractions

The first Mughal emperor, Babur, moved the imperial capital to Agra in the 16th century and today the city is an unpretentious town in Uttar Pradesh with more than its fair share of stupendous Mughal monuments. There are crowded, dusty **bazaars** just outside the Taj Mahal, and some of India's finest hotels open on to streets filled with roadside eateries and vegetable vendors.

Most of Agra's other monuments receive only a dismal trickle of visitors. The best known of these is **Agra Fort**, two kilometres (1.5 miles) west of the Taj Mahal on the banks of the River Yamuna. Built by the third Mughal emperor, Akbar, and added to by his son Jehangir and grandson Shah Jahan, it is an imposing structure with walls of red sandstone almost three kilometres (two miles) long. Entered through the **Amar Singh Gate**, the eastern part of the fort (the only part open to visitors) contains palaces, audience halls and mosques built by all three emperors. The fort presents a good sampling of their favoured architectural styles. Akbar drew on Islamic and Hindu traditions and the result is eclectic. By Shah Jahan's time, the style had become so homogenized that it is impossible to separate the Hindu and Muslim strands. The **Diwan-i-Am** (public audience hall) once housed the fabled Peacock Throne which incorporated virtually all the important gems of the imperial treasury. The beautiful **Diwan-i-Khas** (private audience hall) and the magnificent **Moti Masjid** (Pearl Mosque) were also added by Shah Jahan.

Crossing the River Yamuna by the road and rail bridge and then turning right through the village of **Nagla Kachhpura**, you can get a quiet and uncrowded view of the Taj. Turning left after crossing the river leads to the Aligarh road and three of Agra's least-visited monuments.

The **tomb of Itimad-ud-Daulah** was commissioned by his daughter, the empress Nur Jahan. Like all other Mughal mausoleums, the tomb stands in the centre of a garden and is the first Mughal building constructed entirely of marble. It is lavishly decorated with *pietra dura* inlay work, using mainly jasper with its mottled texture. Because of the medium of its construction and the use of inlay as the chief form of decoration, it is often called the mini-Taj Mahal, but there the resemblance ends, for the tomb of Itimad-ud-Daulah lacks refinement of proportion. It is not without charm, however, and has been accurately likened to a jewel box.

Chini ka Rauza is the only building in India to be decorated exclusively with glazed tile work. The tiny mausoleum overlooking the River Yamuna was the tomb of Afzal Khan, a minister in the court of Shah Jahan. Poor maintenance has resulted in the disintegration of many of the tiles, but enough stylized flowering plants in vivid shades of cobalt blue, yellow and green remain to suggest its original appearance.

Further to the north, just after the Agra bypass turning, is Babur's **Aram Bagh**, sometimes called Rambagh. As one of the first two gardens to be laid out by Babur, it is the earliest prototype of what has come to be known as a Mughal garden. Sprawling along the banks of the River Yamuna, it was Babur's attempt to recreate in Agra some of the lushness of his native Ferghana (in Central Asia). The garden is a skeleton, but the important elements—terraces of varying heights, watercourses and pavilions—are all present. Surrounding the garden on the banks of the river are fragments of the Agra we shall never know: domed cupolas and walls of mansions, reminders of the age of Agra's greatness when nobles vied with one another to build ever more splendid residences on the banks of the river.

The descendants of the craftsmen who worked on the Taj Mahal and the tomb of Itimad-ud-Daulah still practise *pietra dura* marble inlay on table tops, boxes and plaques. The stones used are normally semi-precious (cornelian, jade, mother of pearl, lapis lazuli and malachite) and the motifs are invariably floral. Much skill and labour are involved in producing high-quality and expensive pieces. Agra abounds in showrooms selling inlay work. The more reliable shops will arrange to have bulky items air-freighted home.

Sikandra

Often dismissed as the most curious hybrid of all Mughal buildings, **Akbar's Mausoleum** at Sikandra, ten kilometres (six miles) north of Agra, warrants a visit as the structure befits the emperor's personality as completely as the Taj Mahal does Mumtaz Mahal's. The tomb at Sikandra reflects Akbar's tolerance of all religions, as Rajput, Islamic and Buddhist influences are clearly visible— as disparate elements, however—on the exterior of the building which is a blend of red sandstone and white marble set in an enormous four-part garden where black buck roam. The slender white minarets atop the entrance gateway blend poorly with the other architectural elements but served as an inspiration for the design of the dome of the Taj Mahal.

Fatehpur Sikri

A pleasant 40-kilometre (25-mile) drive west of Agra through open fields takes you to the architectural enigma of the Mughal empire: the ghost city of Fatehpur Sikri.

Fatehpur Sikri is usually given two and a half hours on a whistle-stop tour of Agra, sandwiched in on the trip between Jaipur and Agra. For sheer royal splendour, space and silence, Fatehpur Sikri is worth a full day's outing with a picnic lunch, or even an overnight stop at the government-run tourist complex, the only available accommodation.

Why Fatehpur Sikri was chosen to be a capital of Akbar's Mughal empire and why it was abandoned has never been satisfactorily explained. We do know that Emperor Akbar was troubled by the lack of an heir and consulted Shaikh Salim Chisti, a Sufi saint, who lived at Sikri. When the saint foretold the birth of no fewer than three sons, the emperor transferred two of his pregnant wives to

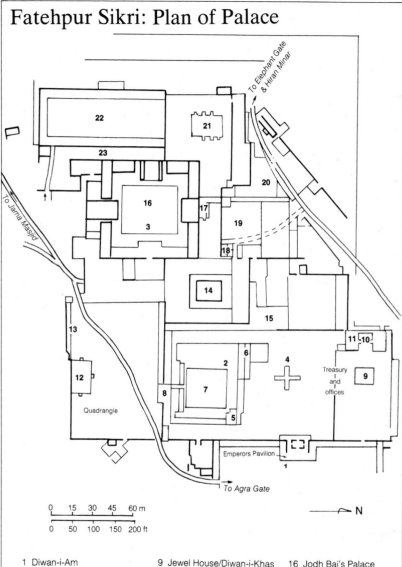

Fatehpur Sikri: Plan of Palace

22

21

23

16

3

17

19

20

14

15

13

12

Quadrangle

11 10

6

2

4

Treasury
and
offices

9

8

7

5

Emperors Pavilion

1

To Elephant Gate & Hiran Minar

To Jama Masjid

To Agra Gate

```
0    15   30   45   60 m
0    50   100  150  200 ft
```

N

1 Diwan-i-Am
2 Daulat Khana
3 Imperial harem
4 Pachisi Court
5 Turkish Sultana's House
6 Abdar Khana
7 Anup Talao
8 Diwan-i-Khas
9 Jewel House/Diwan-i-Khas
10 Ankh Michauli
11 Treasury Kiosk
12 Daftar Khana
13 Maktab Khana
14 Sunahra Makan/Maryam's
   House
15 Panch Mahal/Badgir
16 Jodh Bai's Palace
17 Hawa Mahal
18 Hamam
19 Ladies' Garden
20 Nagina Masjid
21 Birbal's House
22 Minor harem quarters
23 Tosha Khana

Sikri to benefit from the saint's benign influence. As a token of gratitude for his first two sons, the emperor built a mosque and a palace in what was then a mere village.

Soon enough, nobles of the court began constructing residences nearby, and in 1573, after the emperor's conquest of Gujarat, the name Sikri was prefixed by Fatehpur, meaning 'City of Victory'. By this time, the city had been enclosed with a wall, suggesting some degree of permanence. Fourteen years later, Fatehpur Sikri's heyday was over and it has never been occupied since. Why this was so will never be known. The reason most often given—a lack of water—is clearly untenable, for this would suggest that Emperor Akbar's engineers and planners were thoroughly incompetent. It has been suggested that the capital was moved from Fatehpur Sikri to Lahore, strategically located for launching campaigns in the northwest. But this fails to explain why Agra was made the capital when the court moved back from Lahore in 1598.

We have to accept Fatehpur Sikri for what it was: an emperor's whimsy. Inhabited for only 14 years, the ruins of the city are more of a showpiece than a habitation.

In the 19th century Fatehpur Sikri attracted many European visitors who were eager to know how the buildings were used. Local guides, more enthusiastic than informed, invented a series of ingenious explanations. Even the present categorization of the various functions of each building is inspired guesswork rather than documented fact. Thus **Ankh Michauli**, a fine hall near the **Diwan-i-Khas,** was said to have been used for playing blind man's buff (!), whereas it is now believed to have been one of three treasury buildings. The Diwan-i-Khas, which from the outside appears to have two storeys, has only one and a central column with ornate supporting brackets. It remains a mystery how the emperor could have used it as a private audience hall, because if he stood at the place of honour—atop the column—he would have had to turn his back to half his audience, and the other half would have been invisible!

The **Panch Mahal**, so named because of its five storeys, appears open to the elements, but at the time it was built, pierced stonework formed walls behind which the ladies of the royal harem could observe what was taking place in the courtyard below without being observed.

Only one of Akbar's wives, Maryam, had her own palace, the **Sunehra Makan** (golden house), with its vivid wall murals. The other principal wives shared another palace known as **Jodha Bai's Palace**. The neighbouring **Birbal's Palace** provided additional housing for the harem.

South of the palace buildings is the fine **mosque**. The massive doorway, the **Badshahi Darwaza**, which is visible for miles, leads into the huge mosque which surrounds a vast courtyard. Within the courtyard is the small, white marble mausoleum of Sheikh Salim Chisti. Pilgrims of all faiths come to tie strings to the *jali* (pierced stone) work and pray for a child.

Emperor Akbar was concerned with spiritual and religious matters and it was here, in Fatehpur Sikri, that he held his famous discourses with representatives of many faiths. Thus it is only fitting that the architecture of Fatehpur Sikri should be a blend of disparate styles. Hindu and Muslim details occur elsewhere in Mughal and pre-Mughal architecture as part of a unified whole. In Fatehpur Sikri, the two are juxtaposed in a distinct manner not repeated elsewhere.

Lucknow

Straddling both banks of the Gomti River, a tributary of the Ganges, Lucknow is the capital of India's most populous state, Uttar Pradesh. Neglected by most tourists, Lucknow is certainly worth a visit. Modern Lucknow is largely the creation of the nawabs of Oudh and parts of the city still retain an 18th-century flavour. The nawabs were the descendants of the Persian merchant adventurer, Saadat Khan, who was rewarded for his services to the Mughal court with the governorship of the province in 1732. His successor, Safdar Jung, ruled from Delhi and is buried there. The fourth of the ten nawabs, Asaf-ud-Daula, moved the court to Lucknow and turned the city into a centre of Urdu poetry, courtly diction, music and dance. At the beginning of the 19th century, under Ali Khan, the court blossomed. The continued emphasis on the building of palaces and mosques, the pursuit of pleasure in the harem, and the largely incompetent rule led to the province being annexed by the British in 1856. The cult of the sophisticated courtesan was a legendary part of the nawabs' life.

The city is still famous for its cultivated manners and refined urbane culture. It remains the home of light-classical North Indian music and the Kathak school of dance. Each February, the two-week **Lucknow festival** continues the traditions of music and dance made famous by the Oudh court.

Lucknow is the principal Shi'ite Muslim centre in India and the city celebrates holidays and festivals more common to Iran than the other, mostly Sunni, Muslim communities.

Although never an industrial centre—**Kanpur**, 79 kilometres (49 miles) to the southwest, is the great factory town of Uttar Pradesh—Lucknow has traditionally produced silver and bidri work (gun-metal inlaid with silver) and traded in copper, brass and cotton. Lucknow is an important rail junction and has excellent connections with most of northern India. The **Charbagh Railway Station** in the south of the city is an impressive sight and a good place to begin a tour of the city. The architecture reflects both Mughal and European influences. The royal emblem of the nawabs, a pair of fish, still decorates many of the buildings.

Unfortunately, many of the buildings in Lucknow are of brick and some have deteriorated badly. In the city centre, the **Aminabad Market** with its narrow alleys, originally run by women for female customers, is now one of the main shopping areas. The more modern **Hazaratganj** area has wider streets and larger shops. The **Tourist Office** is here.

The extraordinary complex of buildings two kilometres (1.5 miles) east of Hazaratganj which now houses **La Martiniere School** was originally known as Costantia. It was built as the country home of a French soldier, Major-General Claude Martin, who made a fortune as a trader. The general died in 1800 before it was completed, but he left sufficient funds to finish the buildings and endow the school. Constantia is a whimsical mixture of styles incorporating gargoyles and other Gothic details with Corinthian columns. The roof is crowned with a strange collection of statues.

The nearby gardens at **Banarsi Bagh** contain the **zoo** and the **State Museum** (open 10 am–4.30 pm, closed Mondays). Established in 1863, the museum contains an important collection of sculpture, mostly from Mathura. The extensive collection of Kushan, Gupta and Mughal coins can be seen by appointment.

The **British Residency**, built in 1800 and made famous during the Great Mutiny, remains in the state of ruin it was left in at the time of its final relief in November 1857, after two sieges lasting 87 and 53 days left more than 2,000 people dead. The broken walls are still pockmarked with cannonball and shot, and the old buildings are surrounded by well-kept lawns and gardens which at the time of the siege were the site of narrow lanes and streets. The small, dusty museum is open from 9 am to 5.30 pm. The ruined **church** and **cemetery,** containing the graves of those who died during the siege, are nearby.

A kilometre or so west of the Residency are the two fascinating Imambaras. In 1784, Asaf-ud-Daula built the **Bara Imambara**. This great vaulted hall (open

6 am–5 pm), reputedly the largest room in the world, is 50 metres (165 feet) long and its 15-metre (50-foot) high roof is unsupported by pillars. The hall, the great mosque and its two supporting minarets were built as part of a famine relief project. Most of the underground passages are now blocked, but an external stairway leads to the labyrinth on the upper floor known as the **Bhulbhulaiya**. In front of the Imambara is an impressive gateway, **Rumi Darwaza**, built in imitation of Istanbul's Sublime Porte. Beyond the gateway, the **Husainabad Imambara** stands in a large quadrangle in front of an inlaid marble tank. The main building (open 6 am–5 pm) contains the silver throne of the nawabs.

Opposite the Husainabad Imambara is the **Baradari** (summer house) built by Ali Shah and now housing a small portrait gallery (open 8 am–5 pm). The **Jami Masjid** to the west of the Imambara is one of the few in India closed to non-Muslims.

Varanasi (Benares) and Sarnath

Every year tens of thousands of pilgrims visit one of the 2,000-odd temples along the banks of the Ganges at Varanasi and bathe in the river. One of the seven sacred Hindu pilgrimage sites in India, Varanasi is also one of the world's oldest cities, where Shiva is said to have made his permanent home since the dawn of creation. Mentioned in both the *Ramayana* and the *Mahabharata*, Varanasi is to many the religious capital of India.

Varanasi takes its name from its location between the Varuna and Asi rivers which join the Ganges as it makes a broad curve north. The Hindus call the city 'Kashi'—the city of light—after the golden luminescence of the temples, ghats and ashrams in the early morning. The name Benares was used by the British, and before them the Mughals called the town Muhammadabad for a short time.

Pilgrims have come here for over 2,500 years. When the Buddha journeyed here from Gaya, 320 kilometres (200 miles) to the east in Bihar, the city was already an established place of learning. While Varanasi preserves the rituals and traditions of Hindu India, certain contrasts make it a difficult place to understand. The Ganges is the river of life, but the ashes of the dead are poured into its waters.

The Muslims came to Lucknow as conquerers, and successive armies destroyed various temples but not the spirit of the place. Europeans, since Ralph Finch first visited in 1584, have tried to understand the city's importance. Mark Twain wrote, 'Benares is older than history, older than tradition, older even than legend, and looks twice as old as all of them put together.' Although the city has always played a dominant role in the lives of Hindus, it only became the seat of a ruling dynasty in the 11th century. The first sackings of the city by Muslims took place in the12th century and because of successive raids and conquests very little of the city predates the 16th century. During three centuries of Muslim rule, the destruction of temples was often followed by the erection of

A Guru and his Disciples

I went to stay with a guru in a holy city. He had a house on the river in which he lived with his disciples. They lived in a nice way: they meditated a lot and went out for boat rides on the river and in the evenings they all sat around in the guru's room and had a good time. There were quite a few foreigners among the disciples, and it was the guru's greatest wish to go abroad and spread his message there and bring back more disciples. When he heard that Henry was a journalist, he became specially interested in me. He talked to me about the importance of introducing the leaven of Indian spirituality into the lump of Western materialism. To achieve this end, his own presence in the West was urgently required, and to ensure the widest dissemination of his message he would also need the full support of the mass media. He said that since we live in the modern age, we must avail ourselves of all its resources. He was very keen for me to bring Henry into the ashram, and when I was vague in my answers—I certainly didn't want Henry here nor would he in the least want to come—he became very pressing and even quite annoyed and kept returning to the subject.

He didn't seem a very spiritual type of person to me. He was a hefty man with big shoulders and a big head. He wore his hair long but his jaw was clean-shaven and stuck out very large and prominent and gave him a powerful look like a bull. All he ever wore was a saffron robe and this left a good part of his body bare so that it could be seen at once how strong his legs and shoulders were. He had huge eyes which he used constantly and apparently to tremendous effect, fixing people with them and penetrating them with a steady beam. He used them on me when he wanted Henry to come, but they never did anything to me. But the other disciples were very strongly affected by them. There was one girl, Jean, who said they were like the sun, so strong that if she tried to look back at them something terrible would happen to her like being blinded or burned up completely.

Jean had made herself everything an Indian guru expects his disciples to be. She was absolutely humble and submissive. She touched the guru's feet when she came into or went out of his presence, she ran eagerly on any errand he sent her on. She said she gloried in being nothing in herself and living only by his will. And she looked like nothing too, sort of drained of everything she might once have been. At home her cheeks were probably pink but now she was quite white, waxen, and her hair too was completely faded and colourless. She always wore a plain white cotton sari and that made her look paler than ever, and thinner too, it seemed to bring out the fact that she had no hips and was utterly flat-chested. But she was happy—at least she said she was—she said she had never known such happiness and hadn't thought it was possible for human beings to feel like that. And when she said that, there was a sort of sparkle in her pale eyes, and at such moments I envied her because she seemed to have found what I was looking for. But at the same time I wondered whether she really had found what she thought she had, or whether it wasn't something else and she was cheating herself, and one day she'd wake up to the fact and then she'd feel terrible.

She was shocked by my attitude to the guru—not touching his feet or anything, and talking back to him as if he was just an ordinary person. Sometimes I thought perhaps there was something wrong with me because everyone else, all the other disciples and people from outside too who came to see him, they all treated him with this great reverence and their faces lit up in his presence as if there really was something special. Only I couldn't see it. But all the same I was quite happy there—not because of him, but because I liked the atmosphere of the place and the way they all lived. Everyone seemed very contented and as if they were living for something high and beautiful. I thought perhaps if I waited and was patient, I'd also come to be like that. I tried to meditate the way they all did, sitting crosslegged in one spot and concentrating on the holy word that had been given to me. I wasn't ever very successful and kept thinking of other things. But there were times when I went up to sit on the roof and looked out over the river, the way it stretched so calm and broad to the opposite bank and the boats going up and down it and the light changing and being reflected back on the water: and then, though I wasn't trying to meditate or come to any higher thoughts, I did feel very peaceful and was glad to be there.

Ruth Prawer Jhabvala, An Experience of India

mosques on the same site. However, during this time the city continued to flourish as a pilgrimage site. A Hindu ruler recovered power in 1738 and the city was ceded to the British in 1775.

Pilgrims visiting Varanasi must take the **Panchakrosh**, a 55-kilometre (36-mile) road that encircles the sacred city. Starting at **Manikarnika Ghat** and moving south to **Asi Ghat,** the road then circles the city in a clockwise direction, ending at **Barna Ghat**. The trip takes five days on foot and a pilgrim is supposed to visit 108 shrines on the way. Following the road around Kashi is equivalent to circumnavigating the world! If five days is too long, one can go straight to the **Panchakroshi Temple** in the heart of the city.

The river dominates the life of the city. Bathing in the river is a daily act for Hindu residents but the first act of a pilgrim. The ghats are long flights of stone steps that lead down to the river. Along a five-kilometre (three-mile) stretch of the west bank stand many temples and shrines. Only a few of the ghats are used for cremation. Both **Manikarnika Ghat** and **Harishchandra Ghat** are situated alongside the bathing ghats. Death, in Varanasi, is a way of life. To die here is a liberation from the round of *samsara* (the unceasing cycle of life, death and rebirth).

The central **Dashnasvamedha Ghat** is where Brahma sacrificed ten horses. There is a small whitewashed shrine and image of Sitala, the goddess of small-

pox. Nearby is the site of one of Maharaja Jai Singh of Jaipur's masonry observatories. The ghat is always one of the most colourful and crowded each morning. From the Dashnasvamedha ghat a narrow lane lined with shops leads to the Vishwanath Gali and the city's main temple.

The **Vishwanath Temple** has been an important Shiva shrine for over a thousand years. Although the present building dates from 1777, the temple is one of the most important in the city. The precincts are bustling with activity and hundreds of devotees press forward and into the sanctum with its large black *lingam* (a phallic symbol of Shiva). While the main temple is closed to non-Hindus, one can view all the bustling and see the 750 kilograms (1,650 pounds) of gold plating donated

by Maharaja Ranjit Singh, from the roof of a house opposite. Near the Vishwanath Temple and behind the magnificent **Panchagana Ghat** is the smaller of two mosques built by Aurangzeb. The **Great Mosque of Aurangzeb** was built using stone from desecrated temples and has two towering minarets which dominate this stretch of the river.

One of the pleasures of Varanasi is exploring the maze of narrow streets and twisting lanes, each turn leading to another temple or shrine. The lanes are busy and noisy with trading. Shops sell items for *puja* (worship), local brassware and some of the rich silks and brocades for which the city is justly famous.

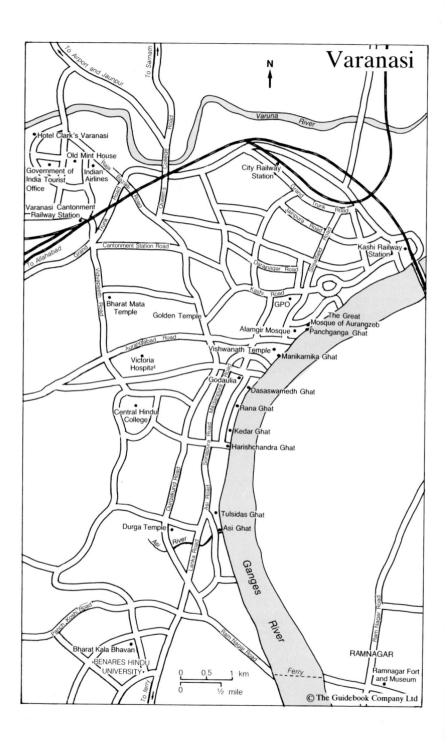

Many of the better hotels are situated in the cantonment area north of the bustling town centre. Among the interesting colonial buildings in various states of disrepair is the fine **Mint House** built by James Prinsep in 1820 and now preserved and used as a carpet showroom. In the south of the city is the large campus of **Benares Hindu University**. The marble **Vishwanatha Temple** is a recent addition but the campus is also home to one of India's great museums. The **Bharat Kala Bhavan** (open 11 am–4 pm, closed Sundays) has excellent sculpture from Mathura, Sarnath, Etah and Khajuraho as well as Varanasi. There is also a fine collection of miniature paintings and manuscripts.

Sarnath

Ten kilometres (six miles) north of Varanasi is Sarnath where the Buddha preached his first sermon and first organized an order of monks, the *sangha*. Known from the *Jataka* stories as 'The Deer Park', Sarnath had always been an important place of learning and pilgrimage until the decline of Buddhism in the tenth century. Among the excavated buildings are monasteries, shrines and the foundations of stupas. The **Dhamekh Stupa**, 30 metres (98 feet) high, dominates the site. The **Dharmarajika Stupa** is now little more than a mound, having been ravished by treasure seekers during the last century. Nearby is the lower part of **Ashoka's Pillar,** the capital of which is in the museum. The excellent **Archaeological Museum** (open 10 am–5 pm, closed Fridays), although small, is one of the most interesting in India. All the pieces are from the site and include the polished sandstone **lion capital** from Ashoka's Pillar, the emblem of India.

Jaunpur

Sixty kilometres (37 miles) northwest of Varanasi is the small town of Jaunpur. Once the capital of a Muslim kingdom, it has many distinctive Islamic buildings from the 14th and 15th centuries. The **Atala Mosque**, just north of the impressive **Akbari Bridge**, was built by Sultan Ibrahim Sharqi on the site of a Hindu temple in 1408, using much of the temple's masonry.

Western India
Rajasthan

The desert state of Rajasthan, southwest of New Delhi on the border with Pakistan, is an area of great physical beauty and contrast; massive forts and magnificent palaces are found in even the remotest part of the state. A drive almost anywhere in Rajasthan will be punctuated by a fort on a distant ridge or a pavilion next to a seasonal pool. The local women wear colourful cotton *lenghas* (skirts) or saris, the men magnificent turbans, each tied in the distinctive style of their region. A thriving folk culture based on heroic legends and local stories is passed on in ballads and traditional puppet plays.

Some of the world's oldest settlements were in Rajasthan: at **Kalibangan**, east of Ganganagar, there are Harappan finds from 3,000–2,000 BC. From the seventh century the warrior caste of Rajputs started to build kingdoms and, despite constant fighting among themselves and with Afghan and Mughal invaders, continued to control the area up to 1947. Over a thousand years of history and myth have been passed on from father to son in the form of stories of valour and love.

The **Aravalli Hills** form a ridge bisecting the desert to the west from the richer agricultural areas to the south and east.

The recent introduction of irrigation by canal from the Himalayas has transformed parts of the northwestern districts of Ganganagar and Bikaner from a subsistence economy to highly productive fruit, vegetable and grain farms. The waters of the Indira Gandhi Canal now reach Mohangarh in Jaisalmer district. The **Chambal River,** Rajasthan's only permanent river, flows north to join the Yamuna and irrigates the rich black soil of Hadaoti.

The great Rajput kingdoms of Mewar (Chittor and Udaipur), Marwar (Jodhpur), Jaisalmer, Bundi, Kota and Jaipur have been absorbed into the modern state of Rajasthan without sacrificing their identity or splendour. The great forts of **Kumbalgarh** and **Ranthambore** are now inhabited by troops of monkeys and the occasional leopard or tiger. The great scrub and thorn forests of northeastern Rajasthan have been reduced to small pockets, two of which now form the **Sariska Tiger Reserve** near Alwar and **Ranthambore National Park**, southeast of Jaipur. Part of the **Thar Desert** southwest of Jaisalmer is now the 3,000-square-kilometre (1,150-square-mile) **Desert National Park.**

Jaipur

Jaipur is quintessential India. Forts and palaces, maharajas and snake charmers, history, colour and pageantry combine to project the dream image of India. Although it is the political centre of Rajasthan and a busy commercial centre, its traditional character survives.

A meticulously planned city, Jaipur was the brainchild of Jai Singh, an 18th-century ruler of the Kachchwaha clan whose traditional stronghold was not at Jaipur but 11 kilometres (seven miles) away at Amber, which had been captured from the Susawat Minas in the 12th century. Amber remained the Kachchwaha capital for over six centuries, with the Minas functioning as hereditary treasurers.

Kachchawaha fortunes took off during Mughal rule, when Akbar won Rajput support and loyalty through marriage alliances. A Kachchwaha princess, Jodha Bai, became Akbar's wife, and the fourth ruler of Amber, Man Singh (1590–1614), his trusted friend and general. Man Singh extended the Mughal boundaries to Kabul in the west and Bengal in the east. In appreciation he was made governor of these areas and allowed to retain part of the treasures of the conquered territories. The fortune thus amassed was put to good use by Jai Singh II (1699–1743), who was accorded supremacy over other clans, having gained the Emperor's confidence. Realizing a hill fort was no longer necessary, Jaipur was conceived.

Amber, built by Man Singh, embodies the Rajput belief that the fort symbolizes the strength of the king. Its commanding view, sheer walls and rock face, and the curved route that leads to the palaces within, all point to a concern with security and defence.

To defend Amber, the massive, brooding **Jaigarh Fort** was built. This also housed the royal treasury, loyally guarded by the Minas. The fort was opened to the public in 1983 after having been minutely inspected by the Indian taxmen, who found in it nothing of value. Puppet shows and the huge Jaivan cannon are some of the main attractions today. Below Jaigarh is the palace and **Amber Fort**, its structures mirrored in Maota Lake which stands adjacent to the Dilaram Garden.

Most visitors to Amber enter from the west, coming into **Jalebi Chowk** with its vendors selling flowers and sweets to be used as offerings at the **Shila Devi Temple**, the most sacred of the Kachchwaha shrines. This image of Kali was brought here by Man Singh from Jessore in Bengal in 1604. With it came the Bengali priests; one of their descendants was the architect of Jaipur.

Through the **Surya Pol** (Sun Gate), one enters another courtyard to the west of which is the **Diwan-i-Am**, built by Jai Singh. The frescos that once adorned the walls were said to have aroused Jehangir's jealousy and so were tactfully covered with plaster.

The private apartments begun by Man Singh in the 17th century and completed by Jai Singh a century later combine Hindu and Mughal styles. Overlooking the Mughal sunken garden is the **Sukh Niwas,** where water from a roof-top cistern flows into the channels below to provide relief from the blistering summer heat. The rich embellishment of the **Diwan-i-Khas** (Private Audience Hall) suits the purpose for which it was built, and the **Sheesh Mahal** (Hall of

Mirrors), its walls covered with tiny mirrors, becomes a dazzling fantasy with the light of a single match. Above is the **Jas Mandir** (Hall of Glory), with its fine alabaster screens set at ground level to facilitate ventilation and provide beautiful views of the plains below. The **Zenana Palace** was exclusively for women.

At the other end of the same ridge is **Nahargarh**, the tiger fort, reached by a ridge-top road approached from the Amber road. Constructed to protect the new city of Jaipur, the fort offers some magnificent views. At the base of the hill is **Gaitor** which contains seven *chatris* (tombs) of uniform style, the earliest and most elaborate being that of Jai Singh II.

Jai Singh's city which sprawls below reflects the myriad facets of his genius. Only 11 when he ascended the throne, and 14 when he won the title of Sawai, he was a warrior and a shrewd and cunning statesman who played his political cards well enough to establish a degree of stability which allowed him to indulge in his other intellectual passions—science and the arts. To enrich the city, Jai Singh encouraged trade and commerce. There was a rich and prosperous trading community, and traditional crafts such as enamelling, metalware, carpet weaving and stonecarving flourished. Many of these survive alongside the city's modern industries—engineering, distilling, glass and sports equipment.

Planned according to the architectural treatise *Shilpa Shastra*, Jaipur consists of seven blocks divided by wide avenues and lanes. The actual planning and execution were carried out by the brilliant scholar engineer Vidyadhar Bhattacharaya, a descendant of one of the Bengali priests brought in by Man Singh. Surrounding these blocks, each devoted to a particular trade or activity, is a crenellated wall with eight gates, enclosing the more interesting districts of Jaipur.

Badi Chaupar (big square) is the nucleus of activity. On a road radiating north towards Amber is the **Hawa Mahal**, a fanciful façade. Popularly known as the Palace of the Wind, it was built in 1799 for Sawai Pratap Singh. The broad pyramidal façade comprises five storeys of semi-octagonal overhanging windows with perforated screens. It was so named, most believe, to allow women in purdah to look out on the world without being observed, while basking in the cool breeze. Others attribute its name to the fact that it has no foundation and therefore supports itself on air *(hawa)*.

The lanes around Badi Chaupar sell traditional handicrafts. **Johari Bazaar** is the jewellery and cotton fabric market where you can buy silver jewellery and precious and semi-precious stones. Opposite the Hawa Mahal are the puppet-makers' shops, and embroidered *jutis (*shoes) are available at **Ramganj.** West of Hawa Mahal are shops selling a variety of textiles including block-printed fabric and embroidered garments. At one corner of this busy square is the **Govinda Deva Temple,** dedicated to Krishna, who is considered the city's guardian deity.

Jaipur City Palace

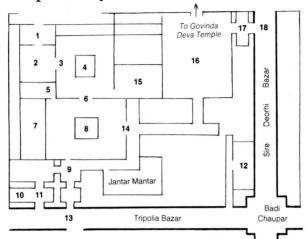

1. Chandra Mahal
   (and Sheesh Mahal)
2. Pritam Niwas Chowk
   (Peacock Courtyard)
3. Ridhi Sidhi Pol
4. Diwan-i-Khas
5. Sileh Khana
6. Sarhad Ki Deorhi
7. Photograph Collection
8. Mubarak Mahal

9. Chandni Chowk
10. Iswari Minar Swarga Sal
11. Atish Pol
12. Hawa Mahal
13. Tripolia Gate
14. Gainda Ka Deorhi
15. Diwan-i-Am
16. Jaleb Chowk
17. Naqqar Khana
18. Sire Deorhi Gate

The **City Palace** is the focal point of the walled city and covers one-seventh of the total area. The Tripolia Gate is for the exclusive use of the maharaja's family. Everyone else must enter from Atish Pol, Tripolia Bazaar or the Sire Deorhi Gate. Construction of this complex, made up of a number of courtyards and buildings, was begun by Sawai Jai Singh II. The central portion is now the **City Palace Museum** (open 9.30 am–4.45 pm), entered through the Gainda Ka Deorhi. The **Mubarak Mahal** (Palace of Welcome), a two-storey structure built as a guesthouse by Maharaja Madho Singh in 1900, served briefly as the royal secretariat. It now houses part of the textiles and costumes section of the museum. Notable among its rich and opulent exhibits is the *atam sukh* of Madho Singh I, a gown tailored to fit his enormous bulk of 225 kilograms (almost 500 pounds). Beyond the Mubarak Mahal is the **Sileh Khana** (armoury) which houses a fine collection of Indian weaponry. The photographs displayed in the next room are the work of Ram Singh II (1835–80) who painted Jaipur pink as a sign of welcome for the Prince of Wales's visit. The beautifully carved gateway of Sire Deorhi is flanked by two marble elephants. Its heavy brass doors lead to a salmon-pink courtyard with the **Diwan-i-Khas** in the centre; the open pavilion on a raised platform was used for ceremonial occasions. Prominently displayed

are two huge silver urns, 160 centimetres (5.3 feet) high with a capacity
of 8,182 litres (1,802 gallons), which
were used to transport River Ganges
water to England for Madho Singh II
when he attended the coronation of
King Edward VII. To the right is the
Diwan-i-Am (Hall of Public Audience), with a large hall open on three
sides, surrounded by verandas with
scalloped arches and delicate screens.
The Diwan-i-Am was the scene of the
historic birth of the state of Rajasthan
in 1949. It is now part of a museum
containing carpets from Herat, fabulous chandeliers and an excellent
collection of miniature paintings in the
Mughal and indigenous Rajput style.

To the northwest, the **Chandra
Mahal** (Moon Palace), a seven-storey
stucco structure that towers above the
surrounding buildings, is decorated with murals and large paintings of Kachchwaha rulers. The gilded ceilings and ivory inlay work are particularly attractive.
The Mukut Mandir which crowns these offers a fabulous view of the surrounding area. Because the Chandra Mahal contains the maharaja's private residence,
only the ground floor is open to the public. The Nakkar Khana was used by
court musicians; it also served as a clock tower. The **Pothi Khana** (library) is
south of the Chandra Mahal. Formerly Durbar Hall, it contains the maharaja's
private collection of paintings and rare manuscripts, outstanding among which
are the *Razmnama,* a Persian translation of the *Mahabharata* done by Abul Fazl,
and miniature editions of the *Gita* and *Lingapurana.*

Adjacent to the City Palace is the **Jantar Mantar Observatory** (9 am–5
pm) a bizarre-looking group of structures that are the result of Jai Singh's
passionate interest in science and astronomy. This was one of the five he
constructed; the others are at Ujjain, Mathura, Varanasi and Delhi. The huge
masonry instruments were used for measuring time and making various astro-
logical calculations.

Beyond the Bapu and Nehru bazaars and outside the walled city is the new
city. Within the **Ram Niwas Gardens** on Jawaharlal Nehru Road is **Albert
Hall**, a combination of Western and indigenous architectural styles designed by
Sir Jacob Swinton as the Central Museum (open 10 am–5 pm, closed Fridays).
The collection includes some superb carpets, metalware, ivory carving, jewel-
lery, textiles, pottery and woodcarving, as well as exhibits on rural life. A few

kilometres further south, **Rambagh Palace** was one of the first royal homes to be converted into a luxury hotel and continues to be one of India's finest. Originally a group of pavilions made into an 18th-century hunting lodge, Madho Singh II transformed it into a royal residence and in 1933 Man Singh II moved there from the City Palace. On the Rambagh property is a golf course and the polo grounds where a festival takes place each March. Overlooking the Rambagh is the **Moti Doongri Fort**.

Excursions from Jaipur include **Galta,** a few kilometres to the east, a place deemed sacred because of the penance of the sage Gwala. There is a sun temple on the hill, and the water in the tanks and springs is said to have curative properties.

The **Sisodia Palace and Garden,** on the Agra road eight kilometres (five miles) east of the city, was built by Maharaja Sawai Jai Singh for his Sisodia queen. This is situated near the **Roop Niwas Gardens** and consists of a hall flanked by verandas, galleries, raised platforms, gardens and bathing pools.

Sanganer, 16 kilometres (ten miles) to the south, has a few Jain temples but is better known for its block-printed fabrics and hand-made paper. The industry is well organized as is apparent from the yards of cloth you see drying on the approach road. Watching these prints being made is a fascinating experience.

Off the Bikaner road 42 kilometres (26 miles) to the northwest is the small village of **Samode**. Nestling beneath a hill fort is a small palace, some of the rooms with excellent mirror work and fine murals. Part of the palace is now a good family hotel.

Bharatpur and Deeg

The small town of Bharatpur lies 56 kilometres (32 miles) west of Agra on the road to Jaipur. Its **Lohagarh Fort** acquired an awesome reputation in the 18th century for its supposedly impregnable defences. Two massive mud ramparts, each encircled by moats, were originally 11 kilometres (seven miles) in circumference. Now only fragments of the inner wall remain, topped by a cannon pointing northeast.

An old brick and stone bridge leads over part of the inner moat to the **Assaldati Gate** and into the fort which contains three palaces and some rather unattractive new buildings. The **Kanra Palace** now houses the museum (10 am -5 pm, closed Fridays). Primarily devoted to archaeology, the museum, founded in 1944, is certainly worth a visit. Most of the sculpture is from local sites and Mathura. East of the museum is **Khas Mahal,** where the royal apartments were located. Many of the rooms are still covered with painted designs, while most of the other buildings in the fort are unadorned. On the ground floor is a set of *hamams* (sunken baths).

Apart from the fort and museum, by far the most important place in Bharatpur is the **Keoladeo Ghana National Park,** five kilometres (three miles) to the south. This magnificent bird sanctuary is one of the world's most important heronries. Originally protected for shooting, the area became a sanctuary in 1956. About a third of the park's 29 square kilometres (11 square miles) is flooded by the monsoon and forms a shallow, freshwater marsh. The remaining dry mixed-scrub forest and grassland supports a range of mammals and birds. By the end of the monsoon in late August, the indigenous water birds have begun to nest and thousands of herons, storks, egrets and cormorants raise as many young. By early October, the first migrants arrive from Central Asia and tens of thousands of ducks, geese and waders settle in for the winter. Raptors and the extremely rare Siberian crane come a few weeks later.

A road runs through the park and although vehicles are not allowed to use it bicycles can be hired. A good network of tree-lined paths along raised embankments gives good cover for bird-watching. From mid-October to early March, boats can be hired to gain access to the marshes. A visit even in the hot summer months is worthwhile.

The road north of Bharatpur to Kosi (on the Delhi–Agra road) goes via **Deeg** (34 kilometres, or 22 miles, from Bharatpur). Formerly the second capital of Bharatpur state, Deeg is now a sleepy, dusty agricultural town but has a magnificent complex of buildings and gardens, the **summer palace**. Built in the mid-18th century, the buildings are set between two large tanks with an older **fort** beyond. This is one of the few palaces open to the public (8 am–6 pm) that remains unspoilt by 'progress'.

Kota and Bundi

The two towns of Kota and Bundi could not be more different although their origins are closely linked. Bundi was conquered by the Hada clan of Chauhan Rajputs in 1241 and Kota was a *jagir*, an estate belonging to the Bundi rulers until 1624, when it became a separate state. A third princely state was formed in 1838 when Jhalawar, 80 kilometres (50 miles) to the south of Kota, was established. These three states occupied a rich fertile region of southeastern Rajasthan known as Hadaoti.

Kota is on the main Delhi–Bombay railway line and there are regular flights to and from Jaipur and Delhi. Its location in the fertile Chambal Valley has traditionally made Kota an important agricultural town. In the last 30 years, the town has become Rajasthan's fastest-growing industrial centre. The Shriram Fertilizer Plant is one of the largest in the country, and hydro and atomic power plants have been established on the Chambal River. But Kota has not totally given itself up to the 20th century. The old town has retained many of its buildings. The **City Palace,** part of the **fort,** is entered through the **Naya Darwaza** which leads into a large square where parades and processions were once held. To the west of the square, the brilliant **Hathi Pol**, or Elephant Gate, leads to the **Rao Madho Singh Museum** (11 am–5 pm, closed Fridays). The fine collection of weapons, textiles and paintings from the 18th-century Kotah school are well maintained by the family trust. Many of the **palace** apartments are open to the public and the **Raj Mahal** in particular has very fine murals depicting hunting scenes, portraits of the Kota rulers and episodes from Hindu legends. The **Government Museum** (10 am–5 pm, closed Fridays) is in the **Hawa Mahal**. Although not as impressive as the Rao Madho Singh Museum, it does have an important sculpture collection, much of it from the ninth-century Bardoli temples, 48 kilometres (30 miles) to the southwest. In 1905, the Maharao (not Maharaja) of Kota moved into a new palace, **Umed Bhawan**, designed by Sir Swinton Jacob and set in beautiful gardens. Nearby, the **Brijraj Bhavan Palace**, formerly the British Residency, is now a private hotel with plenty of atmosphere.

South of Kota the Chambal River flows through a deep gorge with some good views of forested cliffs. On the main line to Delhi, 85 kilometres (50 miles) north of Kota, is **Sawai Madhopur** and a few kilometres further on is the important tiger reserve, **Ranthambhore National Park** (see page 114-116).

Bundi is only 38 kilometres (22 miles) west of Kota, but much of the town has remained as picturesque and romantic as it was when Colonel James Tod wrote about it in 1820. The 'senior' state in Hadaoti, Bundi retains a medieval charm and has been saved from the impact of 'progress'. What the town lacks in infrastructure is compensated for by its atmosphere. The only accommodation is in a government Circuit House or the old, run-down palace guesthouse, **Ranjit Niwas**.

Nestled between rugged hills and dominated by **Taragarh Fort,** Bundi is best explored on foot. The fort was completed in 1354 and commands a marvellous view east across the plains of Hadaoti, the Chambal River and Kota on its far bank. From the ramparts there is a fine view of the town and the rambling palace.

In the centre of the valley the large artificial lake, **Naval Sagar**, reflects images of the palace and fort. An island temple to Varuna, the rain god, is submerged during heavy monsoons.

Exploring the town requires a steady climb. Many of the shops in the town stand up to two metres (six feet) above street level. During the monsoon, when the town's ancient reservoirs inside the fort reach a certain level, warning drums are sounded before the sluice gates are opened, releasing a rush of water that flows past the palace and through the town. This ancient practice has continued for years without loss of life or damage to buildings. A zig-zag road leads up to the palace but it is important to check whether it is open before starting the climb.

The **Bundi Palace** is a series of structures built by successive rulers who gave the buildings their names. A walk up through various gates and courtyards leads to the **Rattan Daulat** (Public Audience Hall) containing a simple white marble throne. Nearby, the living apartments, **Chatar Mahal**, have some beautiful murals, but the prize is the 18th-century **Chitra Shala** on the opposite side. The covered galleries which enclose a small courtyard were built by Rao Raja Umed Singh. The mural and paintings depict a variety of subjects: religious and mythological scenes, court life, processions, hunts and military victories. A small side room has some better-preserved, brightly painted murals which can be seen properly with the help of a lamp or torch.

Don't miss the exquisitely built **Rani-ki-Baori** step-well outside the old city and near the Circuit House. The high arches and excellent carving date from 1700 and are now in urgent need of conservation. A few kilometres west of the town, the new **Phool Sagar Palace** was built around an old pavilion and tank in 1945.

To the north of the town lies the reservoir **Jait Sagar,** with interesting buildings and gardens. The **Sukh Newas** on top of the bund was built in 1773. At the opposite end, the royal **chatris,** many with excellent statues and carving, are in the **Shar Bagh**. In the forest nearby, Umed Singh built a hunting tower, the **Shikar Burj**, where he devoted his life to religious study after abdicating.

Ajmer and Pushkar

Among the many princely states of Rajputana, one area invariably remained under the control of whoever ruled Delhi: Ajmer, strategically placed and originally, along with Delhi, the twin capital of the Chauhans. From its founding and for five centuries until it was annexed in 1556 by Akbar, Ajmer was ruled by a combination of Muslim and Rajput chiefs. Akbar realized the value of its

Tigers

Forget those tamed and shabby tigers. If ever you are lucky enough to see a wild one, you will probably swear off zoos and circuses for life. In its native habitat *Panthera tigris tigris* is uniquely awesome. Steely muscles rippling beneath its tawny striped skin, the animal moves silently on huge soft pads. Those calm golden eyes seem to stare right through you, and the way tigers can vanish into the vegetation with a couple of effortless strides is nothing short of magical.

Riding quietly along jungle tracks in a jeep or on elephant back, you fine-tune your senses for signs that a tiger has passed. Look for fresh pugmarks on soft ground, or telltale claw marks as much as three metres (ten feet) up a tree-trunk. Listen for the barking alarm calls of monkeys and deer, which spread the word when a predator is around. Crows or treepies calling repeatedly from one place could mean that they are perched above a tiger's kill, waiting to hop down and scavenge scraps when the owner leaves. Your nose can help you to locate a carcass, or tell you where a tiger has sprayed its pungent scent on to a tree to mark its territory. It smells like a domestic tomcat, but infinitely stronger.

The way a tiger prepares for the hunt after a day spent relaxing in the shade may also remind you of a pet tabby. In an almost identical toilet routine it licks its paws and washes its face and ears, yawns to show terrifying canines, and finally rises and arches its back in a leisurely stretch. Moving off it looks deceptively casual, but at the first glimpse of potential prey its whole attitude changes. Alert and deliberate it begins its stalk, shrinking impossibly low to become invisible behind the scrappiest cover. Before charging, it crouches, tense as a coiled spring, motionless except for the sharp flicking of its tail-tip, then explodes in an incredible demonstration of raw power. The charge, always short as tigers are sprinters, may not be successful, but if it kills an adult sambar or nilgai there will be food for four or five days. The tiger also attacks other deer species, wild boar, and even monkeys and peacocks if they offer an easy chance.

The privilege of being able to watch the natural activities of both tigers and their prey is a recent one, unique to India and Nepal. Twenty years ago it would have been unthinkable to be able to see a pair of tigers mating, or a wild tigress suckling her cubs. That we now can is a tribute to the protection they have been afforded under Project Tiger. In sanctuaries like the 400-square-kilometre (154-square-mile) Ranthambhore National Park in Rajasthan, whole generations of animals have grown up unpersecuted and without fear of man. Formerly the hunting preserve of the maharajas of Jaipur, who protected it rigorously and held occasional tiger shoots for which they brought their ceremonial elephants from Jaipur, Ranthambhore came under Project Tiger in 1974. The tigers were then completely nocturnal in their habits. By the mid-1980s they had taken to moving around in broad daylight and soon became so accustomed to visitors' jeeps that they even used them as cover whilst stalking their prey.

Ranthambhore looked like one of Project Tiger's most spectacular successes, but the increased number and visibility of the tigers produced a rapid growth in tourism.

Attempts to control traffic have been largely ineffective. A time limit on excursions virtually restricts vehicles to the core area, which in turn disturbs the animals and damages their fragile habitat. At the rumour of a tiger, jeep operators abandon their allotted routes and suddenly a dozen vehicles will be manouvring for a glimpse. Intent on the large tips usually generated by a tiger sighting, drivers often deny their passengers the pleasures of watching birds and other mammals in the park's spectacularly beautiful surroundings.

Such pleasures, however, are restricted to foreigners, comparatively rich Indians and holidaying government officials, and during the 15-kilometre (nine-mile) drive to the park from Sawai Madhopur town, it is hard to believe they exist. The landscape is a desolate semi-desert, mainly because the human and domestic animal populations in the surrounding villages have escalated dramatically. Huge herds of

cattle and goats have chewed the grass down to its very roots. Trees have had their branches amputated for firewood. Unable to feed their livestock or cook their food, poor villagers living on the edge of the park are now driving in their cattle, cutting grass for fodder, and bringing out wood for commercial gain as well as for their own domestic use.

Ranthambhore is not the only Project Tiger sanctuary under severe pressure of this type. It is probably true to say that all 18 Project Tiger reserves and most of India's 280 other national parks and sanctuaries face similar difficulties.

Encroachment and disturbance are widespread. Poaching of tigers for their skins and body parts for traditional Chinese medicines, occurs in some areas. Their prey species are killed for meat or to protect crops. In southern India, timber contractors steal valuable hardwoods like ebony and rosewood from the forest.

But Ranthambhore does have a small new ray of hope. A charitable trust has been set up with the aim of renewing the age-old harmony between man and nature. The Ranthambhore Foundation, which is allied to other non-governmental organizations in India, is helping people in the villages around Ranthambhore to improve their standard of living without further depleting the park's resources. Funds raised in India, together with overseas contributions channelled through the Ranthambhore Society (Grantchester, Linden Gardens, Leatherhead, Surrey KT22 7HB, UK) finance projects including reafforestation, the provision of alternative energy—such as biogas—for cooking, a dairying scheme to replace thousands of unproductive cattle with smaller numbers of high-yield, stall-fed buffaloes, and the development of a local handicrafts industry.

A mobile medical team offering preventative health care and family planning advice is already touring the villages, with a similar educational unit in the pipeline. This will teach both children and adults about the environment and improved agricultural practices as well as provide literacy and numeracy classes for women and girls who do not normally attend school.

The moving force behind the Foundation is naturalist Valmik Thapar. An award-winning documentary film maker, with a degree in social anthropology from Delhi University, Thapar first came to Ranthambhore in 1976 and has since spent several months each year studying the tigers. He has written three books about them, most recently *Tigers: The Secret Life* (Elm Tree Books, London, 1989).

Valmik Thapar is not optimistic about the future of India's forests and their wildlife. Feeling that Project Tiger is in a state of decline due to mismanagement of reserves by staff lacking knowledge and motivation and to its failure to involve local communities, he sees 'little hope of protecting the tiger into the next century' unless radical changes are made.

While the laws regarding the protection of forests and wildlife, and their enforcement, obviously need a strenuous overhaul, organizations like the Ranthambhore Foundation can do a lot to help strike a balance between conservation, which must seem an elitist and ephemeral concept to the average villager, and the needs of the human population.

This is the first such venture to be started around an Indian national park, but it could provide a blueprint for others and a brighter future not only for the tigers but for the world they share with mankind.

Sue Earle

position in controlling the surrounding Rajput kingdoms. He built a royal residence there which was later used by Jehangir and Shah Jahan. After the break-up of the Mughal empire, the Rathores of Marwar (Jodhpur) and the Marathas controlled the city. In 1812, the British finally annexed it and it became the centre of the Chief Commissioner's province of Ajmer–Merwara from where relations with Rajputana were controlled. For many, Ajmer is only a transit point en route to the Pushkar Fair each November, but the town's important history has left equally interesting places to visit. In the heart of the old city, at the base of **Taragarh Hill**, is India's most important Muslim shrine. In around 1191, the Persian saint Khwaja Moinuddin Chishti came to India and established the Sufi order of *Chishtiya*. His tomb, known as the **Dargah Sharif**, is to millions a wish-fulfilling shrine, and each year during the *urs*, or commemoration of his death, thousands of pilgrims come to visit it.

Approach the Dargah through a vibrant **bazaar** and the **Madar Gate** (where shoes are removed) into a large courtyard. On the right is a simple mosque built by Akbar. Nearby are two huge iron cauldrons in which donated rice is cooked with milk, raisins and nuts before being 'looted' and sold to pilgrims as sanctified food. The larger cauldron can hold almost 4,500 kilograms (10,000 pounds) of rice! Near a gateway donated by the Nizam of Hyderabad separating the two courtyards, *qawwalis* (devotional songs) are sung during *urs*. The central courtyard has the saint's tomb enclosed by a silver railing within a domed marble chamber. On the western side of the court is an elegant white marble **mosque** built by Shah Jahan with Persian inscriptions running the length of the building. A short walk beyond the Dargah brings you to the remarkable **Arhaidin-ka Jhompra Mosque**, like the Qutab complex in Delhi, built largely of stone taken from demolished Hindu temples. Originally there was a Sanskrit college built in 1153 on the site; it was turned into a mosque in about 1200, following the sack of Ajmer by Muhammad Ghori in 1193. Much of the building is now ruined, but a marvellous 62-metre- (200-foot-) long row of arches still stands, with Islamic calligraphic inscriptions carved on the main face. Part of the original building, with its distinctive Hindu pillars, lies behind the arches, but the other three sides of the mosque's enclosure have disappeared. Although the mosque is partially ruined, the faithful still come here for prayer on Fridays. From behind the mosque a steep path (about three kilometres, or two miles) leads up to **Taragarh**, or Star Fort, first built by the Chauhans. The fort is also accessible by road through the **Nallah Bazaar**.

Near the railway station is the red sandstone fortified palace built by Akbar in 1570, the **Daulat Khana**. Its central audience hall now houses the **Government Museum** (10 am–5 pm, closed Fridays) with a rich collection of weapons, coins and sculpture. More recent buildings include those of **Mayo College**, one of India's best public schools, founded in 1874 for the sons of the rulers of the Rajput states. To the north of the city is a large artificial lake, **Ana Sagar**, which was created in the 12th century by damming the Luni River. Shah Jahan built a series of pavilions along one bank and the old **British Residency** is now an attractive Circuit House.

The road to Pushkar, 29 kilometres (11 miles) to the northwest, passes Ana Sagar and crosses a pass in the Aravalli Hills known as **Nag Pahar**, Snake Mountain. **Pushkar Lake** is said to have been formed when Brahma dropped a lotus from heaven. The lake is consecrated to him, as is a nearby temple once thought to be the only temple to Brahma in India. Although many temples were destroyed during Aurangzeb's rule, Pushkar has nearly 400. In terms of sanctity the lake is second only to Mansarovar on the Tibetan plateau, and it is a major pilgrimage destination throughout the year. The **ghats** (where photography is prohibited), the temples and thousands of pilgrims give the town a special atmosphere.

During the full moon in the month of Kartik (October/November) the town and nearby dunes become an enormous fairground. A spectacular *mela,* or fair, takes place with thousands of villagers bringing cattle, camels and horses to trade. Nomads and villagers from throughout Rajasthan come together in a mass of colour, competition and entertainment. Pilgrims bathe in the lake on the night of the full moon and the nights preceding and following. Traditional jewellery, naturally dyed fabrics, saris and *lenghas* (Rajasthani skirts) are sold. The fair has rightly become famous yet has retained traditional values. Rajasthan Tourism and a few agents from Jaipur set up large camps adjacent to the main fair for about 12 days. The last four or five days are the most interesting.

There are a number of temples on the surrounding hillocks, from where spectacular views of the town, the fair, the desert and sunsets can be photographed. To the north of the town is one dedicated to Savitri, to the south is one to Gayatri. Both are an easy walk from the town and camps.

Jodhpur

Southwest of Jaipur is the **Thar desert** with Jodhpur at the eastern edge serving as its gateway. The city, 205 kilometres (128 miles) from Ajmer and surrounded by inhospitable scrubland and rocky terrain, was founded in 1459 by the Rathore chieftain Rao Jodha who claimed descent from Lord Rama. After conquering Marwar, Rao Jodha established himself here. Within the high stone wall with its eight gates is the seemingly invincible **Mehrangarh Fort,** rising to a height of 125 metres (393 feet) above the flat plains. Enclosed within are the fabulous palaces, which have now been converted into a **museum** (open 9 am– 5 pm). Inside the exquisite **Moti Mahal** is the Srinagar Chowk (coronation seat) with peacock armrests and gilded elephants. The other sections, the **Phool Mahal**, **Sheesh Mahal**, **Sileh Khana**, **Umaid Vilas** and **Daulat Khana,** display a rich and varied collection of exhibits including palanquins, howdahs (elephant seats, one of them a gift from the emperor Shah Jahan) and the royal cradle. **Umaid Vilas** has a fine collection of Rajput miniatures and Ragmala paintings and a spectacular Mughal tent made of red silk and covered with floral embroidery. The armoury of **Maan Vilas** displays the high level of craftsmanship of the *sikligars* (swordsmiths) and the *dhabadars* (armourers).

While all previous rulers have their *chatris* (cenotaphs) at Mandore, that of Jaswant Singh II, an energetic and successful ruler who spent much time, effort and part of his enormous fortune in various welfare schemes, is at **Jaswant Thada** below the fort. The tombs of four successive rulers adjoin this structure.

The splendour and luxury of the marble and sandstone **Umaid Bhawan Palace** remains in the hotel portion. Conceived to bring employment to over 3,000 people a day during a famine in the 1930s, this 347-room palace is

believed to be one of the largest private homes in the world. An effective combination of indigenous and foreign architecture, and also known as the *chitar* palace because of the particular type of sandstone used, this was the maharaja's second residence, the first being at **Raikabagh.** The museum (open 10 am–4.30 pm) contains an armoury, textiles, manuscripts and Jain images.

Radiating from the central **clock tower** is a maze of lanes with shops selling traditional handicrafts—Jodhpur breeches, *badlas* (zinc water bottles encased in thick cloth), embroidered shoes, tie-dyed textiles and lacquerware.

Mandore, nine kilometres (five miles) from the town, was the original capital of the Parihar Rajputs. The royal *chatris* are in lush and reasonably well maintained gardens. Along one edge of the garden is the 18th-century **Hall of Heroes** with 16 giant figures carved out of a single rock. Jodhpur is a good base from which to visit **Osian**, 65 kilometres (40 miles) to the northwest, once a great trading centre but today famed for its eighth-to-tenth century Brahmin and Jain **temples**. **Nagur**, 135 kilometres (85 miles) from Jodhpur, with its old fort and palace, comes alive during the cattle fair in February.

Jaisalmer

Around Jaisalmer, a rail journey of 330 kilometres (206 miles) from Jodhpur, the impact of the brooding desertscape intensifies. Amidst these stark surroundings, Jaisalmer offers a rich tapestry of exotica: history and legend, fine architecture and colourful people.

The origins of this 12th-century fortress town can be traced to a prophecy by Krishna who predicted that the area would one day be ruled by a member of the lunar clan to which he belonged. In 1156, Rawal Jaisal, a usurper to the throne, shifted the capital of the Bhatti Rajputs from **Lodurva**, 15 kilometres (nine miles) away, to the present site, basing his decision on Krishna's prophecy as related to him by a hermit. Confident of divine protection—he belonged to the lunar clan Krishna referred to—he set about building his capital, undeterred by the oracle's warning that it would be sacked two and a half times.

Jaisalmer's turbulent history was to prove this true. But far from being considered defeats, these events became subjects for traditional ballads eulogizing Bhatti valour and courage. The worst of these periods, during the reign of Alauddin Khaji (1296–1316), lasted for seven long years and ended in *jauhar* (self-immolation) for the women and certain death for the men. Stability came with Mughal rule, and Jaisalmer princesses were married into the Mughal royal family.

Like most desert towns, Jaisalmer is dominated by its impressive **fort** of golden-yellow sandstone, its solid rounded walls and ramparts reinforcing the impression of military might. Jaisalmer is in fact a citadel. Within the outer walls lie the fort and other historic structures, while the modern town has grown up all around. The seven-storey **palace** is approached through a steep winding path that passes in front of the **Temple of Bhawani**, the protectress of the Bhattis. The king met his subjects and was entertained in the **Hall of Public Audience**, close to which is his marble throne and **Jaslu Kuan**, a water source believed to have been created by Krishna. A section of the **Jawahar Mahal** (Jewelled Palace) has been converted into a hotel which effectively recaptures the ambience of the regal lifestyle.

Jaisalmer's strategic position on the overland spice route between India and Central Asia naturally led to the growth of a prosperous merchant community. With ample resources at their command, the merchants vied with one another in building elaborate and ornate *havelis* (residences), utilizing the highly skilled craftsmanship of the *silavats* (stone carvers). The best known, is the **Patwon ki Haveli** built by the five sons of a *patua* (tradesman in brocade, gold and silver) family whose traditional business expanded to include opium, banking and revenue collecting and who had, by the 18th century, established a chain of 300

The Sacred Cows

Srinagar owns a large population of sacred cows and bulls that wander vaguely through the streets, picking up such vegetable garbage, grass, and fallen leaves as they can find. They are small beasts—the half of good-sized English cattle—and marvellously mild. Red rags mean nothing to these little bulls, they can be trusted in china shops—even in nurseries. Liberty, underfeeding and unlimited access to the females of their species account, no doubt, for this surprising gentleness.

But, though harmless, these Hindu totems are passively a nuisance. They will not attack you as you walk or drive along the streets, but neither will they get out of your way. They stand there, meditatively ruminating, in the middle of the road, and no shouting, no ringing of bells or hooting of horns will send them away. Not until you are right on top of them will they move. The fact is, of course, that they know their own sacredness. They have learned by long experience that they can stand in the road as much as they like and that, however furiously the klaxon sounds, nothing will ever happen to them. Nothing; for Kashmir, though its inhabitants are mostly Mohammedans, is ruled by a pious Hindu dynasty. Up till a few years ago a man who killed a cow was sentenced to death. Under a milder dispensation he now gets only a matter of seven years' penal servitude. A salutary fear of cows is rooted in the breast of every Kashmiri chauffeur. And the totems know it. With a majestic impertinence they stroll along the middle of the roads. When one is a god, one does not disturb oneself for the convenience of mere man, however importunate.

It was late in the afternoon when we drove past the Court of Justice. The day's business was over and the sweepers were at work, making clean for the morrow. Outside one of the doors of the building stood a row of brimming waste-paper baskets, and from these, as from mangers, two or three sacred bulls were slowly and majestically feeding. When the baskets were empty officious hands from within replenished them with a fresh supply of torn and scribbled paper. The bulls browsed on; it was a literary feast.

Aldous Huxley, Jesting Pilate

outlets extending from Afghanistan to China. While observing the fine and
delicate workmanship of this *haveli,* it is not difficult to believe that the five
units took over 50 years to build. A similarly high level of craftsmanship can be
seen in **Salim Singh ki Haveli** with its superbly arched roof and in **Nathmalji
ki Haveli**, both residences of former prime ministers. The *havelis* are open between 10.30 am and 5 pm every day.

An important source of water in the past, **Gadisar Lake**, with its gateway
and ghats, is just south of the city wall. The **Badal Mahal** was the former home
of the rulers of Jaisalmer. Nearby, the **Tazia Tower,** built by Muslim *silavats*
who migrated to Pakistan, reflects the religious tolerance of the Bhatti kings. An
extensive complex of Jain **temples** within the fort further substantiates this.
Built by wealthy Marwari merchants, the best known of these are the **Rish-
abdevji** (dedicated to the first Jain *tirthankara,* or teacher), **Sambhavnatwa**
(which has some priceless Jain manuscripts) and the **Ashtapadi**.

Around Jaisalmer it is worth visiting **Bada Bagh**, seven kilometres (four
miles) to the north, where the *chatris* (memorials) of the former rulers are
surrounded by beautiful gardens. **Lodurva**, the former capital, with little to
show of its past aside from crumbling ruins, has relevance today both as a place
of Jain pilgrimage and its association with the tragic love story of Mahendru and
Moomal.

Camel treks into the desert operate from Jaisalmer and go as far as **Sam,** 45
kilometres (28 miles) to the west. Nearby, to the southwest, is **Desert National
Park**, where you can see the great Indian bustard. Permission to visit the park is
obtained from the Forest Department in Jaisalmer.

Like all of Rajasthan, Jaisalmer is best visited in the winter months. At the beginning of January the **Desert Festival** includes camel cart rides, camel races, folk music and dance performances and the sale of Jaisalmer's traditional crafts, silver, leather and cotton fabrics.

Chittor and Udaipur

Chittor and Udaipur are linked by both geography and history. The older of the two, Chittor, which formed part of the marriage dowry of Bappa Rawal, the founder of the Sisodia dynasty in the eighth century, became the capital of Mewar, a fiercely independent kingdom stretching from Gujarat to Ajmer. Chittor was ravaged thrice, first in 1303 by Alauddin Khaji who, according to legend, fell in love with the beautiful queen Padmini and attacked the kingdom in the hope that he could take her as part of the spoils. However, in true Rajput fashion, she committed suicide, preferring a fiery death to dishonour. The second plunder, which took place in 1535, was carried out by Sultan Bahadur Shah of Gujarat. The final attack, by Akbar in 1567, was an attempt to subdue Maharana Udai Singh, the founder of Udaipur. Jehangir finally returned Chittor to the Rajputs in 1616.

At almost every turn of the ruined **Chittorgarh Fort**, tablets and *chatris* (cenotaphs) commemorate acts of bravery and courage. Dotting the surrounding countryside are several towers. Some, like the **Vijay Stambh**, commemorate a victory, while others, such as the **Kirti Stambh**, glorify religion.

The **Palace of Rana Kumbh** inside the fort, believed to be the place where Padmini took her own life, reflects the fine aesthetic sensibilities of its builder. Simpler and distinctly feminine, **Padmini's Palace**, overlooking a large pool, is where Alauddin Khaji first caught a glimpse of the beautiful queen. Another queen of Chittor, Meera, was a mystic, and the temple built in her memory is interesting. Another temple worth visiting is the **Kalika Mata**, originally a Surya or sun temple.

Around Chittor, other archaeological sites worth visiting are **Nagari**, 14 kilometres (nine miles) to the north, which flourished in the Mauryan and Gupta period. **Menal**, 90 kilometres (56 miles) away on the road to Bundi, has interesting temples, while **Deogarh**, 125 kilometres (78 miles) to the south, a 16th-century fort near Pratapgarh, is famous for its palace, murals and Jain temples.

Udaipur is 115 kilometres (72 miles) west of Chittor. In contrast to the masculine character of Chittor, Udaipur is delicate, feminine and incredibly romantic. Founded in 1567 by Maharana Udai Singh, who fled here after the third attack of Chittor, Udaipur is often referred to as the City of Sunrise, for the maharana was the highest ranking of the *Suryavarshi* (solar) Rajputs.

In the centre of Udaipur is **Lake Pichola**. The old city sits on its east bank. There are two beautiful palaces on islands in the lake. **Jag Niwas**, now known as the **Lake Palace Hotel,** is a lavish, plush retreat in a fairy-tale setting. **Jag Mandir** was built as an island retreat for the emperor Shah Jahan. North of Lake Pichola is another lake, **Fateh Sagar**.

Towering over Lake Pichola is the huge **City Palace**, the former home of the rulers of Mewar. Part of it is now an interesting museum. Consisting of four major and several minor palaces built by different rulers, the complex is faultlessly integrated. North of the entrance is the **Jagdish Mandir**.

South of the City Palace is the **Zenana Mahal**. Inside, the **Rang Mahal** has a collection of jewellery and the eastern wing has exquisite inlay work. The current residence of the maharana is at Fateh Prakash. On the Moti Magri hill is the impressive **statue** of Maharana Pratap astride his royal stallion Chetak. Interesting shopping areas include Bara and Bapu **bazaars.**

North of the city is the **Sahelian ki Bari** (Garden of the Maids of Honour), a complex comprising fountains, kiosks, marble elephants and a delightful lotus pool constructed by Maharaja Sajjan Singh. Five kilometres (three miles) west of Udaipur, the **Sajjan Garh Palace** provides a panoramic view of the surrounding countryside. The **Khasi Odi Hunting Lodge** lies to its left. Three kilometres (just under two miles) east is **Ahar,** a prehistoric site with a small museum and cenotaphs to former rulers, who retreated here during the attacks on Chittor.

Eklingi, 22 kilometres (14 miles) northeast of Udaipur on the road to Nathdwara, is a complex of 108 Shiva temples collectively known as the **Shri Eklingi Temple**. The main temple has a huge ornate *mandapa* (pillared pavilion) and a four-faced image of Lord Shiva. **Nagada**, just before Eklingi, has a number of Jain temples, including the notable **Adbhutji** and **Sas Bahu temples**.

The **temple of Shri Nathji** (Vishnu) in **Nathdwara,** 48 kilometres (30 miles) from Udaipur, is one of the principal pilgrimage places in Rajasthan. Stalls here display a variety of handicrafts including *pichwais* (cloth paintings) which are traditionally placed behind a deity and have now become a popular art form. A few kilometres before Nathdwara is a turning to **Haldighati** where in 1576 there was a historic battle between Maharana Pratap and the Mughal forces under Akbar. Today the only edifice that commemorates this is the *chatri* to his horse Chetak.

Though Hindu, the rulers of Udaipur patronized Jain temples in deference to their close association with the Jain community. Aside from the temple at Rishabdeo, a visit to **Ranakpur,** 98 kilometres (62 miles) to the northwest, is a comfortable one-day journey. Situated deep in an Aravalli valley, the main temple is the large 15th-century **Charmukha** (four-faced) **Temple**, dedicated to Adinath. The temple is open to non-Jains every afternoon.

Kumbalgarh Fort, 84 kilometres (56 miles) north of Udaipur, is the most important fort in the area after Chittorgarh and an interesting complex of palaces and temples. **Jaisamand Lake,** 48 kilometres (30 miles) to the southeast, is the second-largest man-made lake in Asia, built by Maharana Jai Singh in the late 17th century. Along its shore are marble *chatris* and the summer palaces of the Udaipur queens. The surrounding area is now a **wildlife sanctuary**.

Gujarat

India's westernmost state is largely ignored by tourists. Gujarat, in turn, is content to move in the direction of massive industrialization and to ignore tourists and, consequently, tourism development. This results in an inadequate tourist transport system and too few moderately priced hotels. On the plus side, Gujarat has numerous archaeological sites and some of the country's finest historical monuments, Hindu and Jain temples and Muslim mosques. For variety there are wildlife sanctuaries and beaches. Gujarat has no nerve-racking swarms of touts, guides and hustlers. Travelling in Gujarat can be amazingly inexpensive and if you stick to Gujarati food, the price of a meal is almost laughable.

Surprisingly, one of India's most industrialized states also produces a wide range of fine handicrafts, including woven woollen shawls, rugs and blankets, tie-dyed silk and wool, embroidered cotton, wool and leather, and block-printed cotton and silk.

Travelling by taxi around Gujarat is by far the most comfortable and convenient way of getting around. Otherwise, try the punctual network of jam-packed state-owned local buses (schedules, destinations, etc. are all in Gujarati script). A slower, less convenient alternative is the railway, both metre- and broadgauge.

Ahmadabad

Four bridges span the Sabarmati River and straddle the two halves of Ahmadabad—the ever-crowded old section, and the modern part which has more or less evolved into India's showcase of architecture, with buildings designed by Corbusier and Kahn, and India's own Doshi and Correa.

An excellent city map for sightseeing is available from the **Gujarat Tourism Office** on Ashram Road.

Ahmadabad's museums are particularly noteworthy—the **Calico Museum** has one of the world's finest collections of textiles. The **Shreyas Museum of Folk Art**, the **Lalbhai Dalpatbhai Museum of Indology**, the **Kite Museum** and the **Utensils Museum** are all private collections belonging to individuals or families. **Vishalla** is not only an excellent Gujarati restaurant; it provides the ambience of rural Gujarat, and should not be missed. It is about eight kilometres (five miles) from the centre of the city in the same complex as the Utensils Museum.

Cross one of the bridges over the Sabarmati and you enter another world. Congested roads lead into labyrinthine lanes, where some of the houses still have ornate, carved wooden facades, and every nook and cranny has a tiny Jain temple or a cul-de-sac with its own wooden gate shutting out the rest of the world. The important temples here are the carved wooden **Swaminarayan Temple** and the Jain **Hutheesing Temple,** made of marble. **Sidi Saiyid's Mosque** has a much-photographed window with stone tracery depicting the tree

of life. The **Jami Masjid** and **Rani Sipri's Mausoleum** are only a few among the scores of Islamic monuments in the city. **Rani ni Hajiro** and **Badshah ni Hajiro** are good places to shop for handicrafts, notably fabrics.

Ahmadabad cannot be done in a day: there is far too much to see and experience. Moreover, it is a convenient base for excursions. **Lothal**, about 80 kilometres (50 miles) to the south, is important archaeologically as the site dates back 4,500 years. **Modhera**, 106 kilometres (66 miles) from Ahmadabad, is not quite as old; the **Sun Temple** here was built a thousand years ago. Overnight excursions might include **Palitana** where there are 863 Jain temples on a hilltop. White-clad Jain nuns, the swirling clouds which envelop the temples, and the continuous chant of prayers make Palitana a spiritual experience even for non-believers. **Patan,** further away from Modhera, is an architecturally important town with many carved wooden buildings. Step wells, seen throughout Gujarat, beautifully carved marble Jain temples, and *patola* weaving are among the other reasons for paying Patan a visit.

Baroda (Vadodara)

If Ahmadabad has a predominantly commercial ambience, Baroda still feels like a princely capital. It was, in fact, the erstwhile capital of the Gaekwad ruler who endowed it with fine buildings and parks, and although the **Laxmi Vilas Palace** and other gracious buildings are not open to the public, Baroda is pleasant enough to warrant a short stop. Perhaps because the former rulers were great patrons of art, Baroda's **College of Fine Art,** housed in a former royal residence, is one of the best in India. Visitors are welcome to walk in and look

around. The **Baroda Museum** and **Maharaja Fateh Singh Museum** are worth
a visit, although the latter is sometimes closed to the public without prior notice.

On R C Dutt Road is an ice-cream parlour serving Vadilal ice-cream, the
best brand in the country and available only in western India.

As in Ahmadabad, three-wheeler rickshaws, the most practical way of
getting around the city, are metered. Drivers carry a card listing the fares
payable according to the meter, though it is usually in the Gujarati script.
Unmetered taxis are available too, so check the prevailing charges.

Champaner, 47 kilometres (30 miles) from Baroda, is a city of ruins. Architecturally significant and distinctive, many of the surviving buildings incorporate local characteristics not found elsewhere in Gujarat. West of Champaner is
the 820-metre (2,700-foot) hill of **Pavagadh**, enclosed by ruined fortifications
and topped by Hindu temples. Champaner and Pavagadh make a very pleasant
one-day excursion from Baroda.

Saurashtra

Part of the fun of travelling around Gujarat is encountering groups of women
exotically attired in traditional embroidered clothing right in the middle of
nowhere. This happens frequently in Saurashtra, enlivening the otherwise dreary
bus rides.

A train leaves Ahmadabad every morning, reaching **Dwarka** by evening.
Dwarka is one of the most important Hindu pilgrimage places because, accord-
ing to legend, Krishna lived here. Non-Hindus are not allowed inside the
Dwarkadish Temple but can admire the exterior, with its lavishly carved spire.

Maharashtra

Maharashtra is one of India's most economically advanced states, with industry concentrated in the urban areas and agriculture spread throughout the rest of the state. Geographically, it consists of the narrow Konkan coast backed up by the Sahyadri range of the Western Ghats, which ascends to the Deccan plateau and a series of river valleys.

In ancient times the region supplied the ports on the western coast and eventually the markets of ancient Mesopotamia and Rome. Vital trade routes influenced its chequered political history. Successive dynasties left a rich artistic and cultural legacy. Numerous rock-cut temples, including the largest in India, are scattered along ancient trade routes. Scores of forts in the Western Ghats testify to the age when a Hindu revival gave prominence to the legendary Shivaji, founder of the great Maratha dynasty which challenged Mughal might and later harassed the British until their decisive defeat in 1818. Royal patronage encouraged the development of various crafts, especially weaving, and nurtured a theatrical tradition that continues today. Buddhist, Hindu and Jain caves, Hindu temples and Muslim shrines scattered throughout Maharashtra recall the various dynasties that came to conquer and stayed to build.

Bombay

Political capital of Maharashtra, and commercial capital of India, Bombay is many cities in one. As the world's largest textiles market, a major industrial centre and the country's busiest port handling over 40 percent of India's maritime trade, it contributes around 50 percent of the national exchequer. The city hums with activity, and its more than eight million residents and three million commuters seem to be constantly on the move. Natural increase and steady rural migration have quadrupled Bombay's population over the last 40 years. The original island of Bombay—consolidating a number of earlier islands—is only 24 kilometres (15 miles) long and some four kilometres (2.5 miles) wide at its broadest point, and has a population density of over 43,000 persons per square kilometre (100,000 per square mile), amongst the highest in the world. Pavement dwellers and slums coexist with modern skyscrapers and gracious colonial buildings, obsolete textile mills with impressive modern factories, Christian churches with Hindu temples—in a medley of contradictions that makes Bombay a product of the Indian past that holds the key to the present and the future.

History

Bombay has no recorded ancient past. Its original inhabitants, Koli (whence 'coolie') fishermen, were largely unaffected by political developments on the mainland. Although Buddhist and Hindu dynasties ruled the region until around the 13th century, there were only scattered settlements on the island. Subsequent Muslim rulers ceded these to the Portuguese, who presented Bombay to the

British as part of the dowry of Catherine of Braganza, bride of Charles II, in 1661. The real development of Bombay commenced soon after under the East India Company and later the British Crown. Recognizing its potential as a centre of maritime commerce, the Company initiated measures which laid the foundation on which the city stands today. Over the next 150 years, the seven original islands were gradually joined together; Parsi, Jain and Muslim merchants and manufacturers from Gujarat were encouraged to settle in the city, and the harbour, docks and industrial base gradually developed. The city received a tremendous impetus with the commissioning of India's first railway in 1854. Its growing cotton trade gained considerably from the American Civil War, which shut off American supplies of cotton to Europe, and later from the opening of the Suez Canal. Bombay's increasing prosperity was reflected in the impressive civic and commercial buildings that went up in the second half of the 19th century. Many of these still stand, giving Bombay much of its character as a grand repository of Victorian architecture. Continuity is further reflected in the names of districts like Colaba, Mahim, Mazagaon, Parel, Worli, Girgaum and Dongri, the seven original islands.

Bombay is a major gateway to India. Dozens of international airlines operate regular flights to and from Sahar, Bombay's international airport. The domestic airport at nearby Santa Cruz caters to an extensive network of domestic destinations. Airport buses and fixed-price taxis operate to all major city locations. The rail network is well developed, with two separate systems. Northern destinations are served by Churchgate (for suburban traffic) and Bombay Central stations of the Western Railway. Services to the south and east and the northern route through central India are provided by the Central Railway at Victoria Terminus. Bus services are extensive.

November to mid-March is the best time to visit Bombay, when temperatures range from 20° to 30°C (68°–86°F). Summers are hot and humid, though somewhat relieved by sea breezes. The monsoon between June and September brings constant heavy rain, cooler temperatures but very high humidity.

Relics of the Raj

Perhaps the appropriate place to begin exploring Bombay's colonial legacy is the **Gateway of India**. Built to commemorate the royal visit of George V and Queen Mary in 1911 but only completed in 1924, the gateway is a combination of European and Indian ceremonial architecture. The last British troops marched out through this gate when India became independent in 1947. Today it is a favourite haunt of tourists. The **Taj Mahal Hotel** opposite the Gateway is an important landmark. It was built in 1903 by Jamshethji N Tata, founder of a prestigious industrial house, to counter a ban on Indians entering the then famous Watson's hostelry. The Taj flourished, becoming the first destination of sea-weary travellers and a world-famous hotel, while Watson's disappeared from the scene before Independence.

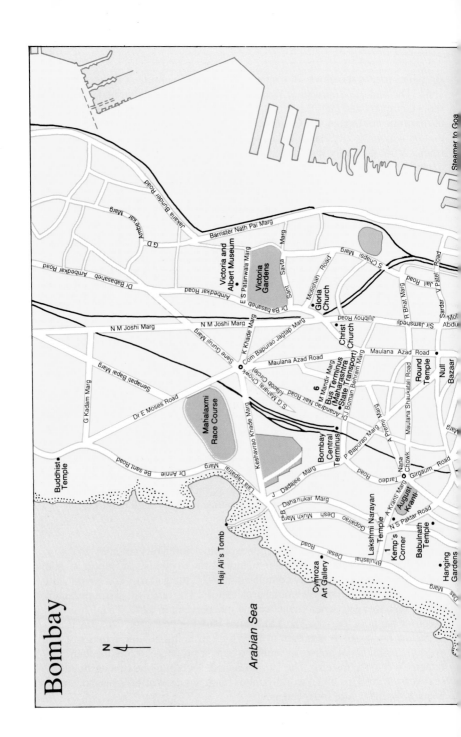

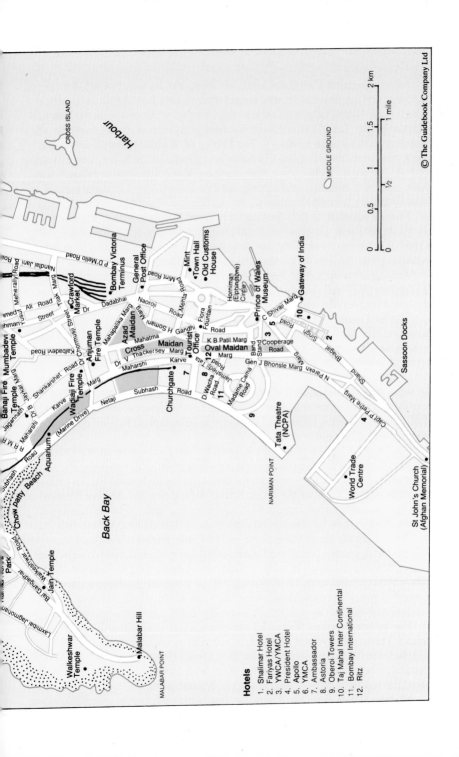

CROSS ISLAND

Harbour

MIDDLE GROUND

© The Guidebook Company Ltd

Nandlal Jani Road

P D'Mello Road

Crawford Market

Bombay Victoria Terminus

General Post Office

Mint Road

Mint
Town Hall
Old Customs House

Mehta Road

Horniman (Elphinstone) Circle

Flora Fountain

Prince of Wales Museum

Gateway of India

Sassoon Docks

St John's Church
(Afghan Memorial)

World Trade Centre

Capt P Petre Marg

NARIMAN POINT

Tata Theatre
(NCPA)

Gen J Bhonsle Marg

Madame Cama Road

Back Bay

MALABAR POINT

Chow Paty Beach

Aquarium

Banaji Fire Temple
Mumbadevi Temple
Wadiaji Fire Temple
Anjuman Fire Temple

Crawford Market

Dr

Dadabhai

Naoroji

Azad Maidan

Cross Maidan

Oval Maidan

Tourist Office

Churchgate

Subhash Road

Netaji

Karve Road

Maharshi

Dr V Thackersey Marg

Mahapalika Marg

Mahatma H Gandhi Road

K B Patil Marg

Cooperage Road

Band Stand

C Shivaji Marg

Shahid Bhagat Singh Road

Shahid Bhagat Singh Marg

Walkeshwar Temple
Jain Temple
Bal Gangadhar
Malabar Hill

Walkeshwar Road

Laxmibai Jagmohan

Hotels

1. Shalimar Hotel
2. Fariyas Hotel
3. YWCA/YMCA
4. President Hotel
5. Apollo
6. YMCA
7. Ambassador
8. Astoria
9. Oberoi Towers
10. Taj Mahal Inter Continental
11. Bombay International
12. Ritz

0   0.5   1   1.5   2 km
0   ½   1   1.5 mile

Many evocative Victorian Gothic buildings can be seen in **Fort**, the central business and administrative area named after the old fort of Bombay, demolished in the 1860s. Of particular interest, close to the Gateway, is the **Council Hall,** once the Sailor's Home, which stands in Byzantine grandeur on the site of Bombay's first British cemetery. The **Prince of Wales Museum**, across the road, commemorates George V's first visit to India in 1905. It is a fine example of Indo-Saracenic architecture, housing excellent collections of Indian sculpture, miniature paintings and Nepali and Tibetan art. There is also a natural history gallery (closed Mondays).

Flora Fountain, at the commercial heart of Bombay, was erected in honour of Sir Bartle Frere, governor of Bombay during the period of dramatic growth (1862–7). A more modern memorial in the same square, dedicated to martyred patriots, gives the area its current official name, **Hutatma Chowk**.

Among other important Bombay landmarks are the extravagant **Victoria Terminus (VT)** and the **Municipal Corporation Building** opposite, both designed by Stevens, and the **General Post Office.** East of Flora Fountain, the simpler **St Thomas's Cathedral** which was once visible from the sea is now surrounded by tall buildings. The classical façade of the old **Town Hall** (1833) nearby now houses the **Asiatic Society** with its marvellous library and cobwebbed statues of forgotten times. A similar façade close by belongs to the **Mint,** built in 1829. Still further east is **Ballard Estate** with office buildings strongly reminiscent of 19th-century London, as is much of Bombay. The **University** with its central clock tower, the Old Secretariat, the High Court, the PWD (Public Works) Office and the Central Telegraph Office are all at the western end of the old Fort.

For Bombay off the beaten track, head for the southern tip of the island, where tree-lined avenues and a pervasive sense of order characterize the modern military and naval enclave built on the remains of a traditional British cantonment. Most relaxing after the hectic activity of the city, the **Afghan Memorial Church** was established here in 1847 and later consecrated to the memory of those who lost their lives in the Afghan Wars. A Koli fishing village still survives along the shore towards the end of **Cuffe Parade**. Wooden boats come in with the day's catch, and the fisherwomen, their saris tucked between their legs in Maharashtrian style, take it to market. A dawn visit to **Sassoon Dock**, now a fishing harbour and fish market, can be a colourful olfactory experience. Before Bombay's present docks were built and modernized, this dock, built by a prominent Baghdadi Jewish family, served regular commercial purposes.

The bazaars north of Victoria Terminus are an exciting medley of colour and sound. There is **Crawford Market**, which sells almost everything; **Mohatta Market**, the mammoth cloth market; the famous **Chor Bazaar**, or 'thieves market', where Victoriana jostles for place with Indian 'antiques'; and **Lal Bazaar**, the red-light district, also known as **Kamatipura**.

Marine Drive, Bombay's most famous boulevard, curves gracefully along **Back Bay** on land reclaimed in 1920. It links the high-rise office complex at

A Life of Luxury

*T*he richer the host, the later dinner was served. Dining late was a
status symbol, like Scotch whisky, five times the price of the
Indian, and the imported car, a particularly costly luxury, that had
brought him here from his hotel. "The first thing those local elites
do—not to mention their presidents or generals or whoever's at the
top—is to get themselves the biggest, latest model foreign cars," he
had been told in his briefing before this trip, "and why not? We
like the way we live. We can't blame them for wanting to live like
us. Besides, it's what makes them ready to buy what we have to
sell."

"Won't you have another drink, Mr Neuman?" his hostess
offered.

"I still have some, thank you."

"It's Scotch."

He raised his hand in polite refusal. The room was remarkable
for its total anonymity. No echo of time past or things to come.
Roses stood stiff and upright on display in a blinding array of
surgically cut, bulk-bought crystal, to judge by the profusion of
vases, ashtrays and bowls all over the room. His host, who had left
the room to answer the telephone, returned, a cherubic face on a
prematurely elderly frame.

"Another drink, Mr Neuman?"

"Not yet, thanks."

"It's Scotch."

"A little later," he said.

His hostess was curled up on the sofa, tiny and elegant in her
airy cotton sari, with decanters and bottles lined up on a trolley at
her elbow. Ignoring his refusal she lifted a hand to press a bell near
her, the bright cluster on her wrist glinting in the lamplight, and
an old white-coated servant hobbled slowly across yards of floor to
refill his glass and present it to him.

Nayantara Saghal, Rich Like Us

Nariman Point with the exclusive residential area of **Malabar Hill**. It is particularly spectacular at night, when its long string of street lights is likened to a sparkling necklace. Towards evening it is a popular promenade. **Chowpatty Beach** to the north also comes to life in the evening. Holy men bury themselves in the sand, others sculpt images of the gods, jugglers and magicians do their bit, fishermen haul in their nets, someone makes a speech, horses gallop along the shore, and the innumerable food stalls do a brisk business.

The **Hanging Gardens** and **Kamla Nehru Park** at the crest of Malabar Hill are pleasant spots, the latter offering a panoramic view of south and central Bombay and, by night, the 'Queen's Necklace' along Marine Drive.

Bombay's many places of worship reflect its cultural diversity. Among the Roman Catholic churches in the city, **St Michael's** at Mahim and the famous shrine of **Mount Mary** in Bandra are particularly well known. The 500-year-old **Haji Ali Mosque** on a tidal island near the **Mahalaxmi Racecourse** attracts numerous worshippers. There is also the relatively new Jain temple on Malabar Hill, its opulence testifying to the prosperity of the Jain community. Hindu temples include the thousand-year-old **Walkeshwar Babul Nath** dedicated to Krishna, **Mahalakshmi** dedicated to the goddess of wealth, and **Mumba Devi** honouring the goddess for whom Bombay is named. Several temples also cluster around the **Ban Ganga tank** at the foot of Malabar Hill, creating an unusual ambience. There are Zoroastrian fire temples all over the city, and on Malabar Hill are the **Towers of Silence** where the Parsi dead are exposed to the elements and the vultures so as to ensure that sacred earth and fire are not polluted. No visitors are allowed.

Trips from Bombay

The beach at **Juhu**, 18 kilometres (11 miles) north of the city centre, is the closest to the city. With donkey and camel rides, performing monkeys, food stalls, lots of people and safe swimming, it is fun. **Marve** and **Madh,** about 40 kilometres (25 miles) away, are more secluded. There is a small fishing village near Marve and the remains of an old Portuguese church at Madh. **Manori** and **Gorai** also have lovely beaches. The fishing village at Gorai and its splendid Portuguese church are worth a visit. The beaches at **Kihim**, **Nagaon** and **Murud** with its island **fort** can be reached by a combination of ferry and bus or by a lengthy but worthwhile drive.

Krishnagiri Upavan National Park, which is 40 kilometres (25 miles) from the city, has reservoirs, a lion 'safari' park, **Film City** and the ancient **Kanheri Caves** established by Buddhist monks in around the second century BC. The **Great Chaitya Cave,** with its long colonnade and magnificent statues of the Buddha, justifies the climb. An elaborate water supply and disposal system is also of interest. There are regular tours, and taxis can be hired from the city or the nearest suburban railway station, **Borivili**.

The rock-cut Hindu temples at **Elephanta**, an island about ten kilometres (six miles) across the harbour, provide an exciting glimpse of Indian sculpture dating from about AD 600. Huge panels depict episodes relating to Lord Shiva,

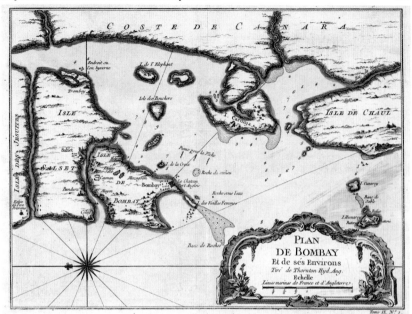

each executed with power, grace and an amazing sense of movement. The central sculpture, a five-metre (16-foot) bust of the god, represents his three aspects as creator, preserver and destroyer. Pleasant walks along forested slopes with spectacular views, especially of the new harbour on the mainland, are a delightful bonus. Launches leave from the Gateway of India every half hour. The one-hour boat ride, past high-prowed fishing boats driven by the wind, oil tankers and merchant ships, modern naval vessels and scurrying tugs, with Bombay's nuclear power plant in the background, is a study in contrasts.

Pune and Lonavala

Although Pune, the historical capital of the Marathas, is the logical beginning for any exploration of Maharashtra state, the hill stations en route are charming diversions. **Matheran,** on a spur of the Western Ghats is closest to Bombay, 64 kilometres (40 miles) away. Shady walks through thick forests, spectacular views and faded elegance combine with an unusual quiet as no vehicles are permitted in the town. The easiest way to get to Matheran is by train from Bombay, via Neral, where a 'toy' train departs regularly for the plateau, taking over two hours for the nine-kilometre (five-mile) ascent. A taxi from Neral is a much quicker alternative.

Lonavala and **Khandala**, on the crest of the Ghats on the way to Pune, are best reached by train from Bombay. Both retain a certain old-world charm and offer a comparatively cool climate conducive to long walks with marvellous views of the valleys below. The **Karla Caves** near Lonavala, built by Buddhist monks in the first century AD, are also worth a visit. Several hilltop forts in the region offer rewarding climbs and exciting panoramas.

Pune (Poona), 70 kilometres (45 miles) from Lonavala, can be reached by either train or road, though twice-daily flights also operate from Bombay. Former capital of the Marathas, Pune became an important cantonment town under the British and is now a burgeoning industrial city. The sights include the hilltop **Parvati Temple;** the 18th-century **Pataleshwar Temple** cut out of a huge rock; **Qamathe Rali Darvesh,** a Muslim shrine with an interesting levitating rock; and **Shinde Chhatri,** (the cenotaph of an important Maratha leader). The **Raj Kelkar Museum** housing a huge private collection of unusual traditional arts is worth a visit. **Simhagad, Raigadh, Torna, Purandhar** and **Shivneri** are some Maratha forts within easy reach of Pune. The city is also a base for excursions to the hill resorts at **Panchgani,** 90 kilometres (55 miles) and **Mahabeleshwar,** 100 kilometres (60 miles), away.

Aurangabad, Ajanta and Ellora

Aurangabad

The take-off point for visiting some of the subcontinent's greatest art treasures at Ajanta and Ellora is Aurangabad. Named for the Mughal emperor Aurangzeb, it was once a major centre of power now recalled by several evocative Muslim monuments. The better known are **Bibi ka Maqbara,** tomb of the empress, an ungainly replica of the Taj; and **Panchakki,** where an old mill and the tomb of an important Sufi saint are set in serene gardens. There is also the **Daulatabad Fort** just outside the city, built by Muhammad bin Tughlaq as an alternative capital to Delhi. Thousands died on the forced march to the new site before the sultan abandoned his plan.

Daily flights link Aurangabad to Delhi and Bombay. Bus tours and taxis are available for visits to the caves at Ajanta, 104 kilometres (65 miles), and Ellora, 28 kilometres (17 miles), away.

Ajanta

Excavated and painted by Buddhist monks between 200 BC and AD 600, the 30 **caves** at Ajanta are decorated with remarkable murals that are universally regarded as some of India's finest artistic treasures. They depict scenes from the life of the Buddha and Buddhist fables with skill and devotion. The technique involved preparing the rock wall with a 10–15 millimetre (half-inch) coating of clay, cow dung, rice husks and animal hair and then covering it with a smooth layer of lime. The composition was then sketched in red and an undercoat applied. Colours were filled in, accents were added and finally the surface was carefully polished.

The finest paintings are found in caves 1, 2, 16, 17 and 19. The magnificent depictions of the bodhisattvas (potential Buddhas who out of compassion renounce the attainment of Buddhahood) Avalokitesvara and Padmapani in cave 1 are particularly well known. The latter, holding a lotus and standing beside his voluptuous wife, is another famous image. In cave 2, ceiling and wall paintings illustrate events associated with the Buddha's birth. A cameo of a woman at her toilet is a universal favourite. Caves 16 and 17 contain some of the finest work at Ajanta. While the pathos of the 'dying princess' is particularly haunting, the sheer variety and exuberance of the visual narrative is overwhelming. The woman painting her lips in cave 18 is also a major attraction.

Although Ajanta is best known for its paintings, the caves contain some excellent sculptures, particularly caves 1, 4, 17, 19 and 26. The magnificent statue of the Buddha in cave 1, the figures fleeing representations of evil in cave 4, the carved dwarfs supporting the pillars in cave 17, the fine sculptures of the Buddha and of a *naga* (snake) king with a cobra hood shading his head in cave 19, and the reclining Buddha and scenes of his temptation in cave 26 are all remarkable works of art.

Ellora

For unknown reasons, Ajanta was abandoned in the seventh century when the artist monks moved to Ellora, 66 kilometres (41 miles) away. Stretching about two kilometres (just over a mile) from north to south, the 34 **cave temples** were carved out of the hillside with hand tools. Only 12 of the 34 caves are Buddhist, but even these incorporate Hindu and Jain themes, demonstrating the gradual decline of Buddhism. They are nevertheless imbued with a sense of serenity. Caves 11 and 12 are among the most ambitious architecturally, with two and even three storeys and lavishly sculpted interiors. In early 1990 the Archaeological Survey of India announced the discovery of 28 additional caves in the upper hills. Possibly dating from the ninth to the 13th centuries, the caves apparently contain Hindu sculpture.

The 17 Hindu caves in the centre are by far the most impressive. Dominating the entire group, the three-tiered tower of the massive **Kailasha Temple** (cave 16) is nearly one and a half times taller than the Parthenon and occupies almost twice its area. It was constructed by excavating approximately 200,000 tonnes of rock and is possibly the world's largest monolithic structure. Working downwards, craftsmen first chiselled the roof out of the rock and then worked the interior, leaving pillars that were decorative rather than functional. Representing Shiva's Himalayan home, the temple is exquisitely sculpted with scenes from Hindu mythology, each pulsing with drama, energy and passion, consummate artistry and immense vitality. The depiction of the demon Ravana shaking Mount Kailash is a masterpiece. Athough the other caves pale in comparison with Kailash, there is also excellent carving to be seen in cave 14 (**Rava Kakhi**), cave 15 (**Das Avatara**), cave 21 (**Ramesvara**) and cave 29 (**Dumar Lena**). The five **Jain temples** to the north mark the latest phase at Ellora. While they are not as spectacular as the Hindu caves, the fine detail of the sculpture is remarkable. Cave 32 (**Indra Sabha**) is particularly lovely, while the **Chota** (little) **Kailasha**, though incomplete, is worthy of inspection.

Front View of the Bisman Kurm, Ellora, 1846 (above)
Prince Vishvantara announcing his banishment, Cave 17, Ajanta (below)

Goa

White sands and blue seas, warmed by the sun; lush tropical vegetation; sleepy villages surrounded by bright paddy fields; leisurely lifestyles amd baroque churches—Goa is all this and much more. More than 1,000 years of Hindu and Muslim rule, followed by five centuries of Portuguese rule, have produced an unusual blend of Eastern and Western culture. About halfway down India's west coast, enclosed by the Western Ghats and the Arabian Sea, Goa became part of the Indian Union only in 1961.

Daily flights link Goa with Bombay, Delhi, Cochin, Trivandrum and Bangalore. Dabolim airport is a 30-minute drive from Panaji (formerly called Panjim), the state capital. Taxis are available at the airport for transfers as well as local transport. Some hotels run their own transport service.

An overnight boat service between Bombay and Panaji can be fun but is hardly luxurious. Unfortunately, the service was suspended in 1989 but should be resumed in 1990.

The peak tourist season in Goa runs from November through February, when temperatures are low enough for a light wrap in the evening. The **carnival**, held three days before Lent at a warmer time of the year, is also an extremely popular occasion to visit. Goa is also pleasant during the monsoon (June to September), though it is wet and fairly humid during these months.

The Beaches

With 130 kilometres (82 miles) of coastline, Goa offers an immense variety of superb beaches, some totally secluded, others with many facilities.

The palm-fringed **Dona Paula**, with its magnificent view of the Marmagao harbour, and the lovely **Miramar** are closest to Panaji. Across the Mandovi River are **Candolim**, the famous **Calangute**, followed by **Baga**, **Anjuna** (well-known for its Wednesday flea market), **Vagator** and, in the extreme north, the little-known **Harmal**. **Siridao**, near the estuary of the Zuari River, is a shell collector's dream. Still further south there are **Bogmalo**, **Valsao** and finally, around eight kilometres (five miles) from Margao, the glorious stretch of **Colva**, virtually deserted except for a few resorts and quietest around **Benaulim** and the **Betul promontory**. Several others are just waiting to be discovered.

When the Portuguese colonized Goa in 1510, **Panaji** was a tiny village on the southern bank of the Mandovi River. It gained importance in the 17th century when the governor's residence was moved there from Old Goa. By 1843, Panaji was raised to the status of a city and named Nova Goa. It became the capital of Portuguese India in 1853 following an outbreak of plague in the old city. Today Panaji has a population of over 40,000.

A Mediterranean flavour is preserved in Panaji's numerous squares, in its broad avenues edged with ornate Latin villas and in old residential areas where narrow cobbled streets meander past old homes with red-tiled roofs and overhanging balconies. And at every corner, innumerable small cafés and bars, integral to Goan life, create a special atmosphere.

As in most Goan towns, life in Panaji revolves around a church, the **Church of the Immaculate Conception**, one of the oldest in Goa. Its impressive entrance, well-proportioned baroque façade and tall towers (once visible from the entrance to the harbour) dominate the square on which it stands. Along the **Campal**, the picturesque riverside boulevard, are some of Panaji's public buildings, including the **Secretariat**, once the governor's residence, built in 1615 on the site of the palace of the Sultan of Bijapur, who lost Goa to the Portuguese.

Velha or Old Goa

Fabulous churches, convents, monasteries and stately mansions once lined the broad avenues of this magnificent 16th-century city. It was then Golden Goa, *Goa Doraida*, the commercial hub of Portugal's eastern empire, with more people than London or Paris, the 'Rome of the Orient', rivalling even Lisbon in magnificence. An old saying went: 'Whoever has seen Goa need not see Lisbon'. Portuguese military reverses and a great plague led to its being abandoned. What remains covers eight square kilometres (three square miles) punctuated by grand churches where Indian craftsmanship merged with Latin exuberance.

The **Cathedral of St Catherine da Se**, one of the most imposing monuments of this period, is the largest church in Asia. Considered the finest expression of religious art in Goa, the **Franciscan Church and Convent,** built in 1521, is the only example of Portuguese Gothic or Manuelne architecture in Asia. Its ornate interior is an effective blend of local and European art. The convent next to the church houses an interesting **museum**.

The focus for many of Goa's visitors, the **Basilica de Bom Jesus** enshrines the mortal remains of St Francis Xavier in a magnificent mausoleum, a gift of the Duke of Tuscany in return for the saint's pillow. An excellent example of Jesuit architecture with a well-proportioned exterior, its interior is perhaps the most richly decorated in Goa. Other religious structures include **St Cajetan's Church**, styled after St Peter's in Rome; the **Chapel of St Catherine**, commemorating the Portuguese conquest of Goa in 1510; and on **Monte Santo**, Holy Hill, are the fortress-like **Church of Our Lady of the Rosary**, one of the oldest in Goa, and the **Church and Convent of Santa Monica**, once one of the largest convents in the Portuguese empire. (It has a crucifix believed to be miraculous.)

Despite its amazing number of churches, Goa is 68 percent Hindu. Portuguese zeal, particularly during the Inquisition, led to the destruction of most of Goa's old temples and mosques. A Hindu flavour endures, however, at **Ponda**, where several temples and shrines survived since it was conquered only in 1763, in a more tolerant era. Among the seven temples in and around Ponda are **Shri**

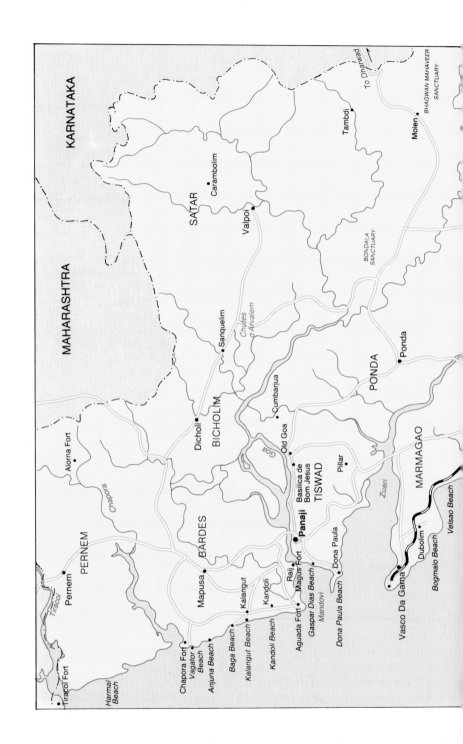

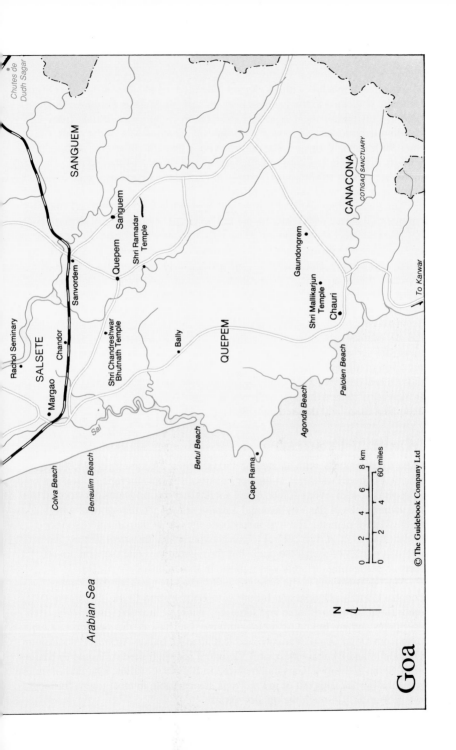

Goa

Arabian Sea

Chutes de
Dudh Sagar

SANGUEM

Rachol Seminary

SALSETE

Margao

Chandor

Sanvordem

Shri Chandreshwar
Bhutnath Temple

Quepem

Sanguem

Shri Ramadar
Temple

Bally

QUEPEM

Gaundongrem

Shri Mallikarjun
Temple

Chauri

CANACONA

COTIGAO SANCTUARY

To Karwar

Colva Beach

Benaulim Beach

Sal

Betul Beach

Cape Rama

Agonda Beach

Palolen Beach

N

0   2   4   6   8 km

0   2   4   60 miles

© The Guidebook Company Ltd

Mangesh, set on a hill with its elegant blue pillars and silver idols; **Shri Shan-tadurga**, dedicated to the goddess Parvati; and the **Nagesh Temple**. All are built in a distinctive local style characterized by ornate interiors and free-standing lamp towers *(deepmals)*. Further inland at the foot of the ghats, the **Shri Mahadeva Temple** is the only surviving example of temple architecture built by the Kadambas who ruled between the 11th and 13th centuries. The more recent **Shri Mahalaxmi Temple** in Panaji, the first constructed under Portuguese rule, was completed in 1818.

Margao, further south, is the second-largest town in Goa and an important commercial centre with a few lovely old homes. The busy port of **Marmagoa** has few historical sights, though its superb harbour was a major factor in the growth of Goa. **Mapusa**, a charming traditional Goan town, comes to life on Friday market day. But it is in the villages that typical Goan life unfolds. Houses are built around an often overgrown central courtyard, surrounded by a deep veranda leading to airy rooms. The feast day of the village patron saint is a major event. The entire village joins the procession, following the brightly decorated image of the saint, and then participates even more enthusiastically in the gay secular celebrations that follow. Feni, the local brew, flows, sumptuous meals are served and there is music and dancing. The annual **carnival** is the cul-mination of all such celebrations. For three days, almost anything goes. Dancing in the streets reaches a frenzied finale on the last day when Momo, the King of Darkness, is carried through the town in an elaborate procession, complete with decorated floats and masked dancers.

Madhya Pradesh

India's largest state, with an area of 450,000 square kilometres (174,000 square miles), Madhya Pradesh is in the very heart of India. Geographically it is a land of contrasts, with river valleys, dense forests and rolling plains overlooked by the ancient hills of the Vindhya and Satpura ranges and the sprawling highlands of the Malwa plateau. The region has been the site of human activity since prehistoric times and its central location explains its turbulent history, reflected in the hundreds of archaeological sites throughout the state that contain art forms representing virtually every phase in Indian history.

Most destinations in the state are well served by air. Two daily flights connect Gwalior, Bhopal and Indore with Bombay and Delhi. There is also a daily flight between Bhopal and Jabalpur. These destinations are also on trunk rail routes and are linked by national highways. Daily flights operate to Khaju-raho from Delhi, Agra, Varanasi and Kathmandu. Indian Airlines links Raipur with Delhi and Bhubaneswar, and Vuyadoot has flights from Bhopal to Khaju-raho, Satna and Rewa. Cars can be hired in Bhopal, Gwalior, Khajuraho, Indore and Jabalpur for trips out of town. Taxis are available in most towns for local transportation, although the quality varies.

The best time to visit Madhya Pradesh is from November through March when temperatures range between 6° and 20° C (42°–68° F). Summers are hot, with temperatures of 30°–45° C (86°–113° F), but the evenings are fairly pleasant, especially at Indore, Mandu, Ujjain and Bhopal on the Malwa plateau, which is famed for its cool summer nights. During the monsoon in July and August, the humidity is high and transportation unreliable. For the more adventuresome, Mandu is at its loveliest during the rains, and wildlife viewing is best in summer.

Gwalior and Shivpuri

The northernmost city of Madhya Pradesh, Gwalior once dominated ancient military and trade routes linking northern and southern India. It was the seat of several great dynasties, each contributing a rich legacy of monuments and extending royal patronage to poets, musicians and artisans. Legend, however, ascribes the origin of the fortress to the miraculous cure of a leper chieftain, Suraj Sen, by the sage Gwalipa, for whom the city is named.

Gwalior's massive hilltop **fort** dominates the city and encloses several interesting monuments. Jain **monoliths** carved into the hillside flank the approach. The **Man Mandir Palace** was built between 1486 and 1517 by the famous Raja Man Singh of the Tomar dynasty. Colourful tiles still decorate its façade and the inner courtyards are richly carved. **Karan Mahal** and **Jehangiri Mahal** are nearby palaces worth visiting. Over 30 metres (100 feet) high, the ninth-century **Teli Temple** combines southern architecture with northern decorative motifs. The twin **Sas Bahu Temples** are graceful examples of 11th-century temple architecture. **Gujari Mahal**, below the fort, built by Raja Man Singh for his favourite queen, is now an **archaeological museum**. Enclosed in stone fretwork, the **Tomb of Muhammad Ghaus**, a Muslim saint, is a superb example of early Mughal architecture. **Tansen**, a disciple of the saint and renowned 16th-century musician, is buried close by. He is remembered here each year at a festival of classical music. The cenotaphs commemorating latter-day Maratha rulers of the Scindia dynasty are also well worth a visit. The **Jai Vilas Palace**, built in the 1800s, combines Tuscan, Italian and Corinthian styles and has imposing interiors.

The medieval town of **Orchha** is just 120 kilometres (75 miles) from Gwalior and 19 kilometres (12 miles) from Jhansi. Synthesizing Hindu and Mughal architecture, its palaces, temples and cenotaphs were built in the 16th and 17th centuries by the Bundela rulers of the area. Situated near the Betwa River, the town has retained much of its character and been little affected by 'progress'.

Shivpuri, one-time summer capital of the Scindias, lies about 112 kilometres (70 miles) southwest of Gwalior on the main Bombay–Delhi highway. The Scindia family cenotaphs in the serene natural setting of the **Madhav National Park** are the main attractions. The nearby **Karera Bustard Sanctuary**, midway

The massive but incomplete **Shiva temple** at **Bhojpur**, 28 kilometres (17 miles) southeast of Bhopal, is a magnificent example of 11th-century temple architecture. Remarkable for its soaring strength of line and elegant sculpture, it houses a huge *lingam*, a ritual phallic symbol.

At **Bhimbetka,** 40 kilometres (25 miles) south of Bhopal, over 500 painted neolithic caves chronicle the life of prehistoric man.

Sanchi, 46 kilometres (30 miles) to the northeast of Bhopal, has some of the finest and most varied examples of Buddhist sculpture and architecture in India. The **Great Stupa**, with its majestic dome built over Buddhist relics, is India's oldest stone structure. An intricately carved railing encircles the stupa, and four magnificently sculpted *toranas*, or gateways, illustrate the Buddha's numerous lives with an intricacy that can only be described as an act of worship. The Buddha is here represented only by symbols: the lotus, the tree of life, footprints, and a throne. The unusually lustrous **Ashoka Pillar** near the southern gateway was originally inscribed with a religious ordinance and surmounted by a lion capital, now the national emblem of India. Of the other *stupas* in the vicinity, numbers 2 and 3 are of particular interest. Only a few ruined monasteries remain. The famous **Begging Bowl**, carved from a single huge boulder and used to collect food for the monks, is near one of these. A poorly designed modern monastery displays two glass caskets containing relics returned to the site by Britain in the 1950s. Other places of interest around Sanchi include the ancient settlements of **Vidisha**, **Udaiygiri** and **Gyaraspur.**

Indore

Planned and built by Rani Ahilyabai of the Maratha Holkar dynasty in the 18th century, Indore was once a major centre of Maratha power. Several temples, palaces and cenotaphs of this period are worth a visit, but the focus of the Indore of today is commerce and industry. It is a perfect base for forays further afield.

Mandu, known in the 15th century as Shadiabad, City of Joy, is about a two-hour drive away. Strategically perched at the edge of the Malwa plateau, about 615 metres (2,000 feet) above sea level, its excellent natural defences are reinforced by massive 45-kilometre- (27-mile-) long fort walls. Dominated successively by Hindu and provincial Muslim dynasties, Mandu later became a favourite monsoon resort of the Mughals. Even today, the monsoon season is the best time to visit. A fine mist shrouds its fairy-tale palaces, and the lakes around which the town is built are planted with masses of lotuses. Almost every structure here is remarkable. There is **Jahaz Mahal**, an elegant two-storey 'ship' palace set between two lakes; **Hindola Mahal**, resembling a swing with its sloping outer walls; **Hoshang Shah's Tomb**, the first marble structure in India and a forerunner of the Taj; **Jami Masjid**, perhaps the finest example of Afghan architecture in India; **Ashrafi Mahal**, once the largest building in Mandu; **Baz Bahadur's Palace**, resonant with legends of his romance with Roopmati; and **Roopmati's Pavilion,** from which she viewed the holy Narmada each morning. A host of lesser but memorable monuments ensure many hauntingly lovely moments.

Ujain, 53 kilometres (33 miles) from Indore, is one of the oldest and holiest Indian cities, with a history dating back to Ashoka (second century BC). It is one of the venues of a mammoth **Kumbh Mela** (religious fair) held every 12 years.

Khajuraho

In 1838 Captain T S Burt, who was working with the Asiatic Society in Calcutta, followed up local rumours and 'discovered' the great temple complex rising above the jungle in Khajuraho. Khajuraho was one of the capitals of the Chandela Rajput kings, and the temples were built during the tenth to 12th centuries. Out of the original 85 temples only 22 survive today. If it were not for Khajuraho's remoteness, there would probably be fewer. The waves of desecration and defacement of Hindu monuments by successive Muslim powers bypassed this remote spot.

Situated in the hot, dry plains of northern Madhya Pradesh, modern Khajuraho caters primarily to the needs of visitors to the temples. There is something incongruous about an airstrip in a village of less than 4,000 people receiving regular Boeing jets, but daily flights connect Khajuraho with Delhi (via Agra) and Varanasi. The nearest railway stations are at Satna (117 kilometres, or 73 miles) and Jhansi (175 kilometres, or 109 miles) which have good connecting bus services. The summers are extremely hot (up to 47°C/117°F in June), making the months between November and March the most pleasant.

The ruins of the original Chandela capital stretch over 21 square kilometres (eight square miles), but very little apart from the temples remains.

The Chandelas traced their descent from Hemvati, the daughter of a Brahmin priest, who fell in love with the moon god while bathing in the River Rati one evening. The son of this union was Chandravarman who founded the Chandela dynasty. From inscriptions found near various temples we now know that Harsadeva was the Chandela ruler in the early tenth century, followed by Yasovarman, then Dhanga who expanded the kingdom, and then the great ruler, Vidyadhara. Each ruler left his mark in successive buildings. Other Chandela centres are mostly to the northwest towards Jhansi, but none compare with the magnificence of Khajuraho. Under Dhanga the kingdom included almost all of modern Madhya Pradesh. During Vidyadhara's reign, the first Muslim invasions of northwestern India took place and were initially contained.

After Vidyadhara's death, the Chandelas moved to hill forts elsewhere in their kingdom, but the religious importance of Khajuraho to the dynasty continued up to the 14th century. Today, six centuries later, the remaining temples can be visited in a leisurely manner, unaffected by the modern world.

The temples are divided into three groups of which the western is the largest and best known. All but three temples, which are built of local granite, are

constructed with hard river sandstone dug from the east bank of the Ken River, 20 kilometres (13 miles) to the east. None of the temples are enclosed; rather they are erected on high masonry platforms, each on an east-west axis.

The oldest temple in the western group is the **Chausath Yogini** situated to the southwest of the **Siva-sagar tank**. The first temple to visit in the western group is the **Lakshmana**. This is complete, with all its outer shrines still standing. The sanctum has richly carved statues of the Vishnu incarnations, Narasimha (man-lion) and Varaha (boar). The frieze around the base of this temple is one of the easiest to study.

At the centre of the western group, the magnificent **Kandariya Mahadev**, built during Vidyadhara's reign, soars 31 metres (102 feet) above its plinth. This, the largest and grandest of the temples, is best visited with a guide who will explain each section. The architecture and sculpture show Chandela art at its peak. The well-preserved main shrine has an exquisitely carved entrance.

It is the sculpture which gives Khajuraho its appeal and importance. Less than a tenth of it can be called erotic, although the postcard sellers try to convince you otherwise. Numerous interpretations have been given for the erotic sculpture, but there is nothing sordid about these inspired carvings showing the beauty and voluptuousness of the female form. Most of the temples are 'banded' by horizontal panels of statues. The *apsaras*, or heavenly dancers, are shown carrying water jars, gazing into mirrors, or engaging in commonplace human activities. The long friezes with scenes of processions, battles and hunting which ring the Lakshmana Temple are some of the best examples of narrative sculpture.

The eastern group is easily reached by rickshaw (cars are also available), with the return journey making a pleasant walk. It comprises mostly Jain temples within a compound. The largest Jain temple is the fine **Parsvanath,** with its famous sculpture of a woman removing a thorn from her foot. The adjacent **Adinatha Temple** has three bands of fine sculpture.

To the south of the village are two temples. The **Duladeo Temple** is close to the Jain group. It was probably the last to be built and much of its sculpture lacks the vitality of the earlier carvings. Three kilometres (two miles) south of the village, near the airport, is the **Chaturbhuj Temple** with its large and intricately carved image of Vishnu.

Eastern India

The seven states of the northeast together with West Bengal, Sikkim, Bihar and Orissa constitute the eastern wing of the Indian Union. These four states offer a rich variety of natural settings, culture and architecture to the discerning traveller: the bustling streets of Calcutta and the quiet inner sanctums of the temples of Orissa; views of the Himalayas from Darjeeling and Sikkim; and the rolling Gangetic plain criss-crossed by rivers with a life of their own. You can visit the sacred bo tree at Bodhgaya in Bihar, where Gautama attained enlightenment and became Buddha; you can relax on the beaches of Orissa and West Bengal, or mingle with the sea of humanity in Calcutta; in the Sunderbans and other wildlife sanctuaries you might get a glimpse of a tiger; in central Orissa and Bihar you can watch tribals dancing and singing; or you can enter the Dickensian world of industrial Calcutta and southern Bihar and watch the process that is destroying the world of both tiger and tribal.

Bihar

Bihar is deeply linked with ancient Indian history. The greatest empires of ancient India built their capital cities here. Buddhism, too, began its triumphant march across East Asia from Bihar. The name of the state is derived from the word *vihar,* which means a Buddhist monastery. Geographically, Bihar falls into two parts, the northern region in the Gangetic plain and, the southern region in the north Deccan plateau area known as Chota Nagpur.

Ancient Sanskrit texts mention four kingdoms in the region but by the sixth century BC, the time of the Buddha, Magadha had established its supremacy under the rulers Bimbisara and Ajatashatru. The latter founded the city of **Pataliputra,** now known as **Patna.** Pataliputra became the chief city of India under the Mauryas and the Guptas, two imperial dynasties which established pan-Indian empires. Now the capital of Bihar state, Patna has a continuous history of about 2,500 years.

The city sprawls on the south bank of the Ganges, for about 20 kilometres (13 miles). The grand **Mosque of Sher Shah Suri,** the brilliant Afghan chief who had chased the Mughal emperor Humayun out of India, dominates the skyline. Nearby stands **Har Mandir**, one of the ten holiest Sikh shrines, built by Maharaja Ranjit Singh to mark the birthplace of Guru Govind Singh, the last of the Sikh gurus. Across the road is **Qulla House**, with its private collection of jade, Chinese paintings and a bed that once belonged to Napoleon. The **Patna Museum** houses an impressive collection of Hindu and Buddhist stone sculptures dating back to the Maurya and Gupta periods. Among the exhibits is the **Didarganji Yakshi**, a Mauryan sandstone statue of a woman, considered one of the great masterpieces of Indian art. At **Kumrahar,** six kilometres (four miles) from central Patna, lie ruins dating back to 600 BC. The main points of interest are the remains of an assembly hall dating back to the Mauryan period and a

Buddhist monastery, **Anand Vihar**. Other places of interest include the unique **Goleghar**, a huge dome-shaped granary built by the British in 1786 which provides a fine view of the city from its top; **Padri ki Haveli**, a Catholic church built in the late 19th century; and the **Khudbaksh Oriental Library,** founded in 1900 and housing rare Arabic and Persian manuscripts and Mughal and Rajput paintings.

Around 90 kilometres (56 miles) south of Patna is the site of the great **Nalanda University**, which flourished from the fifth century AD until the end of the 12th century, when it was sacked by the Afghan invader Bhaktihar Khilji. At its peak the university had more than 10,000 students from all over Asia, and more than 2,000 teachers. Its library held nine million volumes, and legend has it that it burned for six months when it was pillaged. Both the Buddha and Mahavira, the founders of Buddhism and Jainism, visited the university, and Hsüan-tsang, the seventh-century Chinese traveller, spent 12 years there. Excavations over 15 hectares (37 acres) have yielded the remains of 11 monasteries, with student cells, lecture halls, bathrooms, kitchens and libraries.

Close to Nalanda are the major Hindu and Buddhist pilgrim centres, Gaya and Bodhgaya. As a pilgrimage centre, **Gaya** is second only to Varanasi, for Hindus believe whoever makes offerings here will free their ancestors from bondage to the earth. In **Bodhgaya** stands the descendant of the bo tree under which Lord Buddha attained enlightenment. Buddhist pilgrims from all over the world come here throughout the year. The main temple is the **Mahabodhi Temple**, originally erected by Emperor Ashoka in the third century BC but restored only in 1882. Some Buddhist countries have built monasteries in this area in their native styles.

Other places of interest in Bihar are **Vaishali,** 55 kilometres (34 miles) from Patna, and **Rajgir**, about 100 kilometres (63 miles) away, both of which were major cities in ancient India. **Maner,** 30 kilometres (19 miles) from Patna, is the most sacred Muslim shrine in Bihar. **Sonepur,** 22 kilometres (14 miles) from Patna and across the Ganges, is the site of a famous **cattle fair**, beginning on the first full moon of November *(Kartik Purnima)* and lasting over a fortnight. In **Saurath**, in the Madhubani district, a marriage market is held in June. Mithila Brahmins from all over the country gather to arrange the unions of their children.

Southern Bihar is very different from the north. Rich in minerals, it was originally inhabited predominantly by the Santal, Bedia, Bihor and Munda tribes, but the last few decades have seen a dramatic transformation of the region from a peaceful, pastoral backwater to what a tourist pamphlet describes as the Ruhr of India. The main towns in this region, **Ranchi, Jamshedpur** and **Dhanbad**, are all industrial towns. Ranchi is still a quiet place and sometimes considered a minor hill station. At 651 metres (2,135 feet), it has a more pleasant climate than much of the state during the monsoon and winter months. Jamshedpur, further to the south near the border with Orissa, is India's industrial showpiece. A well-managed industrial town has grown up around the huge TISCO and TELCO plants, belonging to India's two biggest companies which are part of the enterprising Tata group.

Orissa

South of Bihar, on the shores of the Bay of Bengal, industrial India is left behind. Green plains, river valleys, mountains, waterfalls, forests and beaches constitute the landscape of one of India's most thoroughly rural states. The whitewashed mud village houses stand amidst bright green paddy fields and there are sandy and unspoilt beaches as well as lakes. The **Chilka lagoon** is the largest brackish lake in Asia and has rich birdlife.

Orissa offers the gourmet a variety of seafood: lobster, prawns and crab, all of which the Oriyans transform into delectable creations. The Oriyans are fond of good food and bake delicious *chakuri*, *kakara monda* and *arisa* cakes; *rasa-goolas* and *chenapodopitha* (cottage cheese steamed over a slow fire) are among the favourite Oriyan sweets.

The hill forests of central Orissa are a tribal area and the home of wild animals, including tigers and elephants. Some 62 distinct tribal groups have been identified as living in the state. Many of them still survive by hunting and gathering. They make excellent carvings of wood and soapstone, exquisite silver filigree jewellery and children's toys, and also colourful votive paintings on canvas—the famous *pattachitra* folk paintings. Most of Orissa's horn work, brass and ironware, silk and handloom products—the Sambalpuri and Cuttack saris, for example—owe their fineness to a rigorously developed folk handicraft tradition. Orissa has its cities, too; not industrial nodes or purely administrative centres, but beautiful temple cities where pilgrims come to worship and to celebrate festivals. The chief attractions of Orissa—Bhubaneshwar, Puri and Konarak—form a compact, easy-to-visit triangle.

The seventh to 13th centuries were the great age of Orissan temple building, the age of Brahmin resurgence under the Kesari and Ganga kings. Before that, we hear not of Orissa but of the kingdom of Kalinga where in 262 BC, after a bloody war, the Mauryan emperor Ashoka converted to Buddhism. From then until the fourth century Buddhism and Jainism held sway, but after the seventh century Hinduism reasserted itself. Orissa managed to preserve its distinctive identity for several centuries, but with its occupation by the Mughals in the 16th century and Europeans making inroads from the 17th century onwards, the villages and towns of Orissa seem to have lapsed into silence.

Bhubaneswar

Of the innumerable temples built here over the centuries, some 500 still stand. Built around **Bindu Sarovar**, a tank believed to receive waters from all the holy rivers of India, the temples follow a common architectural pattern. Each has an entrance *(jagmohan),* a sanctum for the deity *(deul),* a dancing hall *(natya*

First Day on the Job

Adams led me first to his own court, a large roughly-furnished room full of native clerks sitting on carpets on the floor, who all rose and saluted, bowing almost to the ground as we entered. Here I was sworn in with the oaths which it was still the custom to administer in those days, and signed a certificate to the effect that I had that day in the forenoon assumed charge of my office. Then he took me into another room similar to, but smaller than, his own, pointed to a small group of clerks who were all bowing elaborately and said in his sharp, jerky way, 'This is your court, and these are your amlà, now go to work,' and before I could open my mouth to ask him a single question he had turned and abruptly left the room! This was throwing one into one's work with a vengeance! Here was I, as ignorant of the whole business as a child, with a hundred questions to ask, and no one to ask them from. I had heard from Elliot and from other men that it was customary to allow a man on joining his first district to sit on the bench beside one of the older Magistrates for a few days so that he might gradually pick up some ideas of how to do the work, and I had expected something of the kind myself. But Adams had told me as we walked along that the work was so heavy he could hardly get through it, so I suppose he had no time for teaching beginners. My stock of available knowledge consisted of Persian and Hindustani, the latter language I already spoke fluently and tolerably correctly. Of law and procedure I, of course, knew nothing.

However, no time was to be lost; the people were already staring at me rather wonderingly as I hesitated for a minute, so I took my seat at a plain and rather dirty table separated from the rest of the room by a plainer and dirtier railing. The amlà took their seats, some *on a form beside the table, others on carpets on the floor, and the head man of them a young, slight Musulman named Mushtak Ali, who I afterwards learnt was my sarishtadar, rose and pointing to a pile of papers covered with writing in the Persian character, said in beautiful Delhi Hindustani with many courteous periphrases, 'These are the cases on your Honour's file for trial—what is your order?' I said as by instinct, 'Call up the first case,' though what I was to do with it I knew as little as the man in the moon. Mushtak Ali smiled and looked round at his fellows as who should say, 'Guessed right the first time'. Then he mentioned some names to a six-foot-high Sikh with a turban as big as a bandbox, armed with sword and shield, who went out into the veranda and bawled loudly for some minutes. Then entered a dirty, greasy shopkeeper, the plaintiff, who was sworn by the tall Sikh, and had a wooden tablet given him with the words of the oath written on which he held tight all the while he was making his statement. I was furnished with a printed form and requested to fill in what the greasy man said in a certain column, other columns being intended for the statements of the defendant and witnesses. The defendant was next sworn and deposed. He was a big, powerful zemindar, i.e. peasant with a long black beard. Both these people spoke Panjabi, of which I could not understand one word, but the sarishtadar translated it into Hindustani as they spoke, so I got on wonderfully well. By four o'clock I had disposed of all my cases and went back to Adams's house where I spent the evening pleasantly with him and his wife, picking up a great deal of information about the place, the people and the work. I went to bed intensely tired but very much interested in, and pleased with, my day's experience.*

John Beames, Memoirs of a Bengal Civilian, *1896*

mandir), a hall of offerings *(bhoga mandapa)* and rising above all, a beehive-shaped tower *(sikhara)*. Carvings abound —flowers, animals, gods and humans are all sculpted with tremendous verve and delicacy. The single female figures of later centuries are particularly seductive and sensual.

Completed in the early 12th century, the **Lingaraja Temple** is one of the most prized examples of temple architecture in India. Devoted to Lord Shiva, it is located in a huge walled compound with its tower, built without mortar, rising to a height of 39 metres (127 feet). The inner walls of the sanctum, housing the *lingam* of Shiva, are unadorned; the outer walls are sculpted with deities, nymphs and amorous couples. Scattered around the compound are little temples and shrines devoted to various Hindu gods and goddesses. Entry to the temple is restricted to Hindus.

The **Rajrani Temple** owes some of its glory to its setting, in splendid isolation amidst green paddy fields. Beautifully proportioned and sensuously sculpted with, smiling nude nymphs and embracing couples, it is striking for its attention to detail. It is among the last temples built during the great era of construction.

In a mango grove, 'the Grove of the Perfect Being', amidst the ruins of about 20 temples, lie some of the oldest of Bhubaneswar's temples, the Parasurameswara, Kedareswara and Mukateswara temples. **Parasurameswara** is the oldest temple in Bhubaneswar. Latticed windows, dancing dwarfs, a four-armed Ganesh and a two-armed Kartikeya mounted on a peacock and killing a snake, are all the products of seventh-century temple architecture.

Kedareswara Temple is known primarily for the two-and-a-half-metre- (eight-foot-) tall statue of the monkey god Hanuman and another of the goddess Durga standing on a lion.

Mukateswara Temple stands out for its finely sculpted gateway and the diamond-shaped latticed windows of its *jagmohan*. Notice the wonderful figures on the walls—elephants, monkeys, maidens and *nagins* (snake deities).

The sanctum of the **Vaital Temple,** with its oblong roof and figures of Durga's incarnations, and next to it the **Sisireswara Temple,** with figures of lions, elephants, Ganesh and Kartikeya, are worth visiting, while the **Ananta Vasudeva Temple** may be visited as one of the few in Bhubaneswar belonging to the Vaishnava cult of Vishnu.

Around Bhubaneswar

At **Dhauli,** eight kilometres (five miles) away, are a set of edicts that the Mauryan emperor Ashoka engraved in stone—the earliest-known inscribed records in India—commemorating his conversion to Buddhism. A little further on is the village of **Pipli**, famed for its appliqué work. West of Bhubaneswar lie the two hills of **Udaygiri** and **Khandagiri,** with rock caves that were occupied by Jain monks as early as the second century BC.

Nandanakanana, 20 kilometres (12 miles) from Bhubaneswar, is a large
recreation park in the middle of Chandka forest, with many animals in their
natural habitat. A botanical garden in the park is an added attraction. **Cuttack,**
Orissa's former capital which is surrounded by rivers, lies 29 kilometres (18
miles) from Bhubaneswar and is one of the state's oldest towns. Here the ruins
of the 13th-century **Barabati Fort** may be seen. In the centre of the city a
Muslim shrine, **Kadan Rasul,** contains relics of the prophet Muhammad.

To the northeast of Cuttack lie the hills of **Ratnagiri** and **Lalitagiri** forming,
together with the **University of Puspagiri,** an ancient Buddhist complex. West
of the town are the Buddhist weaving villages of **Muniabandha** and **Na-
vapatna.** Further on is the lush green forest of **Tikarpara.** The magnificent
Mahanadi gorge teems with wildlife.

Sixty kilometres (40 miles) to the south of Bhubaneswar is **Puri**, one of the
four holiest places in India and the site of the 12th-century **Jagannath Temple.**
With a tower 65 metres (211 feet) high, surmounted by the mystic wheel or
chakra, and the flag of Vishnu, the main temple building stands in a 200 by 194

metre (656 by 630 foot) compound. There are many wardens and pilgrim guides. In all, 20,000 people are economically dependent on the temple, which houses images of Lord Jagannath, Lord of the Universe, his brother Balbhadra and sister Subhadra. Non-Hindus are not allowed to enter, but models of the curious images carved in wood are sold in the shops.

Each June, pilgrims flock to Puri for the **Rath Yatra** or Car Festival. On that day, the gods leave their temple in their chariots. Lord Jagannath has an enormous yellow-striped canopied chariot, 14 metres (45 feet) high and 11 metres (35 feet) square, on 16 wheels, each two metres (seven feet) in diameter. Subhadra has a red chariot, Balabhadra a blue one. All three are pulled by thousands of pilgrims, who vie with one another for this honour, from the temple to **Gundiacha Mandir**, 1.5 kilometres (one mile) away. The procession commemoraes of Krishna's journey from Gukul to Mathura. The enormous chariots are difficult to get rolling, but once they start it is almost impossible to stop them. It is these chariots which have given the English language the word 'juggernaut'. The procession generates incredible frenzy and excitement. Until

recently, it was not uncommon for pilgrims to throw themselves under the wheels of Jagannath's chariot in the belief that the Lord would bless them for dying in this manner.

But Puri can be quietly charming, too. Pilgrims are seen throughout the year, but when the festival is over the town takes on a lovely seaside atmosphere, especially in the late evening when the lights come on and the streets of the bazaars become crowded. The best place to be at this time is Puri's marvellous sandy beach.

Even in its present state of dilapidation, the **Sun Temple** at **Konarak,** located about 30 kilometres (19 miles) inland from Puri, is splendid. It is said to have been built by the ruler Narasimha in the 13th century as a glorious tribute to Surya, the sun god. Only the large audience hall has survived, but it is so impressive that the mind boggles trying to of conceive the grandeur of the architect's overall conception. Had the dancing room and the immense tower survived, Konarak would surely rank as one of the wonders of the world.

The temple was conceived as the sun god's own chariot, standing on 12 pairs of eight-spoke wheels and drawn by seven straining horses. The horses represent the seven days of the week, the wheels the 24 fortnights of the Indian year, and the eight spokes of each wheel the periods into which the ancients divided day and night. The surviving structure has carvings of foliage, animals, mythical beings, musicians and dancers, as well as war, hunting and court scenes. Two lions guard the pyramidal entrance and on each side of the temple there is a colossal war elephant and a war horse trampling foreign soldiers. The most striking sculptures are the erotic figures, some of them larger than life.

Further south you leave behind the Oriyan cities. An inland sea, dotted with islands (such as Nalabar) and abounding in fish and birds, **Chilka Lake** is a natural formation much of which forms part of a wildlife sanctuary. Still further south is **Chatrapur**, standing on high ground above the sea amidst pine groves. And then **Gopalpur**, still a quaint fishing village but slowly becoming a modern seaside resort. A little west of Gopalpur, at **Tatapani**, there are hot sulphur springs.

Most of the state's tribals live in southern inland Orissa. They include the Mundas, the Gadabas, the Koyas and the Bondas, a tribe of Tibeto-Burmese origin. Southern Orissa also presents the traveller with a marvellous landscape.

The 2,750-square-kilometre (1,061-square-mile) **Simlipal National Park** in northeastern Orissa is one of the 18 Project Tiger reserves in India. The area is lush and rich in wildlife. There are two waterfalls here, **Bavehipani** which has a 400-metre (1,300-foot) cascade, and **Jorndda**, a 150-metre (500-foot) drop.

The 10th-century town of **Khitching**, 45 kilometres (28 miles) from Joshipur west of the park, is interesting because the **temple** here is built in a style quite different from that of Bhubaneswar, Puri and Konarak. There is a small museum next to the temple with some excellent sculpture, including a seated Shiva and Parvati.

West Bengal

West Bengal is 'the gateway to the exotic east'. Its capital, Calcutta, is well connected by air and rail with the rest of the country and the world and is an excellent springboard for visits to Darjeeling and the Sunderbans, Konarak, Puri and Bhubaneswar, Patna, Nalanda and Gaya.

West Bengal is made up of the delta of the lower Ganges and the other rivers which join it to form the Sunderbans, and the mountainous region in the north—first the Duar Hills and then the great Himalayas. The best time to visit this region is September through March.

The British played a major role in shaping modern Bengal. They established their first base as a ruling power at **Plassey**, about 170 kilometres (110 miles) north of Calcutta, after they won a crucial battle in 1757, the year which traditionally marks the beginning of direct British rule. When the British withdrew in 1947, they left a divided Bengal: East Bengal, with its Muslim majority, became the eastern wing of Pakistan and eventually Bangladesh; the rest of the province remained with India and is now the state of West Bengal.

The name 'Bengal' derives from Vanga, a kingdom mentioned in ancient Sanskrit texts. The Pala dynasty ruled Bengal from the eighth to the 12th century and was succeeded by the Senas who in turn were displaced by Muslim rulers in the latter half of the 13th century. Though the British influence is most clearly in evidence, especially in Calcutta, the Palas, Senas and Islamic rulers have each left their distinctive mark.

Calcutta

Calcutta forces you to examine all your earlier notions of human potential. If you want something more than romantic palaces and charming handicrafts and can move both within and outside yourself, Calcutta is an experience not to be missed. Here no attempt is made to hide or romanticize the all too evident extremes of wealth and poverty, the good and the bad, the ugly and the beautiful. There are museums, palaces, gardens and buildings worth visiting in Calcutta, but above all what is on display here is the piece of work called mankind—in all his glory and infirmity.

The human body dominates Calcutta. If you arrive by train, the pandemonium at **Howrah Station**, almost a city in itself, can serve as an excellent introduction to the city proper. Located on the west bank of the Hooghly River, the station houses an enormous establishment with a seemingly permanent population living on the platforms. Amidst the cries of vendors, newsboys, pedlars of sweets, fruits and tea, shouting porters, hooting locomotives and announcements booming on the loudspeakers, you can see entire families serenely cooking, eating and sleeping.

The crush, the press and the bustle of the railway platform is multiplied a hundredfold on **Howrah Bridge**, just a few metres away. The traffic on this

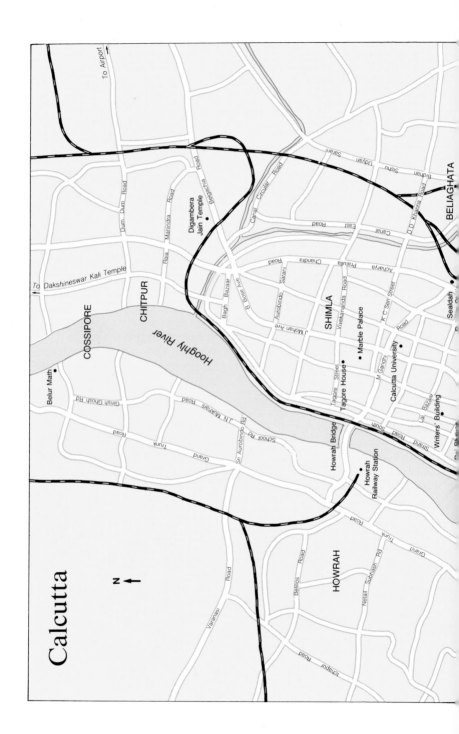

© The Guidebook Company Ltd

Canal South Road

Tapsia Road

Mother Teresa's Mission

Bose Street

Ripon Street

Chandra

Jagdish

Acharya

Ramakrishna Mission Institute of Culture

Ochterlony Monument

Oberoi Grand

New Market

Park Street

Rossell Street

Middleton Street

Shakespeare Sarani

Birla Academy of Art and Culture

Dr Meghnad Saha Sarani

Indian Museum

St Paul's Cathedral

Ballygunge Road

Euell Gardens

Jawaharlal Nehru Road (Chowringhee Road)

Victoria Memorial

Birla Planetarium

Bose Road

Chandra

St Peter's Church

Fort William

Race Course

Maidan

Kidderpore Road

Acharya Jagdish

Ashutosh Mukharji Road

Kali Temple

Second Hooghly Bridge

Kidderpore Docks

Zoo

Taj Bengal Hotel

National Library

Belvedere Road

Alipore Road

Kalighat Road

Tollygunge Circular Road

Tollygunge Club

To Botanical Gardens

0   0.5   1   1.5 km
0   ½   1 miles

huge web of girders across the muddy Hooghly has to be seen to be believed. Cars, trucks, buses, tramcars, rickshaws, scooters, bicycles, ox-carts, people, cows, goats, donkeys—all jostle their way across its 1,500-metre (one-mile) span. Some three million people are said to cross the bridge every day. While planning your itinerary, try to avoid crossing the bridge during the morning and evening rush hours.

If you arrive by plane, your car or bus will move through the seemingly endless suburbs of Calcutta until suddenly you find yourself in the heart of the city. Sprawling over more than 725 square kilometres (280 square miles), and with a population of more than 11 million, Calcutta is the largest city in India. As you journey across it, you will be struck by its two salient features: the great Victorian buildings whose crumbling masonry still manages to reflect its former colonial grandeur, and the masses of people crowding the streets and the pavements.

Calcutta is not an old city. Just 300 years ago this vigorous giant was a tiny, insignificant village known as Kalikata. In 1690, Job Charnock, chief of the East India Company's factory in Hooghly, looking for new factory sites, selected and leased the three tiny villages of Sutanati, Govindpuri and Kalikata from Emperor Aurangzeb. Six years later the company built the first **Fort William** and later, in 1773, rebuilt it in its present form. From then until 1911, when the capital was shifted to New Delhi, Calcutta remained the economic, industrial and political centre of India.

Calcutta suffered greatly from the partition of India in 1947. Millions of Hindus flooded the city, fleeing their homes in the new Muslim-majority state. In 1971, yet another human tidal wave, consisting of the refugees from Bangladesh, engulfed the city. However, over the years, the city has displayed an amazing ability to accommodate immigrants from the Bengal hinterland, and, if the excessive population creates social and civil problems of vast magnitude, it also spurs individuals to meet them head on. The indomitable spirit and abounding love of modern-day saints like Mother Teresa and her Sisters of Mercy is as much an aspect of this bewildering and bewitching city as the *bustees* (settlements) of the poor and the families on the pavements.

Calcutta's sights are scattered far and wide and the traffic is slow, so a bit of planning is essential. The golden rule is to start as early as possible and to avoid the rush hours. Also, to conserve energy and time, plan your itinerary on the basis of the proximity of the places to be visited.

When the British rebuilt Fort William in 1773, they cleared a huge expanse of land around it to give their guns a clear line of fire. This exposed area is now the **Maidan**, Calcutta's 'lung'. Here Calcuttans play cricket and football, organize their political rallies, 'take the air' while munching the delicious snacks hawked there and even let their cows loose to browse on its grass. All day the place pulsates with activity. The best time to go for a walk in the Maidan is in the late afternoon or in the evening when the sun sets over the Hooghly.

At the southern end of the Maidan is the **Victoria Memorial**. This huge marble museum is a combination of classical European architecture and Mughal motifs, often described as an unhappy British attempt to build their version of the Taj. It was Lord Curzon's idea to create a museum that would tell the story of the British Empire in India, and this the Victoria Memorial succeeds in doing remarkably well. It was opened to the public in 1921. An imposing, rather severe-looking statue of Queen Victoria by George Frampton fronts the museum, and inside there are portraits, busts and sketches of all the key figures of the Raj days. The good paintings by British artists include a large collection of pictures by Thomas and William Daniell, Burne-Jones's portrait of Rudyard Kipling and several examples of Zoffany's best work, including *Warren Hastings and his Family*. There is also a fine collection of Indian and Persian miniatures. A brief, informative guidebook is available at the site.

One of the largest and most impressive museums in India, the **Indian Museum,** is situated at the junction of Sudder Street and **Chowringhee**. Founded in 1814 on the basis of the collection of the Asiatic Society, its widely varied exhibits include such oddities as a roomful of meteorites and a number of (stuffed) man-eating crocodiles. It has an impressive archaeology and sculpture department with a superb collection of Gandharan Buddhist art, as well as works from Khajuraho, Bhairat and many other important sites.

There are more than 30 other museums in the city, many specializing in a single topic. The **Asutosh Museum** on the Calcutta University campus, for example, concentrates on the rich artistic heritage of eastern India. The **Marble Palace** on Muktaram Babu Street, presents an eccentric collection of statues and paintings, including works by Reubens and Sir Joshua Reynolds. The collector, Rajendra Mallick, never left India and his collection gives a remarkable insight into the hybrid culture of the nouveau riches of Calcutta who thrived under British influence. The **Academy of Fine Arts** on Cathedral Road displays contemporary Indian art. The **Ethnographic Museum** in the New Secretariat Building on KS Roy Road is run by the Tribal Welfare Department of the Government of West Bengal. **Birla Planetarium** at the end of Chowringhee is one of the largest in the world. It shows programmes in various languages, including English. The **Royal Asiatic Society of Bengal**, on Park Street, has a fine library of books and manuscripts.

Octherlony Monument, one of Calcutta's most prominent landmarks, now officially called **Sahib Minar,** stands at the northern end of the Maidan. Its 48-metre- (15-foot-) high column was erected in 1828 and named after the hero of the Nepal wars. It has an Egyptian base, a Syrian column and a Turkish capital!

The picturesque **Eden Gardens** at the northwest corner of the Maidan has an exquisite little Burmese pagoda set in a small lake. The Calcutta **cricket stadium** is in these gardens.

The imposing **St Paul's Cathedral** was built between 1839 and 1847. It stands just east of Victoria Memorial at the southern end of the Maidan. It is the first Church of England cathedral to be built in the British Empire. It was designed by Major Forbes and the Burne-Jones stained-glass west window merits a visit.

Kali Temple, also known as **Kalighat**, is about two kilometres (just over a mile) south of the cathedral. It is an important centre of Hindu pilgrimage and has the distinction of being one of the few prominent buildings of the city which is of wholly Indian origin. It was built around 200 years ago.

The **Botanical Gardens** occupy 109 hectares (269 acres) on the west bank of the Hooghly, south of Howrah. They were founded in 1786, and the famous Assam and Darjeeling teas were developed here. The prime attraction now is a 200-year-old banyan tree with roots spread over an area 400 metres (a quarter of a mile) in diameter. The garden is about 19 kilometres (12 miles) from Chowringhee.

Darjeeling

This jewel of a town nestles in the Himalayas some 700 kilometres (435 miles) north of Calcutta. One of the great train journeys of India is the overnight *Darjeeling Mail* which leaves Sealdah Station in north Calcutta in the evening and reaches **New Jalpaiguri** early the next morning. The last leg of the journey, the 52 kilometres (32 miles) from New Jalpaiguri, can take over six hours as the 'fairy-tale' toy train twists and winds its way up from the plains.

Everest is 140 kilometres (88 miles) from Darjeeling and, if the sky is clear, it is possible to see the peak. The real presence in Darjeeling, however, is that of

Kanchenjunga. You can see the world's
third-highest peak on a clear morning.
The best time is at sunrise, as its snowy
peak emerges from darkness into light.
The city is a fascinating place where you
can go for a walk in a tea garden, ride on
a chairlift which takes you down 2,050
metres (6,600 feet) to the valley below,
or trek to a high-altitude spot. The other
attractions in Darjeeling are its exquisite
Buddhist monasteries and colourful
markets. The most famous is the **Ghoom
Buddhist Monastery** located about eight
kilometres (five miles) from town. Entry
to the shrine is open to all.

Two other mountain towns worth
visiting are Kalimpong and Gangtok.
Kalimpong is a small, quiet bazaar town
at an altitude of 1,250 metres (4,062
feet). The 38-kilometre (24-mile) drive
from Darjeeling following the Teesta
River is interesting. Kalimpong has two Buddhist **monasteries** and a very fine
view of the surrounding landscape.

Gangtok, the capital of Sikkim, is a five-hour drive from Darjeeling. Places
of interest here include the **Tsuk-La-Khang**, the royal chapel, with fine wooden
carvings and many impressive images of the Buddha on decorated altars; the
Institute of Tibetology (open 10 am–4 pm, closed Sundays), which promotes
research into the traditions of Tibet and Mahayana Buddhism; the **Orchid
Sanctuary**, where most of the 454 species of Sikkim orchids can be seen; and
Enghey Monastery, near the tourist lodge, which is 200 years old.

Across the Ranipod Valley to the southwest of Gangtok is the **Rumtek
Monastery**, a reconstruction of the original in Tibet. It is now the seat of the
Kagyupa sect of Tibetan Buddhism. The monastery is always open and the
lamas are happy to receive visitors. The bus from Darjeeling leaves in the
afternoon, returning the next morning, necessitating an overnight stay. However,
cars are available in Gangtok and the 24-kilometre (15-mile) journey each way
can easily be done in a day.

At present, permits are required to visit Darjeeling and Kurseong Districts in
West Bengal and Sikkim. These can be obtained from Indian embassies and
high commissions abroad but take six or more weeks to process. They are also
available from Foreigners Registration Offices (see page 241). Permits are
usually valid for 15 days and can be extended locally. Sikkim permits often take
longer to process.

Northeastern India

Prior to Independence, the seven northeastern states—Assam, Meghalaya, Arunchal Pradesh, Nagaland, Manipur, Mizoram and Tripura—belonged to Assam province or the North East Frontier Agency. The entire region covers a very small area yet the people living here have been able to preserve their distinctive ways of life. From food and dress to language and dance, local ways persist, making travel in these parts a rich experience. Similarly varied are the flora and fauna of the region.

How has the northeast preserved so much that is local and traditional? Much of the area is mountainous and there is little contact among the different groups. Geographical isolation from the rest of India is another factor. Finally, living in relative harmony with the environment, the local cultures have evolved independently, respectful of nature's heritage.

Two factors give the area a certain unity. First, this is the chief tribal area of India. Secondly, the northeast has a high percentage of Christians. This notwithstanding, differences rather than similarities mark the conduct of everyday life, even today.

Assam and Meghalaya are inhabited by the Garo, Khasi and Jaintia tribes. The Garos are of Tibetan stock while the Khasis, related to the Jaintias, are in turn related to the Shaans of Burma. In Arunachal live 82 Mongoloid and Tibeto-Burmese tribes. The **Nagas**, the tribes of Tripura, and the **Meithis** of Manipur all have Tibeto-Burmese origins, while the **Lushai, Hmars** and **Pawis** of Mizoram are related to the Shaans. The Assam and Meghalaya tribals still commemorate their dead by erecting *mewbynnas,* stone monoliths.

Traditional folk festivals are celebrated throughout the northeast with tremendous enthusiam, but once again, the charm of these occasions lies in their local flavour. The Jaintias dance their celebrated *Laho,* while the *Kuallam* and *Chiraw* are the distinctive folk dances of the Mizos. Nagas still perform war dances wearing bright costumes and war paint and wielding bamboo shields and spears. The Manipuris excel in a spear dance *(Takhousarol)*, but are better known for having developed *Joqoi*, a Manipuri school of Indian classical dance.

For various reasons, the northeast is considered a sensitive area by the government of India, resulting in restrictions on entry. One reason is that it borders on Bhutan, China, Burma and Bangladesh. Secondly, for almost a decade the entire area has been politically troubled. There have been great changes in the situation recently and it is hoped that the area will soon be open to foreign tourists. Currently, entry is possible only with special permits, given freely for visits to Guwahati and Kaziranga National Park in Assam and to Shillong in Meghalaya. Applications to visit these areas take six to eight weeks to process and must be made through Indian embassies or high commissions abroad or the Ministry of Home Affairs (Foreigners' Wing), Lok Nayak Bhawan, Khan Market, New Delhi.

Meghalaya

Meghalaya means 'Abode of the Clouds'. The state was created in 1971, with its capital at **Shillong**. At an altitude of almost 1,500 metres (4,500 feet), the town is built in an area of pinewoods and meadows. Because of its topography, the British in India often described Meghalaya as the 'Scotland of the East'.

Since Shillong originated as a market town, perhaps the best place to begin exploring it is **Bara Bazaar**, the hub of the old city. Hill people come here with their local wares, utensils and baskets, vegetables, chickens, fish and spices.

Ward Lake, well-landscaped and set in the **Botanical Gardens,** is close to the township, as are **Lady Hydari Park** and the **mini-zoo**. The park is landscaped and the pine trees here resemble Himalayan *chir* but are in fact a native species.

Green downs and conifers make a perfect setting for some wonderful golf on Shillong's 18-hole **golf course,** while the **archery stakes,** which probably evolved from some ancient tribal custom, is an interesting sport to watch.

Above the town rises **Shillong Peak** from which the township got its name. There are numerous **waterfalls** in the vicinity. Shillong has two interesting museums: the **Meghalaya State Museum**, housed in the State Central Library building, has a collection of jewellery, handicrafts, weapons, costumes, musical instruments and coins. The **Butterfly Museum** has a good display of beetles and butterflies from the region and other parts of India.

Cherrapunji, 56 kilometres (36 miles) south of Shillong, is reputed to be the wettest place on earth, receiving 1,150 centimetres (450 inches) of rainfall a year. Cherrapunji produces an exquisite orange-flavoured honey; orchids grow here; and the three-metre (ten-foot-) long baskets made by the locals are fascinating creations. Above all, the drive to Cherrapunji offers wonderful views.

At **Jakrem** there is a **hot spring,** and 16 kilometres (ten miles) away on the Shillong–Guwahati road lies **Lake Umiam**. Perhaps the most interesting destination is **Mauphlang**, 24 kilometres (15 miles) along the road to Cherrapunji, where there are numerous **monoliths,** possibly erected as a form of ancestor worship.

Assam

Guwahati

Guwahati, capital of Assam, is an ancient settlement. As the main airline centre in the northeast, it is a convenient point of entry into the Brahmaputra Valley in which the state is cradled. Impressive in its immensity and enchanting in its beauty, the Brahmaputra in flood is an awe-inspiring sight. When the rains come and the river rises, little can be done to check its fury. When the waters recede, however, they leave behind fertile soil for a rich harvest of jute, rice and mustard.

Southern India

The four southern states of Andhra Pradesh, Karnataka, Tamil Nadu and Kerala are separated from North India by the east–west Vindhya Range. South India encompasses arid plains, humid jungles, cool hills, deserted beaches, fertile farmlands and broad rivers. Despite ethnic, religious and linguistic differences, the people of these four states are bound together by a certain homogeneity.

For centuries the northern borders of South India were under constant threat. The south has only been able to preserve its monuments and culture because these borders were never sufficiently weakened to permit an invader to affect life and society. The battles for the southern kingdoms were internal, thus allowing local philosophies, traditions and arts to evolve in a consistently sympathetic environment. In the north, where almost every aspect of life has been touched by outside influences, the visitor often finds echoes of his own culture: Islamic architecture is only one example. The south, on the other hand, has retained its individuality in such a way that Indians from other parts of the country are amazed by its unique rhythms and lifestyles. In South India, foreigners are welcomed with warmth and sincerity by people eager to reveal the beauty and treasures of their land and culture.

Andhra Pradesh

The character of Andhra Pradesh, the largest of the southern states, has been formed by its landscape, history and religion. Physically, it is rich in contrasts: ancient rocks loom in the arid valleys and plateaux of the southwest; India's rice-bowl lies in the fertile deltas of the Krishna and Godavari rivers; a wealth of teak grows in the hills that teem with wildlife around Srisailam; and Golconda's apparent barrenness has yielded some of the world's most fabled diamonds, including the legendary Koh-i-noor.

Although Andhra Pradesh is known as the 'Gateway to the South', its geography and history have imbued it with elements of northern, mostly Muslim, culture. When the Mughal emperor Aurangzeb conquered Hyderabad in 1687 he merely replaced a Muslim dynasty that had ruled there for seven generations. The influence of Islamic culture on architecture, food and language was enormous. Buildings have arches, domes and minarets; rich biryanis and spicy kebabs have the flavour of Mughlai cooking; and the courtly northern language of Urdu is as much the *lingua franca* as the more Dravidian Telegu. The medieval power struggles between the Hindus and Muslims were bitter and unrelenting but did not stop the followers of these faiths from building magnificent monuments. The richest Hindu temple in India, the **Venkateshwara** at **Tirupati**, is in Andhra Pradesh, as is one of Asia's largest mosques, the **Mecca Masjid** in **Hyderabad**. Buddhists have also left magnificent evidence of their devotion at **Amaravati** and **Nagarjunakonda**. Skilled craftsmen continue to create a wide variety of handicrafts, and although musicians play in the classical, Carnatic style common throughout South India, dancers move to the rhythms of Andhra Pradesh's own dance form, the energetic *Kuchipudi*.

Hyderabad

Although Hyderabad is now the capital of Andhra Pradesh and one of India's largest cities, its days as the capital of the Qutb Shahi dynasty, as a centre of the Mughal empire and as the seat of the wealthy Nizams have left an indelible mark. Regardless of Hyderabad's increasing importance in modern India, the city most people are drawn to is the Hyderabad of history. It is the only large South Indian city whose architecture, history and culture are all predominantly Muslim and it is this image which endures. Although the older generation will tell you that nothing is left of the grace and culture of the past but ruins and memories, it is they who preserve the dying echoes of bygone magnificence.

The first dynasty to make an impact here was that of the Qutb Shahi kings who rose to power in the 16th century. Until they moved to Hyderabad in 1590 they ruled from the nearby fortress at Golconda. Upon arrival in Hyderabad they promptly built the city's most famous landmark, the **Charminar,** commemorating the end of a plague epidemic in 1591. The Charminar, with a mosque on its upper floor, looms over the heart of the city.

During the day it wears a tired and weary look as all forms of Indian transport hurtle around it; only at night, when the four delicate minarets are illuminated, does it take on a youthful and more romantic appearance.

The **Mecca Masjid,** near the Charminar, is one of the world's largest and most impressive mosques, accommodating 10,000 of the faithful at one time. The entrance arches and colonnades were made from huge slabs of granite which required more than 1,400 bullocks to haul from the quarry 11 kilometres (seven miles) away. The Mecca Masjid has been both a witness to and a silent participant in Hyderabad's history. During its construction the Qutb Shahi kingdom was annexed by the Mughals and, although building began under Abdullah Qutb Shahi in 1614, it was not completed until 1687 under the reign of Aurangzeb.

Seven Qutb Shahi kings were followed by seven Mughals and then by seven Nizams, whose personalities and legendary wealth have contributed to the Hyderabad mystique. The last Nizam, Sir Osman Ali Khan, was officially addressed as His Exalted Highness (and was the only Indian prince the British allowed to use such an elevated title) but was universally referred to as 'the richest man in the world'. He was an eccentric miser who dressed shabbily and smoked cigarette ends but kept a diamond the size of an ostrich egg on his desk—wrapped in newspaper. He also founded the local Osmania University which specializes in Persian, Arabic and Urdu studies.

Although a Hyderabadi nobleman built the **Falaknuma Palace** for himself, he had little choice but to give it to the Nizam after he had admired it, particularly its lavish European-style interior. The Nizam added this beautiful palace to his list of residences but hardly ever visited it. The sumptuousness of the **Purana Haveli**, another of the Nizam's palaces, can be gauged by a single wardrobe; the silks, brocades, damasks and fine muslins it once bulged with have gone but it still stretches for 800 metres (half a mile). The royal women lived in strict purdah, secluded from prying eyes in the adjoining **Zenana quarters**.

The 3,500 objects in the **Salar Jung Museum** were all acquired by one of the Nizam's prime ministers, Mir Yusuf Ali Salar Jung III. Fabulously wealthy in his own right, he was an acquisitive and insatiable collector, whose agents haunted the world's salerooms. Although much of what was brought back to Hyderabad was of inferior quality, recent reorganization of the museum has resulted in the discovery of several outstanding works. Many European artists are represented, but few by their better work. Although there is a fine Canaletto, it is the jewels, ornaments, ivories and manuscripts of the North Indian court that are so outstanding. Of particular interest are the jewelled swords and daggers of the Mughal emperors and the thrones and turbans of Tippu Sultan.

Golconda

The deserted ruins of **Golconda Fort,** crowning a hill 11 kilometres (seven miles) west of Hyderabad, still throb with the might of the Qutb Shahi kings. Golconda's recorded history dates from 1364 when it was no more than a small mud-walled fort. By 1518, when the Qutb Shahi kings rose to power, the fort had been enlarged and rebuilt in hard granite with huge iron spikes in its massive gates to repel battering war elephants.

Invasion was a constant threat and the measures taken to prevent it included cordon walls, high ramparts, huge semicircular bastions, a wide moat and a balcony from which boiling oil could be poured on would-be invaders. Although the fort withstood many attacks, it fell in 1687 after a siege of eight months. Ironically, it was the treachery of a Qutb Shahi general that brought defeat, not inadequate defences. The extraordinary acoustics for which Golconda is rightly famous also played a part in its protection; the entry gate and the summit's citadel were designed so that the guards on the lower level could easily be heard at the top.

But Golconda also has a softer side. In addition to its massive defences there are also the palaces and mosques of its kings and nobles and the lovely pavilions, gardens and Turkish baths of their queens, princesses and favourites. The exquisitely decorated rooms of the **Rani Mahal** once sparkled with precious jewels and were surrounded by gardens and fountains.

But death has its place here, too. Mortuary baths were built where special attendants washed the royal dead who could be interred only after a ceremonial cleaning. Many of the Qutb Shahi kings are buried at Golconda in massive **tombs** inscribed with their names and the dates of their reigns. Amongst the dead is Taramati, the favourite of Abdulla Qutb Shahi; the delicacy of her tomb recalls a courtesan whose sweet voice the wind once carried all over the hillside.

The Muslim kings were tolerant of the beliefs held by their many Hindu subjects. Near the Royal Palaces is a small **temple** dedicated to the goddess Kali. One Hindu official incurred royal displeasure when he appropriated money to renovate a Golconda temple. Apprehended and found guilty, he was incarcerated in the prison that now bears his name, **Ramdas Kotha**. The idols he made of his favourite god Rama and Rama's consort and brother can still be seen here.

Supplying water to the rocky aridness of Golconda required sophisticated engineering. The problem was solved with a system in which 'Persian wheels' raised water through cooling clay pipes into canals and storage reservoirs. The system made it possible to create and maintain beautiful gardens.

In its heyday Golconda, literally the 'Shepherd on the Hill', was famous throughout the known world. Visitors were drawn by reports of its glorious wealth and the fabulous bazaars that traded in precious stones. The great Koh-i-noor diamond that now graces the British crown was mined here.

Karnataka

Karnataka has also been touched by Islamic culture but has absorbed it less
deeply than Andhra Pradesh. Most of the ruling dynasties of Karnataka were
Hindu, and although Bijapur, the stronghold of the Adil Shah Sultans, is typi-
cally Muslim, and two of Karnataka's most famous rulers, Hyder Ali and Tippu
Sultan, were devout Muslims, the region reflects the softer lines of Hindu
culture.

Many of the kings who rose to power in South India ruled over all or part of
Karnataka, and their legacy is in the extraordinary range of monuments they
have bequeathed to posterity. Almost all of these kings sought to proclaim both
their secular might and their religious devotion by housing their gods in magnificent stone temples. The Chalukyas led the way in the fifth century, creating
Aihole, Badami and Pattadakal; the Hoysalas belie their tribal origins with the
ornateness of Belur, Halebid and Somnathpur; and the great Vijayanagar kings
have, at Hampi, given the world one of its greatest architectural and archaeological treasures.

Karnataka's great architectural heritage is matched by its great natural
beauty: the coastline running from Mangalore to Karwar, the foaming waters at
Jog Falls, the national parks and sanctuaries at Bandipur and Nagarhole, and the

green tapestry of wooded valleys and paddy fields in Coorg. Karnataka is the home of many of India's most eminent musicians, writers, poets and dancers and her folk drama, *Yakshagana,* is gaining worldwide recognition.

Aihole, Badami, Pattadakal and Bijapur

In Karnataka's northern district of Bijapur, four archaeological sites—Aihole, Badami, Pattadakal and Bijapur—span 1,000 years of history. Visited in chronological order, they demonstrate how the earliest experiments in Hindu architecture matured, but also include some remarkable examples of Muslim architecture. Aihole, Pattadakal and Badami are only a few kilometres apart. Badami is on the railway line 125 kilometres (78 miles) south of Bijapur. As local transport is difficult to arrange, it is best to drive there from Bijapur, Hubli or Hampi.

Aihole

Aihole, 50 kilometres (32 miles) from Badami, is the site of the first capital of the Chalukyas, who reigned in the fifth century. The original inhabitants built 50 temples inside their fort walls and another 50 outside before moving on to Badami, leaving behind mute monuments which reveal nothing of these people's way of life or the reasons for their departure. The temple known as

Lad Khan, dating from AD 450, is probably Aihole's oldest building. It was sometimes used as an assembly hall for royal marriages, and is named after a mysterious Muslim prince who later converted it into his residence, leaving the Hindu images untouched. Lad Khan has an upper sanctum with images of Vishnu and Surya, the sun god, carved on its walls. From here you can view the village of Aihole, known locally as Aivalli and historically as Arya-Hole (the city of the Aryans).

Aihole is architecturally important because its temples are prototypes for both North and South Indian styles. Compared with the grandeur of later Hindu temples, Aihole's are modest. Without them, however, there would be neither the massive magnificence of Madurai nor the powerful majesty of Bhubaneswar.

Near the fort wall is the **Temple of Durga,** laid out like a Buddhist temple but with a unique semicircular apse containing high-relief carvings of Hindu deities: the all-powerful goddess Chamundi Devi is overcoming a buffalo demon, whilst the bold eyes of Narasimha, the half-lion god, confront the onlooker, and the great Shiva reveals himself in many beautiful poses.

The Chalukyas seem to have had no sectarian preferences. Their temples honour not only a great number of Hindu deities but also those revered by the Jains and Buddhists. In the

Huchimalli Temple we find the three great Hindu gods: Shiva, Vishnu and Brahma. Lower down the hill, there is a **Buddhist temple** whose dark interior shields hordes of squeaking bats and a serenely detached figure of the Buddha. One of the finest temples, the **Ravana Phadi**, is carved out of sandstone and is remarkable for the vigour and energy sculpted into the high-relief figures of Shiva.

Badami

In around AD 550 the Chalukyas shifted their capital from Aihole to Badami, remaining there until they were ousted by a Pallava king a century later. Badami nestles amongst hills which enclose the healing waters of **Bhuthanatha Lake**. Several temples cluster on the shores and in the natural gorge that leads into the city. While these deserve a visit, it is the gigantic carvings on the walls of the four **cave temples** that have made Badami famous.

Cave 1: Although this cave contains an image of a four-armed Vishnu, the deity who dominates is Shiva. Attended by his servant, the dwarf Ganas, he is shown in many forms: as Nataraja, the Lord of the Cosmic Dance; as Ardhanaresvar, a half-man, half-woman aspect; as Bhuthanatha, the God of Souls; and as a *lingam* protected by a hooded cobra.

Cave 2: Two stone doorkeepers guard the entrance to this cave dedicated to Vishnu. The huge sculptures portray him in some of his incarnations, including that of Krishna.

Cave 3: Here the theme of Vishnu's incarnations continues. There are also some very beautiful, though faded, frescos.

Cave 4: Probably later than the others, this cave honours Jain deities. The meditative figure in the shrine is Mahavir, the founder of Jainism. There is also an enormous carving of the Jain saint, Parsanatha.

Pattadakal

Pattadakal, on the banks of the Malaprabha River, 30 kilometres (19 miles) from Badami, was the last Chalukyan capital and the place where the Chalukyas crowned their kings.

Although Pattadakal flourished from the seventh century, the earliest building, a brick-pillared pavilion, dates from the third or fourth century. The Chalukyas have left a scattering of fine temples, all built with the local pink sandstone. The eighth-century **Virupaksha Temple** is a huge stone structure with sculptures depicting scenes from both the *Ramayana* and the *Mahabharata*. There is also a famous carving which appears to be either an elephant or a buffalo. The exteriors of both the **Mallikarjuna** and **Papanatha temples** are decorated with detailed scenes from the epics. The latest building, the ninth-century **Jain temple,** has two beautifully sculpted stone elephants.

Bijapur

The great monuments built by the Muslim rulers of Bijapur, the Adil Shah sultans, are masterpieces of Islamic architecture. They represent a contrast to the region's Hindu temples but nonetheless make as powerful an impact.

Standing on the formidable fort walls that enclose the 'City of Victory' is the great cannon known as the **Malik-e-Maidan** (King of the Plains). It took the combined muscle of 400 bullocks and ten elephants to drag this 54-tonne war trophy from distant Purandar. So loud were the explosions which roared from its huge mouth, which takes the form of a lion devouring elephants, that the gunner had to submerge himself in water. Cast in an alloy of copper, tin and iron, this massive cannon remains cool even in the blazing sun and gives off a hauntingly gentle sound when tapped.

Built by Adil Shah I (1557–80), the interior arches of the **Jami Masjid,** one of India's largest and most beautiful mosques, are designed to give an unobstructed view of the pulpit. Although the mosque's awesome vastness is crowned by a huge onion dome, the overall effect is lightened by graceful minarets and the golden calligraphy of Koranic verses.

During the lifetime of his queen, Taj Sultana, Ibrahim Adil Shah II (1580–1626) began to build her palatial tomb. The **Ibrahim Roza** is said to have inspired the Taj Mahal. Its lyrical and symmetrical grace is achieved with delicate minarets, and although verses from the Koran are inscribed on the outer walls, the dynasty's religious tolerance is apparent in the panels carved with crosses and lotuses. In the mosque that forms part of the complex, the acoustics amplify the muezzin calling the faithful to prayer, but make him inaudible near the tombs. Ibrahim Shah also lies here, having died before his queen.

The **Gol Gumbaz**, the great mausoleum of Ibrahim's successor, Muhammad Adil Shah III (1626–56), is also an acoustical marvel; in the **Whispering Gallery** of its vast dome the softest sound will carry 75 metres (246 feet) and more. Walls three metres (ten feet) thick soar up to the huge dome unsupported by even a single pillar, an architectural feat second only to St Peter's in Rome. The Gol Gumbaz houses the tombs of Muhammad Adil Shah, his wife, daughter and favourite court dancer.

Hampi and Vijayanagar

Four centuries ago, the Portuguese chronicler Domingo Paes wrote after visiting Vijayanagar, 'City of Victory': 'All the sights were so beautiful that I felt as if in a dreamland.' At the time of his visit the Vijayanagar empire was at the height of its glory due to the efforts of its most famous king, the warrior-poet Krishnadeva Raya.

After a reign of 20 years, Krishnadeva died in 1529 and the Hindu empire began a steady decline. The final death knell was sounded in 1565 when the city was looted and passed into Muslim hands, and gradually it was forgotten. But it was a temporary slumber; now known as Hampi, the city has reawakened and its splendours are once again on display.

As you approach Hampi, 13 kilometres (eight miles) from Hospet in central Karnataka, the gentle landscape gives little indication of what lies ahead. But suddenly great boulders rear up, huge and smooth, perched precariously on top of each other. And tucked between two great rocks you discover a small pavilion, and then another, and then a shrine! By the time you arrive at the centre of all this magnificence, you are in the ancient Vijayanagar capital.

Hampi is perfectly positioned for defence. It is rimmed on three sides by natural rock ramparts and on the north by the Tungabhadra River. Despite being naturally enclosed, it sprawls across a 27-square-kilometre (ten-square-mile) site.

The endless procession of Hindu pilgrims to the **Virupaksha Temple** in the heart of Hampi has never been interrupted by secular events. The temple, with its 11-storey gateway, is the core of the city. The shops and eating-houses which line the eastern approach conceal the ancient capital's main **bazaar**, the famous street that once dazzled medieval visitors.

Although the temple throngs with devotees on festival days, it is often a place of serenity. Virupaksha is another name for Shiva. Images of his mount, the devoted bull Nandi, can be seen everywhere, always facing the dark inner sanctum where the most sacred image is installed. Just inside the towering gateway is an unusual three-headed Nandi. Virupaksha was already a thriving centre of worship when Krishnadeva Raya came to the throne. The king was an enthusiastic patron of the arts and made numerous additions to the temple, including the three-storeyed gateway that leads to the inner courtyard where the temple's mischievous elephant is often tethered. There is also lovely pavilion with well-preserved frescos.

Grouped together on the sacred hill behind the temple are the **Hemakuta temples**, some dating to the ninth century. Although they are no longer used for worship, a few are still used by *sadhus* (ascetics) for yoga and meditation. From Hemakuta Hill there is a fine view of the Virupaksha complex and the city.

Although images of Ganesh appear all over Hampi, there are two unique idols on the southern side of Hemakuta Hill that are designed to impress. The smaller is affectionately and ironically known as the 'mustard-seed' Ganesh, **Sasivekalu Ganesh**, and stands almost 2.5 metres (eight feet) tall. Nearby is an even larger image, a 4.5-metre- (15-foot-) high statue, hewn from a single granite boulder and called, in the same vein, the 'gram' Ganesh, **Kadalkalu Ganesh**.

Images carved out of a single rock are a feature of Hampi; the most spectacular is that of the man-lion god **Narasimha.** Originally Narasimha's consort, Lakshmi, sat lovingly on his left thigh but she, along with his four arms, have now vanished.

To the right of this startling image is a small shrine with a crumbling roof

containing a three-metre (ten-foot) *lingam*.

The buildings designed for the kings and their courts lie to the south. The queens once bathed in the perfumed waters of the large square pavilion known as the **Queen's bath**. The women of the court lived in their own separate walled area, the **Zenana enclosure**. Here is the almost perfectly preserved **Lotus Mahal**, a two-storeyed open pavilion with a ceiling. A staircase leads to more arches and vaulted domes where the balconies and windows were once decorated and ornamented and the empty niches filled with religious figures.

The **King's Palace** is now little more than a flight of stairs going nowhere, although the richness of the remaining base, covered with exquisitely carved processions of elephants, horses and dancers, suggests its former grandeur. The **Audience Hall** of the kings, close by the palace, was once one of the grandest buildings in Hampi, but is now devoid of its upper storey; only the staircases used by the court ladies to reach their secluded vantage points still exist. To the east of the Audience Hall is the building which Domingo Paes called the **Hall of Victory** since it was built by Krishnadeva Raya after a successful campaign. Also known as the **Khanavami-Dibba**, it was used primarily to celebrate the annual Dussehra festival.

The Vijayanagar kings were famous for their great armies of elephants. They used them both to lead their soldiers into battle and to impress their subjects on ceremonial occasions. Near the Zenana enclosure are the domed **elephant stables**.

The Vijayanagar rulers were devoutly religious and housed their gods in magnificent temples. One of the most ornate, the small **Hazararma Temple**, is carved with scenes from the great Hindu epic, the *Ramayana*. Further south, beyond the city's imposing walls, is the **Pattahirama Temple** where the main shrine stands in the centre of a courtyard, surrounded by a series of pillared colonnades.

If you have time for only one Hampi building, see the celebrated **Vitthala Temple**, dedicated to Vishnu. A pillared colonnade decorated with elephants runs around the inside of the enclosing wall which faces on to several pavilions. Each of the 56 pillars in the central pavilion yields a different pitch when tapped, and every surface of the pavilion is carved with dancers, drummers, musicians, gods, goddesses, elephants, horses, demons, flowers and parrots. In the centre, facing the main shrine, is the famous **stone chariot**, with wheels that revolve. It is modelled after the wooden chariots used in South India to take the gods out in festival processions and houses an image of Vishnu's eagle, Garuda.

Bangalore

Bangalore's history began when a local chieftain called Kempegowda received land from his overlord, the Vijayanagar emperor. Although construction of the city began in 1537 with a simple mud fort, Kempegowda set its boundaries, which he marked by four watchtowers, some distance away. Four hundred years later, Bangalore (literally 'still marches forward') is Karnataka's state capital and a vital centre of science, aeronautics and electronics.

Kempegowda's Bangalore was enlarged and developed by two Muslims, Hyder Ali and his son Tippu Sultan, the famous Tiger of Mysore. Its present appearance, however, owes more to the British who came here after Tippu's fall. Attracted by the pleasantly cool climate, the Raj made Bangalore its southern headquarters and developed the cantonment area into an important military base, a post-Independence position it still holds. Bangalore was popular with the British as a summer resort and they often referred to it as a pensioner's paradise. It is this rather British emphasis on pleasant relaxation, golf, horse-racing, gardens and flowers, clubs, restaurants and fine shopping that gives Bangalore its singular character and appeal.

Although Bangalore is now called India's Science City, it still justifies the older epithet of Garden City. One of India's finest botanical gardens is the **Lalbagh,** laid out in 1760 by Hyder Ali and developed by his son Tippu Sultan. The lofty **Glass House** in the centre of the Lalbagh is built on the lines of the Victorian Crystal Palace in London and is used for various exhibitions, notably the flower shows held in January and August.

Bangalore's reputation for gardens is further enhanced by the lawns and flowering trees of **Cubbon Park**, which is now officially called **Jayachamara-jendra Park.** The park's namesake is Lord Cubbon, a 19th-century British representative in Bangalore. Laid out in 1864, it has a natural, almost wild appearance when compared with the more manicured Lalbagh, yet it is situated–all 121 hectares (300 acres) of it–in the heart of the city. It contains the magnificent Gothic architecture of the **Public Library**, the **Visvesvarya Industrial and Technical Museum** and the **Venkatappa Art Gallery.**

Although Kempegowda's original mud **fort** was rebuilt in more durable stone by Hyder Ali and Tippu Sultan, some remnants of the earlier defences can still be seen. The military purpose of the fort is slightly tempered by the beautifully carved Islamic architecture of the arches and the **Hindu temple** just inside the fort. Dedicated to the elephant god Ganesh, it has episodes from the life of Krishna carved on its exterior walls. Also within the fort enclosure is the **summer palace,** a two-storey building begun by Hyder Ali in 1778 and completed by Tippu a year later. Its many elaborate arches and minarets closely resemble another summer palace, the **Dariya Daulat** at **Srirangapatna** near Mysore (see page 196). The ground floor of the palace has been converted into a small **museum** which reconstructs events in the lives of this famous father and son.

Kempegowda is credited with having built the **Bull Temple.** Undoubtedly one of Bangalore's oldest temples, it is dominated by the large figure of a bull carved from a single grey granite boulder that has been darkened by polishing with a mixture of oil and charcoal. Slightly to the west of the Bull Temple are four **watchtowers**, also by Kempegowda.

The **Vidhana Soudha,** built in 1956, is Bangalore's most impressive modern building. Bordering Cubbon Park's northern side, its five storeys house the state

Body Language

Nowhere else on earth, perhaps, is the human head such a versatile instrument of non-verbal communication as in the Indian subcontinent. Other cultures may be content to let the head rest inert atop the spinal column in a straight axis from crown to toe, as prosaic as an umbrella knob. But in India, the noggin is expected to loll, to shake, to nod, to all-but fibrillate as part of normal discourse.

One of the most basic yogic exercises is a 360° rotation of the head to limber up the topmost vertebrae. You can see people practising it in parks any morning, just as automatically as they clear their throats before uttering the first words of the day. Indian posture—anything but ramrod-straight—leaves the head free to go its own way, according to the exigencies of conversation.

This non-vertical carriage, with its attendant latitude for head gestures, seems to date back to Vedic times, judging from the figures in ancient temple friezes. It remains embedded to this day in the Indian aesthetic, as attested by the chorus kewpies in Hindi movies or the classical dancers of Bharata Natyam, Mohiniattam and Kathakali.

No coincidence, then, that these dance forms feature a complete and well-defined repertoire of head gestures to move the narrative along. A favourite piece of Indian tourist kitsch is a six-inch moulded plastic model of a Kathakali dancer with his green-painted face framed in a conical headdress. The head is spring-loaded to emphasize every cranial twitch. Suitable for mounting on the dashboard. Works best on pot-holed Calcutta roads.

If what you are after, though, is not a studied ambiguity but rather a guide to sorting out the bewildering array of subcontinental head gestures, a few pointers might prove helpful:

• As soon as you get used to the idea that a sideways shake of the head does not necessarily mean 'no', as in the West, it is all too easy to assume the opposite, that it means 'yes'. More likely, in fact, is that it signifies the oft-heard 'atcha', which can denote anything from enthusiastic agreement to merely 'I have heard you'.

• A slow shake of the head, however, usually indicates approval of something. This gesture is seen at concerts, after a particularly brilliant riff, accompanied by a murmur of 'kya baat hai' (How about that!).

• A rapid oscillation, often in a figure-eight pattern, can mean very good. It is the gesture of cricket fans when the home team scores. If you see diners waggling like this in a restaurant, by all means go on in.

• A head cock—an oscillation arrested in mid-swing—implies a question: 'Oh, yeah?' or 'How's that?' or 'Maybe'.

• Nor should you forget, as you run through the lexicon of exotic possibilities, that a brisk swing of the head just might turn out to mean a simple 'no' after all.

'Talking' heads are by no means the only vehicle of non-verbal communication on the subcontinent. The celebrated subcontinental 'lip point' offers an instance to the contrary. So when you ask, say, 'Which way to Victoria Terminus?' your informant will cock his chin in the appropriate direction and purse his lips. The distance is roughly proportional to the extent of the lip action. A real platypus pucker means you still have quite a way to go.

Nor is orienteering the only public non-verbal use of the subcontinental kisser. In crowded, noisy places like bazaars, you may be startled to hear loud, plashy osculations over the din. If you trace the sound to its source, you're likely to find nothing more salacious than a porter seeking right-of-way. It simply means "Hey, you", or "Heads up". The degree of urgency is proportional to the juiciness of the smack. Ignore it at your peril: you might wind up in a stinking nullah. An equally elaborate repertoire of hand gestures enlivens conversation. They, too, find their analogues in the *mudras* (formal hand poses) of temple art and classic dance.

Whatever hand gestures subcontinentals make, they use their right hand only. Left hands are reserved for a very particular function suggested by the almost universal absence of toilet paper. The left hand may be used to support the right when giving or receiving an object, as a mark of particular politeness, but never on its own.

Both hands figure in the Hindu 'namaste' greeting, pressed together at chest level, fingertips pointing upwards. The full translation of this gesture is supposed to be 'The deity within me greets the deity within you'. To Muslims, such an idea is idolatrous. Greet them instead with a 'salaam'—glancingly touch first your forehead and then your heart. Even a handshake can be followed with a touch of the heart as a sweetener.

If you bump into somebody or step on their toes, you can mitigate things with an open-palmed gesture towards the offended party followed by a glancing touch of your own heart. Don't try this, though, in the middle of one of India's ubiquitous crowds: on a rush-hour bus, for instance, your mitigation might well compound the original fault.

One of the most versatile gestures features the fingers slightly spread, palms facing the speaker and hands rotated at the wrists. It means, generically, 'What's up?' But connotations vary vastly according to the intensity of the question, which is conveyed by the height of the hands and the speed of the wrist rotation.

Nosy bystanders will gesture this way at about shoulder level. As hysteria mounts, the *mudra* moves up to ear level and higher. But a single desultory twist of the wrists around the chest level denotes a dismissive 'What's with you?'

If a palms-inward gesture suggests anxiety, its opposite—a 'pattycake' *mudra* with the palms facing away from the speaker and pointing upward—means something like 'just so'. At waist level, fingertips splayed outwards, it's like 'Well, that's settled' or simply 'bas' (enough). When enough is really enough, a more polite way to say 'no thanks' is to start with a 'namaste' then turn it into a 'pat-tycake' with the palms facing out.

Satiety is hardly the dominant message of subcontinental body language, one feels after a stint in a few of the grimmest cities. Rather, the gesture more often seen there signals ravenous, bottomless want. The beggar's *mudra*, cupped hands thrust outward, speaks for itself. It is so ingrained in the poorest of the poor that many times, if you see a beggar sleeping, his hands will naturally fall into this pose.

legislature and the Secretariat. Although India's national symbol of three lions crowns the largest, central dome, the overall design reflects the architecture of the palaces of Mysore. The building is floodlit on Sundays and public holidays. Opposite is the long, low **High Court**, built in 1868 and recently rescued from demolition.

Belur and Halebid

Over a thousand years ago a *sadhu* (ascetic) was attacked by a tiger. Seeing a tribal warrior nearby he called out for help: 'Hoy Sala! Sala!' Without hesitation a man, named Sala, rushed towards the tiger and plunged his spear into its side. Legend credits this courageous man with being the founder of the South Indian dynasty which took its name from the sadhu's cry ('Hoysala') and adopted the symbol of a man killing a tiger as its emblem. The Hoysalas are the least known of South India's kings, whose only enduring legacy after they outgrew their tribal and warlike beginnings were the temples at Belur and Halebid near Hassan, 180 kilometres (112 miles) west of Bangalore, and at Somnathpur, 45 kilometres (28 miles) east of Mysore. No other form of Indian art or architecture is as ornate and intricately decorative as theirs, nor, perhaps, as suggestive of languorous sensuality.

Belur

In 1116, King Bittiga repudiated Jainism and returned the Hoysalas to the Hindu fold, renaming himself Vishnuvardhana. In the same year he defeated the mighty Cholas and, to celebrate this victory, ordered a temple erected at Belur, 38 kilometres (24 miles) from Hassan, in honour of Channakesava, an incarnation of Vishnu.

The temple took 103 years to build and is a classic example of the Hoysala style. It rises, like a rococo wedding cake in stone, from a star-shaped plinth, one of the hallmarks of Hoysala building design. From the base upwards, there is an extraordinary wealth of decorative detail; every available inch is crammed with intricate carvings. Line upon line of friezes form bands around the temple, each depicting scenes from Hindu mythology. In one frieze, 650 elephants jostle one another in a continuous line.

All the Hoysala temples are constructed of a kind of soapstone which when freshly quarried is soft and yields easily to the chisel but which hardens after exposure—a characteristic that made it possible for the stonecarvers to achieve a remarkable degree of detail. Many people, however, find the Hoysala style florid and over-decorated.

The tradition of anonymity that conceals the identity of Indian craftsmen is absent at Belur (and Halebid). The name of its architect, Jakanachari, has come down to us, as well as the signatures of his craftsmen.

Many of the figures of full-bosomed women depicted at Belur are believed to be portraits of King Vishnuvardhana's queen, Shantala Devi. She was a famous dancer, a woman of great wit and intelligence, and there is a stone portrait of her just inside the temple's eastern entrance. Her husband, the king, stands beside her, mustachioed, bejewelled and justifiably proud.

Halebid

The Halebid temples and palaces that the visitor sees today were once part of the last Hoysala capital, located 16 kilometres (ten miles) east of Belur. In 1310, a Muslim army swept down from Delhi on a rampage, brutally killing its citizens and looting its treasures. Any hope that the city might be rebuilt was crushed forever in 1326 when a second onslaught wrought greater destruction and brought the Hoysala empire to an end.

And yet the remains are magnificent. The main temple is dedicated to Shiva and, as at Belur, was built by King Vishnuvardhana. It conforms, with its star-shaped base, to the pattern of all Hoysala temples but is the most intricately decorated. Only in the darkness of the inner sanctum where the stark black *lingam*, the symbol of Shiva, is still worshipped is there any suggestion of simplicity.

Elephants are believed to denote stability and perhaps it is their sturdy support that has helped the temple to weather the centuries, for an intricately carved line of them winds around the base. Above them are many bands of finely detailed friezes, each with extraordinary examples of superb craftsmanship.

The two-metre (six-foot) *dvara-palikas*, or door guardians of the temple are imposing in height, but what holds the eye is the unbelievable lace-like fineness of the carving. At Halebid the eye can easily become confused by the wealth of ornate carving on the temple and it requires an effort to focus on small details. As at Belur, it is the celestial women who have the greatest appeal. Saraswati, the Goddess of Learning, is shown dancing and Shiva dances too, as Nataraja, the Lord of the Cosmic Dance. Krishna himself dances, but on the great rearing hood of a demon serpent.

Surprisingly, the temple is unfinished. Stonemasons and sculptors laboured for 86 years and stopped suddenly for reasons unknown.

Sravanabelagola

The huge 17.7-metre- (58-foot-) high **monolithic statue** of Gommateshvara Sravanabelagola stands on the summit of the 143-metre (470-foot) granite Vindhyagiri Hill. The site was established in the ninth century and remains one of the most important Jain pilgrimage sites in southern India. Every 12 years (next in 1993) the great statue is given a ritual libation. The town is 170 kilometres (106 miles) from Bangalore and 60 kilometres (37 miles) southeast of Hassan.

Mysore

The Mysore of legend takes its name from a famous demon called Mahishasure, a great warrior who ruled as a tyrant until he was killed by the goddess Chamundeshwari. The Mysore seat of history was the capital of several imperial dynasties and later of the princely state of Mysore, the seat of the Wodeyar maharajas. Today there is no trace of the battle between the goddess and the demon and the great dynasties have vanished, the splendour of the maharajas has faded, Mysore state has been renamed Karnataka—and redefined on a linguistic basis—and the capital shifted to Bangalore. For generations the Wodeyar maharajas worshipped the goddess Chamundeshwari as their family deity and were strict observers of religious practices. They attracted scholars to their court and acted as generous patrons of the arts. They built much of the Mysore we see today and a portion of the city's most famous landmark, the imposing **Royal Palace**. The palace stands on the foundations of an earlier palace gutted by fire in 1897. The most magnificent room is the **Durbar Hall**, particularly splendid during the Dussehra festival (late September/early October) when the maharaja's jewel-studded gold throne—weighing 200 kilograms (440 pounds)—is on display.

For more of Mysore's opulence, go to the **Jaganmohan Palace.** Built in 1861, part of it was shortly afterwards converted into the **Sri Chamarajendra Art Gallery** by a former maharaja. It displays portraits of the royal family in all their ceremonial regalia as well as work by both Indian and Western artists. There is also a sizeable collection of furniture, glass and china along with sculpture and decorative arts from around the world.

The **Chamarajendra Zoological Gardens** were opened in 1892, with much effort being put into providing the inmates with near-natural habitats. The zoo houses several rare species, many of which have been bred in captivity, including India's most magnificent snake, the king cobra.

The gleaming steam engines on display at the **Railway Museum**, opened in 1979, are emblazoned with the royal insignia of the maharajas, and the private coaches, in which they travelled with their families and vast retinues, recall bygone splendour. Although the maharajas had nothing to do with building **St Philomena's Church,** its architects were possibly affected by the grandeur of the royal buildings.

Thirteen kilometres (eight miles) outside Mysore is **Chamundi Hill,** whose 1,000 stone steps, carved by a 17th-century maharaja, bring you to the **temple** of the goddess Chamundeshwari. About halfway up is a huge granite monolith of Nandi, Shiva's divine bull. Next to the hilltop temple is a huge statue of the demon Mahishasura brandishing a viciously curved sword in one hand and a rearing cobra in the other.

The ideal time to visit Mysore is during the **Dussehra festival** (late September/early October). The citizens of Mysore celebrate with faith and fervour, for the festival honours the goddess Saraswati and their own Chamundeshwari. The festival climaxes on the tenth day when a magnificent procession sets out from the Royal Palace. A majestic elephant carries the idol of Chamundeshwari

through the crowded streets. She is seated in a golden howdah and regally attended by priests, musicians, caparisoned elephants, horses and camels.

Srirangapatna

Set between the two arms of the Cauvery River just 16 kilometres (ten miles) north of Mysore is the imposing **temple** of another great Hindu deity, Ranganath, an aspect of Vishnu. The island town of Srirangapatna (City of Lord Ranganath) dates back to the early 13th century. Two centuries ago the island was the capital of Hyder Ali and his son Tippu Sultan, the 'Tiger of Mysore'. Both waged constant war against the British and Tippu Sultan was defeated and killed by them at Srirangapatna in 1799. His remains now lie in a magnificent mausoleum, the **Gumbaz,** near those of his father. Father and son both left many fine buildings; Hyder Ali, a devout Muslim, even built an addition to the Hindu temple. The splendour of Tippu Sultan's summer palace, the Dariya Daulat, must have provided him with a peaceful refuge even though the murals depict his battles with the British. A less restful building, enclosed by stone walls and a moat, is the **fort,** with dungeons used to imprison captured British officers. Situated within the fort is a mosque from whose high walls Mysore can be seen.

Ranganathittu Bird Sanctuary

A few kilometres from Srirangapatna is the Ranganathittu Bird Sanctuary, which spreads across a series of small islets in the River Cauvery. Although a wide variety of birds—including some migrants from faraway Siberia—can be seen, it is the vast numbers of spoonbills, herons and egrets which breed here that make it famous. Their chicks usually hatch between July and August and the season is from May to November.

Somnathpur

In India, a place where two rivers converge is usually considered sacred. Somnathpur, some 45 kilometres (28 miles) east of Mysore where the Kabini flows into the Kaveri, is no exception. The small town was named after its founder, Somnath, an officer in the court of the Hoysala king Narasimha III. What makes this town famous is its magnificent **temple**, built by Somnath in 1268.

As at Belur and Halebid the temple stands on a star-shaped base. However, it differs from the others in that its triple shrine stands in the centre of a courtyard surrounded by a cloister-like enclosure. The temple is dedicated to three aspects of Vishnu; Kesava, Janardhana and Venugopala. The overall effect at Somnathpur is less ornate and elaborate than the other Hoysala temples and the carving is more restrained. Nonetheless, the wealth of detail in the stories told in stone is almost overwhelming. Scenes from the great Hindu epics, the *Ramayana* and the *Mahabharata*, flow across the walls, with the end of each chapter or scene marked by a closed or half-closed door. No fewer than 74 separate sculpted images of unparalleled beauty compel us to marvel at the conception of the chief architect, Jakanachari, and the skills of his craftsmen.

Mangalore and the Coast

A benevolent and powerful goddess called Mangala Devi has given her name to Mangalore. Set near palm-fringed backwaters formed by the confluence of the Netravathi and Gurupur rivers, Mangalore has a pleasant climate all year round. Its importance as a seaport is increasing, continuing a tradition dating back to when Mangalore traded with Mesopotamia and Greece. Decorative tiles from Mangalore are used all over India and the manufacture of *bidis*, cigarettes rolled from a single tobacco leaf, is a popular cottage industry; it is also an important centre of the cashew and coffee trade. Although the city is named after a Hindu goddess, it has one of India's largest Christian communities, and several churches date from the 16th century; the earliest, the **Church of the Most Holy Rosary,** was founded in 1526. But Mangalore has little to offer of architectural or historic interest; its attractions are its relaxed atmosphere, lush greenness and location as a good starting point for the journey up the coast to Karwar.

Between the waves of the Arabian Sea and the rising grandeur of the Western Ghats lies a strip of land—no more than 65 kilometres (40 miles) wide at its broadest—which runs for almost 600 kilometres (350 miles). Only when the rivers that rise in the Western Ghats rush towards the Arabian Sea during the monsoon (July to September) does travel become, if not difficult, uncomfortable. This is not a place to hurry. Rather, one should just drift up the coast, enjoying the scenic beauty of some of the best and least-known beaches in India, as well as the wonderful cuisine.

There is little to distinguish one seaside village from another. Only at Udipi, 58 kilometres (36 miles) from Mangalore and slightly inland, and at Gokarna, 55 kilometres (34 miles) from journey's end at Karwar, does the atmosphere change. **Udipi** is one of South India's most important Hindu centres and the seat of Dwaita, a system of Hindu philosophy. The 13th-century exponent of this philosophy, Sri Madhava-Acharya, installed the beautiful idol of Krishna in Udipi's famous **temple**. As the town is also the home of eight *mutts*, or Hindu monasteries, the streets are always bustling with devout pilgrims. All over India Udipi Hotels are a familiar sight and a byword for inexpensive, strictly vegetarian, no-frills restaurants whose proprietors and staff hail from this small town.

Gokarna is one of India's most sacred places. Overlooking the sea, the temple dedicated to Shiva, the **Mahabaleshwar**, is said to be second in sanctity only to the Viswanath Temple in Varanasi. After the death of a close relative, Hindus come here to perform their obsequies. A belief held by the people of Kerala is that the Nagas, the underworld snake gods, spend part of the year here. The **festival of Shivaratri** in late February/early March draws large crowds.

The Bengali poet Rabindranath Tagore declared that **Karwar** had the loveliest beach in the world, but the truth is that the whole coastline is dotted with beautiful beaches and the traveller can choose his favourite for himself.

Tamil Nadu

Tamil Nadu is a living museum where cultures and traditions that developed over 2,000 years ago still flourish. Perhaps more than any other Indian state, Tamil Nadu displays not only the great antiquity of its culture, but also the viability—even the necessity—of this culture in today's rapidly changing society.

The Dravidian culture of Tamil Nadu is as ancient and complex as any the world has known. Among the great dynasties of the south that held sway here, the Chola kings are synonymous with power and compassion, magnificent temples and the delicate bronze images of their deities.

Madras

In the early 17th century, the Cooum and Adyar rivers flowed towards the Coromandel Coast and into the Bay of Bengal with only a few fishermen to witness their progress. Today the area between the two estuaries is the centre of India's fourth-largest city and the capital of Tamil Nadu, Madras. Despite its size and importance Madras is a city that never hurries. Compared with India's other major cities, Madras is a quiet backwater, conservative in its ways, with considerable importance placed on old-fashioned values and traditions. More women wear the traditional sari here than anywhere else in India; Brahmin men in finely woven white *dhotis*, their foreheads smeared with sandalpaste and sacred ash, go happily about their business, and every woman, regardless of status, has flowers in her hair. On the day in late August when the Brahmins change the sacred thread that denotes their caste, you can see hundreds of men on scooters going to the temples in crisply laundered and elaborately tied *dhotis* and wearing crash helmets!

For all this, Madras is a clean and efficient city. It has an excellent public transport system; its auto-rickshaw scooters are all new and well maintained and its airport is modern and well planned. There are some unexpected contrasts: the garish Tamil film posters decorating sections of Mount Road; the massive cutouts of politicians; and the hysteria of political meetings are just a few. Although Madras presents fewer of the hassles and tensions common in other Indian cities, the main shopping centres are always throbbing with life. Try the T Nagar area, where you will not find a single quiet or uncrowded spot; yet the general mood is relaxed. The people of Madras smile easily, have time for each other and are helpful to visitors. Most speak excellent English.

The growth of Madras began when the British made it a bastion of the East India Company in 1639 and built **Fort St George** a year later. Part of this fort, which now houses the Tamil Nadu State Legislature and Secretariat, is an excellent **museum.** Robert Clive, later known as Clive of India, started his career here as a writer—a lowly clerk—with the East India Company.

Next to the fort is **St Mary's**, consecrated in 1680, India's oldest Anglican church. Two famous men were married in it: Robert Clive and Elihu Yale, an Englishman born in Boston who became the governor of Madras and later founded Yale University. The **Ice House** on Marina Beach near the aquarium is an unusual relic of the British era. Ice, brought all the way from America in ships, was stored here to cool the thirsts of Company men.

Amongst Indian Roman Catholics there is a popular belief that one of the Twelve Apostles, St Thomas, arrived in Malabar (Kerala) in AD 52. He converted some Brahmins and founded India's oldest Christian community, the Syrian Christians, before moving on to preach the gospel on the eastern coast of South India. Here he was received less warmly and was eventually martyred on a small hill near the present airport, now called **St Thomas Mount,** where a small church called Our Lady of Expectations stands in his memory. Although no positive proof exists, many claim that he was buried in another church he founded, the imposing **San Thome Cathedral Basilica.** The church that originally stood on this site was much smaller.

Although Madras is only 350 years old, the region has been sacred to the Hindus for many centuries. The **Parthasarathy Temple** at Triplicane, dedicated to Krishna, was built in the eighth century by one of the Pallava kings, with later additions by the rajas of Vijayanagar in the 16th century. Another great temple, **Kapaleeswara,** which is dedicated to Shiva, is located in the suburb of Mylapore where its majestic gate towers, covered with hordes of painted stucco figures of gods, goddesses and semi-divine beings, are a local landmark. Several legends surround this temple; one concerns a Tamil saint who brought a dead girl back to life there. These are wonderful places to watch temple life: newly married couples offering prayers, old women lost in devotion, priests hurrying to the gods they serve, garlands being woven, musicians playing, women gliding by in silken groups.

At the end of March the 11-day **Arupathumoovar festival** is centred around the **Mylapore Temple**. Crowds of ecstatic devotees gather to witness the ritual pageantry of the gods being taken out in spectacular processions. Late December sees the start of the **Madras Music Festival**, featuring performances by the best southern artists as well as musicians from other parts of India. Classical music is important in Madras; concerts are well-attended by knowledgeable audiences and it sometimes seems that a new *sabha* (music hall) opens every other week.

One of the finest venues for music and the traditional arts is the auditorium at the **Kalakshetra** in Adyar, founded 40 years ago by Rukmini Devi, a pioneer in the field of dance and music who rescued *Bharata Natyam* dance from the depths.

Off Kodambakkam High Road is a **memorial** to a second-century poet and saint, Thiruvalluvar, who lived near the Kapaleeswara Temple and wrote a revered Tamil classic. The monument, in stone, is in the shape of a temple

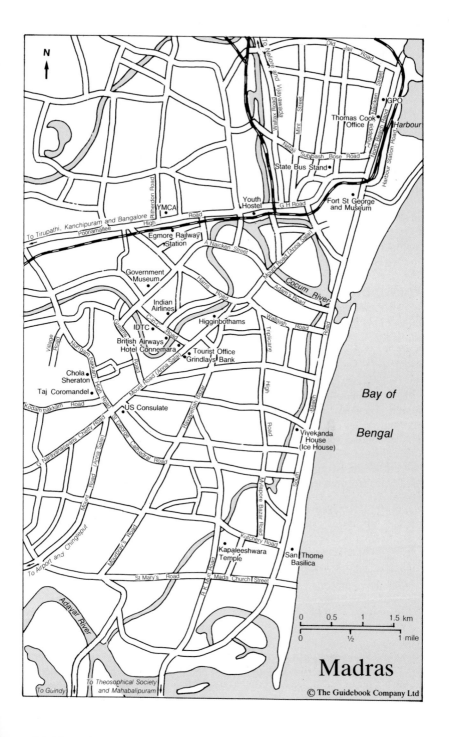

Madrid

© The Guidebook Company Ltd

chariot with long and colourful cylindrical banners hanging from its roof and swaying in the breeze.

Close to the banks of the Adyar River is the headquarters of the **Theosophical Society**, established in 1882 seven years after the Theosophical movement was founded in New York. The sprawling complex with its famous banyan trees provides an atmosphere of great peace and tranquillity in which to meditate.

Guindy National Park is a large open area designed for relaxation. It includes a **Children's Park** and **Deer Park,** but the most interesting section is the **Snake Park.**

The **Government Art Museum,** on Pantheon Road, established in 1851, has sections devoted to natural history and anthropology, but the finest displays are of the sculpture of South India's great dynasties, the Pallavas, the Cholas and the Pandyas. The one gallery not to be missed is that devoted to the museum's fine bronze collection.

Mahabalipuram (Mamallapuram)

Sixty kilometres (38 miles) south of Madras is Mamallapuram, the city the Pallava king Mahendra Varman built as a seaport to connect his empire with Southeast Asia. The road from Madras passes the fishing village of **Covelong,** with a fine beach and the excellent Fisherman's Cove Hotel. Near Covelong is a private **crocodile farm** and snake project. Mamallapuram was once an important Pallava city, second only to the capital Kanchipuram, 65 kilometres (40 miles) away, but they and the dynasties that succeeded them have vanished and there is no evidence of former maritime importance. Today it is little more than a coastal village, with its fame resing on a series of rock-cut shrines and a serenely beautiful shore temple.

The world's largest bas-relief, called both **Arjuna's Penance** and the **Descent of the Ganges**, was carved at Mamallapuram during the reign of Narasimha Varman (670–715). Some say that the mass of delicate figures rendered in profusion on the whale-shaped rock depict Shiva releasing the sacred River Ganges from its heavenly source and sending it down to earth; others believe that it shows the great archer, Arjuna, doing penance to persuade the gods to give him a special bow with which to overcome his enemies. The fact that water once flowed down the central fissure lends more weight to the Ganges legend. Accordingly, the emaciated standing figure in the left-hand section above the small square shrine of Vishnu and to the right of the large figure of Shiva is Bhagirath, the sage who asked Shiva to direct the Ganges down to earth.

Behind 'Arjuna's Penance' is a series of rock-cut **cave temples** with their inner walls carved with bas-relief scenes of great beauty. The most famous is the **Mahishasuramardhini Shrine,** where the goddess Durga surges forward on a roaring lion and attacks the much larger but already cowering buffalo demon with a battery of weapons in her eight hands. The adjoining panel is a rendering of Vishnu reclining on the coils of Shesha, the thousand-headed snake, as he floats blissfully on the cosmic ocean. In another cave, Krishna is shown holding a mountain over his devotees to protect them from the wrath of a storm sent by Indra. A less-benign aspect of Vishnu is shown in a third cave where, as Varha the boar, he rescues the earth goddess and seats her on his knee.

At Mamallapuram's southern limits are the **Five Rathas,** small shrines hewn out of hard granite that take their names from four of the five Pandava princes, heroes in the *Mahabharata* epic, and their common wife Draupadi. The divine status of the figures carved on the *rathas*, particularly the **Dharamaraja Ratha,** is obvious; some of the most graceful images are those of Shiva. A beautiful bas-relief panel of the goddess Durga in the sanctum of the **Draupadi Shrine** shows her as a wide-hipped woman flanked by kneeling attendants.

Over the centuries Pallava architects evolved their techniques. From cutting into rock to create their temples, they began to use the same rock for building. The first, and most perfect example of this development is the **Shore Temple**, the sole survivor of seven such temples. A modern boundary wall destroys its isolated grandeur but protects it from the pounding waves. The twin-towered temple stands within a courtyard surrounded by a wall topped with rows of sitting bulls rendered featureless by erosion. The damaged basalt *lingam* of Shiva was originally designed to receive the first rays of the morning sun and stands within a shrine decorated with bas-relief panels of the god and his consort. Another shrine shows Vishnu deep in his cosmic sleep.

Kanchipuram

Seventy kilometres (44 miles) west of Madras on the road to Bangalore, Kanchipuram is in many respects a typical South Indian town. But as one of India's seven sacred cities, this city of a thousand temples is a major centre of Hindu worship.

Kanchipuram was the capital of successive south Indian dynasties, beginning with the Pallavas. Their earliest temple, the **Kailashnatha,** was built by Rajasimha in about 725; he was also the builder of the Shore Temple at Mamallapuram. Dedicated to Shiva, whose guardian bull, Nandi, faces the sanctum from outside, the temple is built of sandstone.

The next temple chronologically is the **Vaikuntaperumal,** dedicated to Vishnu and built by another Pallava king. It is famous for its bas-relief scenes of battles and its ancient inscriptions. These two temples are perhaps of more interest to the lover of history and architecture than to the devotee. Hindu pilgrims usually visit other temples.

One of these, the **Ekambareswara** dedicated to Shiva, received the attentions of the Pallavas, the Cholas and the Rayas of Vijayanagar. It has one of the tallest (57 metres, or 186 feet) gateway towers in India. A vast complex of halls, corridors and enclosures, it has a huge tank full of sacred fish and, deep within its holy precincts, a thousand-year-old mango tree, the fruit of which is said to impart knowledge.

An Exemplary Wife

In the Dravidian country is a city called Kanchi, where lived
Shaktikumara, the multi-millionaire son of a merchant. As he
approached the age of eighteen, he anxiously reflected: "There is no
true happiness for a man without a wife, or with a wife who lacks the
appropriate virtues. Now how could I find a virtuous wife?"

So, diffident of the problematical satisfaction in a wife recommended by others, he became a fortune-teller, tucked a measure of rice
in his garment's hem, and roamed the earth. Now those who had
daughters exhibited their daughters to him as a man who could
interpret stigmata. But whatever the stigmata, he would say when-
ever he saw a girl of his own caste: "My good girl, can you feed me
properly with this measure of rice?" As a result, he wandered from
house to house, ridiculed and rejected.

In a city on the right bank of the Kaveri in the Shibi country, he
one day inspected a maiden presented by her nurse. She was meagrely
begemmed, for she with her parents had run through a great property, though still possessing a dilapidated mansion. When he set eyes
on her, he thought: "In the case of this girl, not a single member is too
fat or too thin, too short or too long, lacking in symmetry or purity of
outline. The fingers have a tinge of pink; the hands are marked with
many stigmata of fortune—the barley-corn, the fish, the lotus, the
bowl, and others. The ankle joints are even; the feet plump, not
stringy. The calves have a classic curve; and the knees slip almost
unobserved into the swell of the thighs. The hips are balanced,
regular, sweetly set, and shaped like chariot wheels. The navel has
elegance, flatness and depth; the lower body is adorned with three
plicatures. The breasts, with emergent nipples, give a broad-based
beauty to the entire chest. The graceful arms are marked with the
lines that promise money, grain, and numerous sons; there is a
daintiness in the slope of the shoulder, and an absence of knobbiness
at the joints. The slender neck shows the conchshell's curve . The lip
has a slight pout and an even colour; the charming chin does not
retreat; the cheek is full and firm; the brows unite to form a black,
soft, wavy line; the nose resembles a half-blown sesamum blossom;

the great, gentle eyes have a sweet and modest glance, yet flashing with three colours—pure black, white, and the pigmented part; the brow charms like the crescent moon; the curls are bewitching as a mine of sapphires; each lovely ear has double decoration, its ring and the winsome line of a drooping lotus stem: the whole face is like a lily. Her hair is abundant, long, curly (not kinky), not fading even at the end, of a smooth, glossy black throughout, and fragrant.

"Such is her person; the character must correspond. Besides, I love her. So I will apply my test and marry her. For endless regrets are the certain portion of the heedless."

So, with an affectionate glance, he said to her: "My dear young lady, are you by any chance competent to convert this measure of rice into an adequate meal for me?"

Hereupon the girl signalled with her eyes to the old serving-woman, who took the measure of grain from his hand, washed the girl's feet, and seated her in a spot, carefully sprinkled and swept, before the house door. The girl trampled the fragrant rice, dried it a little at a time, turned it repeatedly in the sun, put it on a hard, level spot, struck it very gently with hollow stalk, and extracted the kernels without crushing the husks. "Mother," she said to the nurse, "jewellers find a use for these husks, which serve to polish gems. Take them these, and with the pennies earned buy firewood—solid sticks, neither too moist nor too dry—a modest kettle, and two saucers."

When this had been done, in a shallow, wide-mouthed, pot-bellied mortar of urjoon *wood, with a long, heavy acacia pestle, plated with iron at the head, smooth in the body, and with a perceptible tenuity in the waist, she caused the grains to rise and fall with the busy grace and skill of her arm; repeatedly made them hop and sink with her fingers; stripped them of awns in the winnowing sieve; rinsed them a number of times; then—having paid honour to the fireplace—dropped them into quintessential boiled water. As the grains softened, hopped, and swelled, she collected the fire, fitted the lid to the kettle, and strained off the scum. Next, she sprinkled with water such fagots as were only scorched and sent the charred, but no longer burning, sticks to the retailers with the command: "For the pennies you get for these, buy as much as you can in vegetables, butter, curds, oil, emblic, and tamarind."*

When the nurse had done this, she provided a couple of hors d'œuvres; *then, remarking that the scummy broth should be set in a new saucer planted in moist sand, she cooled it with a gentle breeze from* a palm-leaf fan, added sufficient salt, and let the smoke from the wood fire scent it; she also ground the emblic fine to bring out its odour, sweet as a lotus; next, by the lips of the nurse, she invited him to take a bath. This he did thoroughly, receiving oil and emblic from her after she too had bathed.

After his bath, he seated himself on a plank set on the pavement (sprinkled and swept), and fingered the two saucers of liquid served on the quarter of a greenish white plantain leaf clipped from a tree in the courtyard. Then she set the rice gruel before him. He drank, relaxed, felt happy; and satisfaction pervaded his frame. Next, she served him two ladlefuls of rice, and brought a little butter, soup, and a relish. The following course was the rest of the rice, with curds, powdered spices, and fragrant, refreshing buttermilk and clotted cheese.

The man enjoyed his meal to the last morsel, then asked for water. She let it spout a continuous stream from a new pitcher; it was rich with the odour of incense, perfumed with fresh trumpet flowers, fragrant with full-blown lotuses. He set the saucer to his lips. His eyelashes were tinged and granulated by clinging drops, cool as snow; his ears took delight in the trickling sound of the stream; his cheek tingled and thrilled at the delicious contact; his nostrils expanded to the rushing gush of fragrance; his sense of taste was entranced by the exquisite flavour: he drank the pure water in great gulps. Then, in obedience to a nod, the maiden gave him a gargle from another vessel. Finally, the old nurse cleared the table; and on the pavement, freshly cleansed with cow dung, he dozed for a time, wrapped in his ragged cloak. Greatly pleased, he married the girl with all due ceremony and took her home.

After marriage, however, he neglected her and kept a mistress, whom the wife also treated as a dear friend. Her husband she served as a god, indefatigable in personal attention, indomitable in household duty, winning the devotion of domestics by inexhaustible considerateness. Subjugated by her merits, the husband subordinated the entire household to her, made her sole mistress of life and person, and thus enjoyed virtue, money, and love. And that, I may say, is how good wives please the soul.

Dandin (circa 600-700 AD) ,
The Ten Princes, *translated by A W Ryder*

The other important temple is the 12th-century **Varadaraja Vishnu Temple,** featuring a hundred-pillar hall and a huge chain carved out of a single piece of stone.

Kanchipuram produces some of India's most beautiful and sought-after silk saris. All over the city the clacking of looms can be heard as weavers work in pairs creating these silken masterpieces.

Pondicherry

Just a few kilometres from Pondicherry is **Arikamedu** where in the early years of the Christian era Roman merchant ships loaded their holds with muslins, silks, spices and timber in exchange for gold, wine and slaves. The Romans left fewer traces than later European visitors, particularly the French, who arrived in the early part of the 18th century and attempted to establish themselves in Pondicherry, formerly known as Vedapuri, Poduke and Puducherry. Initially they were thwarted by the British, and constant battles for possession marked the early years of their occupation. Although almost always under French rule, Pondicherry could not really be considered French until 1763, when they obtained it from the British as part of the Treaty of Paris, and it remained in French hands until 1954. It is now part of a Union Territory that includes three other small formerly French colonies: Mahe (Kerala), Karaikal (Tamil Nadu) and Yanam (Andhra Pradesh).

It is easier to travel the 115 kilometres (72 miles) from Madras to Pondicherry by road, rather than take the train to Villupuram, 38 kilometres (24 miles) west of the town, from where there is a branch line and a bus service.

Although the French influence is gradually fading, Pondicherry retains a few Gallic accents. The old French quarter, once divided by a canal into the **Ville Blanc** for the French and the **Ville Noir** for the Indians, still has its cobbled streets; the street signs are blue and white as in France; and policemen continue to wear uniforms modelled on those of the French gendarmes.

Pondicherry's main sights are the **Rai Nivas** (the official residence of the Lieutenant Governor), the **Sacred Heart Church** and the **Sri Aurobindo ashram**. The ashram retreat was founded in 1926 by Sri Aurobindo after whose death the spiritual authority passed to one of his disciples, a French woman known as 'The Mother'. The ashram's many activities include the making of perfumes, soap, incense and hand-made paper.

The Mother was also instrumental in founding the 'City of Dawn', **Auroville**, ten kilometres (six miles) from Pondicherry. Its original charter aimed at creating a city of the future where people from India and abroad could live and work together in a spiritual environment. Despite these laudable intentions, the dream began to sour soon after The Mother died in 1973.

Dissatisfaction and disputes with the local people led to clashes and, in 1980, the Indian government stepped in and took over. The futuristic buildings of Auroville were designed by the French architect Roger Auger. The vast **Matri Mandir** serves both as a meditation hall and the spiritual centre of Auroville.

Tiruchirapalli (Trichy)

Close to the centre of Tamil Nadu on the River Cauvery is Tiruchirapalli, known better as Trichy. An ideal base from which to explore the temple towns of South India, Trichy boasts two extraordinary temples of its own. The town is well connected with daily flights to and from Madras and there are less frequent services to Madurai and Colombo. Trichy is on the main Madras–Madurai railway line, with connections to Chidambaram and Tanjore.

Historically, Trichy's prosperity was linked to the fortunes of South India's ruling dynasties. Although the city is generally associated with the Cholas and the Pallavas, Pandyas and Nayaks have also left their imprint. During the Carnatic Wars of the 18th century Trichy was often in the forefront of events. A massive outcrop of rock, 83 metres (273 feet) high, rears abruptly out of the plains, as if to guard the city. On the summit is the **Rock Fort Temple**, dedicated to Ganesh, the Remover of Obstacles. Pilgrims making the ascent pass two cave temples dating from the seventh-century Pallava era and a temple dedicated to Ganesh's father, Shiva.

North of the city, between the Cauvery River and its tributary the Kollidam, is an island where Trichy's two great temples are located. The largest, the remarkable **Srirangam Temple,** and the surrounding secular buildings are enclosed by seven great walls. One of the largest temples in South India, Srirangam was originally built by the Cholas in the 13th and 14th centuries. Later kings added to it to honour the god Vishnu and to display their own wealth and power. In the **Horse Court** each pillar is carved with a great rearing horse and intricate gatherings of men and gods are sculpted around the base.

Two kilometres (just over a mile) east of Srirangam, there was once a simple shrine under a *jambu* tree where, so the legend goes, an elephant used to worship Shiva. This shrine is now the splendid temple of **Tituvanaikkaval**—also called **Jambukeswarwaram**, after the *jambu* tree.

Tanjavur (Tanjore)

After leaving Trichy the Cauvery River flows east through Tamil Nadu's rice-growing region and 55 kilometres (34 miles) away it arrives at Tanjavur (Tanjore). South Indian culture has always revolved around temples. In Tanjavur the centre of such activity is the Chola temple, the **Brihadeshwara**, built by Rajaraja I (985–1016), the greatest of the Chola kings. Suffering from leprosy, Rajaraja learned from his guru that he would be cured if he built a temple to Shiva. It took 12 years for the work to be finished, but when he finally took a bath in the temple tank, he was immediately cured of his affliction.

A colonnaded cloister runs the length of the enclosing walls where you can see some of the famous **Tanjore frescos** (the oldest and most fragile are preserved elsewhere) depicting religious myths and courtly pursuits. Guarding the central shrine is a gigantic carving of the bull Nandi, the second-largest in

India. The soaring **vimana tower** is unusual in that it is higher than any of the outer gate towers. Nearly 65 metres (202 feet) high, it is crowned with a huge cupola carved from a boulder that is estimated to weigh over 81 tonnes. To raise the stone it was necessary to haul it along a ramp six kilometres (3.7 miles) long. A small **Archaeological Museum** inside the temple compound gives an interesting overview of the temple and its restoration.

Close to the temple is the **palace,** parts of which date back to the mid-16th century. The **Saraswathi Mahal Library** has an important collection of Indian and European manuscripts. The Chola bronzes in the **Art Gallery** (open 10 am –1 pm, 2–5 pm, closed Wednesdays) should not be missed.

Madurai

The name 'Madurai' is said to be a corruption of *mathuram,* 'nectar', a name given to the city after a drop of nectar fell from Shiva's hair. Madurai is a temple town; everything physically, emotionally, culturally and commercially revolves around its great temple, the **Meenakshi**. Here, also, the last of the three great Tamil *sangams*, or academies of learning, flourished around 2,000 years ago.

The temple complex is one of the largest and most impressive in India and its soaring towers, the tallest over 48 metres (157 feet) high, are visible for miles around. The temple is dedicated to Shiva, known here as Sundareswara, and his consort, the 'fish-eyed' goddess Meenakshi. Their marriage is celebrated during the ten-day **Chithirai festival** (late April/early May). The **Avanimoolam festival** (late August/early September) is another holiday in honour of Sundareswara's coronation. The eastern part of the city celebrates the beautiful **Float festival**, when the gods sail across the waters of Teppakulam Tank on a raft decorated with flowers and lights (late January/early February).

Madurai was once the capital of the Pandyan kings who are credited with having built the temple and the town. The temple is enclosed by high walls set with five elaborately decorated *gopurams* (gate towers), with the main entrance on the eastern side. You can climb up the inside of the tallest tower, the southern one, and gaze down upon the temple complex, the surrounding streets and the countryside.

One important feature of the temple is the **Golden Lotus Tank**, where the merits of Tamil books were tested by throwing them in and observing whether they would float or sink. In the heart of the temple are the twin shrines of Sundareswara and Meenakshi. Although non-Hindus are not permitted inside them, the rest of the temple is open to all (and can be photographed when the temple closes for worship between 12.30 and 4 pm on payment of Rs5). Not to be missed is the **Thousand-pillared Hall**. Actually there are only 997, each carved with a dragon, although their symmetry has been somewhat spoiled by the presence of the worthwhile **Temple Art Museum.** A much-stressed feature of the group of pillars located near the museum exit is that they sound different musical notes when tapped.

The Pandya dynasty was followed, in the early part of the 16th century, by the Nayaks who maintained the tradition of patronizing both Tamil literature and the Meenakshi Temple. Just a short distance from the temple is a **palace** named after one of their rulers, Thirumalai Nayak, a prodigious builder. Constructed in the early 18th century, it was nearly destroyed by the end of the same century and has suffered considerably from both the passage of time and the uses to which it has been put. Even so, its Indo-Saracenic architecture and the sheer scale and grandeur of the huge arched passageways, supported by the carved and painted pillars that surround the great courtyard full of trees, still impress.

In 1959 Jawaharlal Nehru opened the **Gandhi Museum** here, situated to the north of the Vaigai River. The museum contains a wealth of information about the Mahatma in the form of letters, photographs and personal possessions.

Madurai is also famous for its textiles, and much of the activity in its well-planned streets revolves around this industry. Its vast cottage industry weaves distinctive, brightly coloured saris.

Kanya Kumari

Many centuries ago, according to Hindu legend, a virgin goddess fell in love with Shiva. Unfortunately for her he was lost in meditation and ignored both her beauty and her presence. Believing that if she performed an arduous penance she would attract his attention, the goddess subjected herself to harsh austerities. Although Shiva did eventually acknowledge her devotion and agree to marry her he insisted they wait until a later incarnation. Furious, she hurled the already prepared wedding feast into the sea.

Kanya Kumari, at the extreme southern tip of India, is named after this goddess. As the presiding deity of the **Kumari Amman Temple** by the sea, she is now a symbol of unity and devotion. Hindu pilgrims believe that the beach's multi-coloured sands are the washed-ashore remnants of her wedding feast.

In India, where every confluence of water is held to be sacred, Kanya Kumari is especially regarded, for it is the meeting place of the Arabian Sea, the Indian Ocean and the Bay of Bengal, and here Mahatma Gandhi's cremated ashes were brought immediately after his assassination in 1948. Before they were scattered upon the seas, the urn that contained them was placed on the spot where the **Gandhi Memorial** now stands. On 2 October every year, Gandhi's birthday, the rays of the sun fall on the black marble marker that indicates the precise positioning of the urn.

In 1892, one of India's greatest religious philosophers, Vivekananda, came to Kanya Kumari before leaving to address the World Congress of Religions in Chicago. The **Vivekananda Memorial,** built in 1970, now occupies a rock on which he meditated and has been designed to incorporate various strands of Indian architecture. The Virgin Goddess was an earlier penitent there and in a separate shrine the faithful can see her footprint on the hard rock.

Kanya Kumari is noted for its magnificent sunrises and sunsets. It is also the only place in India where, when the moon is full, it can be seen rising as the sun sets.

Kerala

Kerala, the smallest of the South Indian states, presents something of an enigma. Temples lack the elaborate ornamentation found in the other states, and people dress in pristine white cotton. The most literate state in India, Kerala leads the country in a number of areas such as family planning and health care. It also earns a high proportion of India's foreign exchange, through exporting spices. In 1957, Kerala elected the free world's first communist government. Christians have thrived here since just after the crucifixion, and centuries ago tolerant Hindu kings welcomed both Muslims and Jews to these shores.

Kerala is also one of India's most beautiful states. The endless patchwork of green paddy fields, the cool mist-filled High Ranges, the palm-fringed beaches and the timeless tranquillity of the Backwaters should satisfy all lovers of natural beauty.

Kerala contributes generously to India's cultural heritage. In music, song, dance and mime the great dance-drama *Kathakali* recreates episodes from the Hindu epics. Kerala's own female dance form, *Mohiniattam*, has a lyrical and sensual fluidity that befits the dance of an enchantress, and *Kudiyattam* and *Krishnattam* are classical dance dramas. *Theyyam,* found in northern Kerala, is a spectacular act of worship where elaborately costumed and made-up dancers become possessed by the spirits of the gods. *Kalaripayattu* is Kerala's own martial art. The state's most spectacular temple festival is the **Pooram** at **Trichur**, when the district's presiding deities are honoured with processions of caparisoned elephants and thundering drums.

Trivandrum

When in 1750 the legendary Travancore maharaja's kingdom was threatened by a vast army, he took an oath: if his enemies were vanquished he would give his kingdom to Vishnu. Eventually victorious, he placed his sword before the sanctum of the deity and from that day onwards he and his successors, ruled as the *dasas* or servants of Vishnu. Although Trivandrum is now the state capital of Kerala, it has remained the city of this god.

Trivandrum is built on seven hills. Long ago, when the area was still a forest, an idol of Vishnu was found on the highest hill. The humble shrine that housed the idol eventually grew into the **Sri Padmanabha Swamy Temple.** Even the name of the city acknowledges its connection with its presiding deity: Trivandrum is an Anglicized form of Thiru Anantha Puram, the 'Sacred Abode of Anantha', the divine, thousand-headed serpent in whose coils Vishnu reclines when he sleeps on the cosmic ocean. The sacred precincts of the temple are closed to non-Hindus, and twice a day when the Maharaja of Travancore pays his respects to his god, even ordinary Hindus may not enter.

The **Government Art Museum** with its slightly surreal architecture displays an interesting array of Kerala's arts and artifacts: bronzes, antique

jewellery, woodcarvings, musical instruments, ritual objects and handicrafts. In the same complex is the **Sri Chitra Art Gallery,** best known for its collection of paintings by a 19th-century Kerala artist, Raja Ravi Varma, a member of the royal family who painted Victorian portraits and scenes inspired by ancient Hindu myths. The gallery also houses the collections of the Travancore maharajas, Mughal miniatures, Tanjore paintings and works by a Russian *émigré,* Sveteslav Roerich.

Several years ago, murals showing brown-skinned men teaching martial arts to the Chinese were found in northern China. This discovery supported a long-held claim that the martial arts originated in Kerala. The claim is still disputed, but Kerala's martial art, *kalaripayattu,* is at least as ancient, fast and deadly as the other, better-known schools.

Take a walk through **Connemara Market** by passing under an imposing archway whose British design is at odds with the bustle you will find inside.

Kovalam

Kovalam, 16 kilometres (ten miles) south of Trivandrum, is most people's idea of paradise: a lazy blue sea lapping against golden sands fringed by swaying palms. You can sail into the sheltered bay in a catamaran or swim in the clear waters—but not too far out as there are strong currents. Centuries ago, India's natural system of medicine, called *ayurveda,* was developed in Kerala. At the **Health and Yoga Centre** you can enjoy a soothing *ayurvedic* oil massage.

Padmanabhapuram Palace

Some 37 kilometres (23 miles) from Kovalam (53 kilometres, or 33 miles, from Trivandrum) is the 16th-century Padmanabhapuram Palace (closed on Mondays), once the seat of the Travancore maharajas. The palace is in fact now in Tamil Nadu, midway between Trivandrum and Kanya Kumari. It is a grand version of a traditional feudal house built mainly of dark teak. Murals depict the Travancore rulers' deity asleep on the sacred snake; there are great dining halls capable of holding a thousand people; the floors are polished to a mirror-like finish using an unlikely mixture of charcoal, egg white and coconut shells; and there is a bed given to a maharaja by the Portuguese made of 64 different kinds of wood.

Cochin

'Queen of the Arabian Sea' and the 'Venice of the East' are titles applied to Cochin. For centuries Kerala has supplied the world with pepper, cardamom, cinnamon; nutmeg and more recently tea, coffee, coir products, rubber and seafood, all shipped out from Cochin.

Cochin has assimilated aspects of the Arabic, Chinese, Portuguese, Dutch and British ways of life. The Arabs did not settle here, but from the seventh

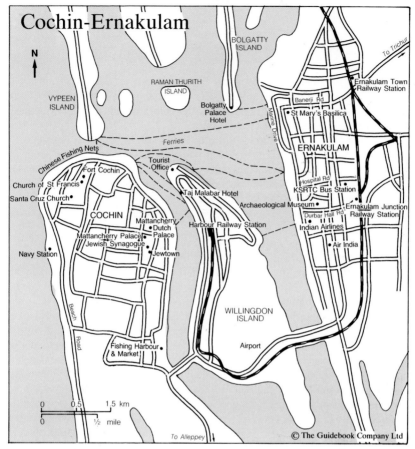

Cochin-Ernakulam

N

BOLGATTY ISLAND

RAMAN THURITH ISLAND

VYPEEN ISLAND

To Trichur

Ernakulam Town Railway Station

Banerji Rd

Bolgatty Palace Hotel

Marine Drive

St Mary's Basilica

Ferries

Chinese Fishing Nets

Fort Cochin

Tourist Office

ERNAKULAM

Church of St Francis

Santa Cruz Church

Taj Malabar Hotel

Hospital Rd

KSRTC Bus Station

COCHIN

Mattancherry Dutch Palace

Archaeological Museum

Mattancherry Palace Jewish Synagogue

Harbour Railway Station

Durbar Hall Rd

Indian Airlines

Ernakulam Junction Railway Station

Navy Station

Jewtown

Air India

Beach Road

WILLINGDON ISLAND

Fishing Harbour & Market

Airport

0   0.5   1.5 km

0   ½ mile

To Alleppey

© The Guidebook Company Ltd

century onwards the muezzin's call has been heard and their trading dhows have been a familiar sight in the harbour. The Chinese fishing nets that rim the shore, particularly in the **Fort Cochin** area, recall Eastern trade links. The Portuguese were the first Europeans to settle in Cochin and the first to settle in India. The oldest European church in India, so it is believed, is the **Church of St Francis,** which the Portuguese built in 1510. Services have been conducted according to the rituals of the Catholic Church (for the Portuguese), the Dutch Reform Church (for the Dutch), the Anglican Church (for the British), and today they are under the aegis of the Church of South India. Although the mortal remains of Vasco da Gama are now entombed in Lisbon, where they were taken 14 years after his death in 1524, the gravestone under which he originally lay can still be seen.

In exchange for certain trading rights and concessions, the Portuguese built the **Mattanchery Palace** in 1557 and presented it to the Cochin rajas. Its more popular name, the **Dutch Palace**, was acquired sometime after 1663 when the Dutch ousted the Portuguese and the same year enlarged and renovated the palace. Neither the Portuguese, the Dutch nor the British ever lived there, but the rajas of Cochin occupied it, mostly for ceremonial occasions. It is now a **museum** (open 10 am–5 pm, closed Fridays) housing a small collection of royal costumes and weapons. Don't miss the 17th-century murals depicting scenes from the *Ramayana* and other Indian epics.

In 1744, the Dutch built the **Bolghatty Palace** for themselves. A simple and elegant building that is now a hotel, it is situated on **Bolghatty Island**, overlooking the busy waterways. The Dutch were more tolerant than the Portuguese (they abolished slavery) and the cool restraint of the Bolghatty Palace's airy rooms suggests a people more at ease with their surroundings. They were, however, a temporary presence, finally giving in to their great rivals, the British, in 1796.

The British presence lasted nearly 150 years but produced nothing of any great architectural interest. Their enduring legacy lies in the construction of roads and railways and their influence on language, education, government and the law.

Today the community whose presence arouses the most interest is the Cochin Jews. Although there is evidence of 'Black' Jews being in Kerala as early as AD 68, the origin of the 'White' Jews of Cochin is shrouded in mystery and the subject of endless debate. For the Jews, Cochin must have seemed a real haven, for they were welcomed by the Hindu ruler. He granted them extensive privileges and donated land adjoining Mattanchery Palace and the Hindu temple on which to construct a synagogue. Ironically, the only time these Jews were persecuted was during the Portuguese era. The **synagogue** is in **Jewtown** at the end of a series of narrow cobbled streets and was built in 1568. Recent emigration to Israel has reduced the once-thriving community to around 30 people, but a Torah and the copper plates recording the privileges granted to their ancestors by the rajas can still be seen. From the ceiling hang clusters of lovely oil lamps, and the floor is paved with hand-painted Chinese tiles, each with a different design.

The Backwaters

The traveller in Cochin can move by air, sea, rail or road. But another choice unique to Kerala is the Backwaters. Although Kerala's entire coastline is 550 kilometres (340 miles) long, her navigable inland network of rivers, canals and lakes totals 1,920 kilometres (1,200 miles). The system stretches south from Cochin to Trivandrum and forms one of India's most beautiful regions, with narrow canals, wide rivers and vast expanses of water such as **Vembanad Lake.**

Amongst the boats that ply the blue-green waters are Chinese-style junks and country-boats with thatched roofs. At one time the bulk of the region's produce was transported by boats piloted by singing boatmen, but today the faster roads take most of the traffic. One of the most beautiful stretches lies between **Alleppey** and **Quilon**; it takes nine hours to cover the distance by local ferry. Alleppey, 58 kilometres (36 miles) south of Cochin, has more canals than roads and is the starting point for Backwater excursions.

Although a languid atmosphere is the hallmark of the Backwaters, the festival of **Onam** (late August/early September) sees a complete change of pace. This is when the **snakeboats** race down the rivers, echoing the ancient rivalries of warrior kings. The best-known race is the Nehru Cup, held at Alleppey on the second Saturday in August.

The High Ranges and Periyar

The popular image of Kerala is of a lush coastal region whose swaying palm trees, lazy backwaters and golden sands bake in the sultry climate of a tropical paradise. This is an accurate enough image in many respects but one which ignores another—and quite different—Kerala: the Kerala of the hills and High Ranges; the Kerala that possesses some of India's most beautiful scenery and has a cool, bracing climate far removed from the coast's humidity. This Kerala starts at Ponmudi, a mere 60 kilometres (38 miles) from Trivandrum.

Ponmudi is a tiny hill station, set at an altitude of 325 metres (1,066 feet) amongst forest-covered hills. The two-hour drive from Trivandrum takes you along a winding road, past small villages, through the **Golden Valley** and up into another world. As you climb, the hairpin bends provide ever-changing aspects of the hills, every curve in the road revealing an even more breathtaking

'I'm Out of Society'

hen the Youghals came into the station, Strickland—very gravely, as he did everything—fell in love with Miss Youghal; and she, after a while, fell in love with him because she could not understand him. Then Strickland told the parents; but Mrs Youghal said she was not going to throw her daughter into the worst paid Department in the Empire, and old Youghal said, in so many words, that he mistrusted Strickland's ways and works, and would thank him not to speak or write to his daughter any more. 'Very well,' said Strickland, for he did not wish to make his lady-love's life a burden. After one long talk with Miss Youghal he dropped the business entirely.

The Youghals went up to Simla in April.

In July Strickland secured three months' leave on 'urgent private affairs.' He locked up his house—though not a native in the Province would wittingly have touched 'Estreekin Sahib's' gear for the world—and went down to see a friend of his, an old dyer, at Tarn Taran.

Here all trace of him was lost, until a sais or groom met me on the Simla Mall with this extraordinary note:

DEAR OLD MAN,—Please give bearer a box of cheroots— Supers, No. 1, for preference. They are freshest at the Club. I'll repay when I reappear; but at present I'm out of society.— Yours,

E. STRICKLAND

I ordered two boxes, and handed them over to the sais with my love. That sais was Strickland, and he was in old Youghal's employ, attached to Miss Youghal's Arab. The poor fellow was suffering for an English smoke, and knew that, whatever happened, I should hold my tongue till the business was over.

Later on, Mrs Youghal, who was wrapped up in her servants, began talking at houses where she called of her paragon among saises—the man who was never too busy to get up in the morning and pick flowers for the breakfast-table, and who blacked—actually blacked—the hoofs of his horse like a London coachman! The turn-out of Miss Youghal's Arab was a wonder and a delight. Strickland—Dulloo, I mean—found his reward in the pretty things that Miss Youghal said to him when she went out riding. Her parents were pleased to find she had forgotten all her foolishness for young Strickland and said she was a good girl.

Strickland vows that the two months of his service were the most rigid mental discipline he has ever gone through. Quite apart from the little fact that the wife of one of his fellow-saises fell in love with him and then tried to poison him with arsenic because he would have nothing to do with her, he had to school himself into keeping quiet when Miss Youghal went out riding with some man who tried to flirt with her, and he was forced to trot behind carrying the blanket and hearing every word! Also, he had to keep his temper when he was slanged in the theatre porch by a policeman—especially once when he was abused by a Naik he had himself recruited from Isser Jang village—or, worse still, when a young subaltern called him a pig for not making way quickly enough.

But the life had its compensations. He obtained great insight into the ways and thefts of saises—enough, he says, to have summarily convicted half the population of the Punjab if he had been on business. He became one of the leading players at knuckle-bones, which all jhampánis and many saises play while they are waiting outside the Government House or the Gaiety Theatre of nights; he learned to smoke tobacco that was three-fourths cowdung; and he heard the wisdom of the grizzled Jemadar of the Government House grooms. Whose words are valuable. He saw many things which amused him; and he states, on honour, that no man can appreciate Simla properly till he has seen it from the sais's point of view.

Rudyard Kipling, Plain Tales from the Hills, *1888*

view. Either you are gifted with the sight of a lovely green valley—almost certainly mist-filled if you are early—or a glimpse of pristine natural beauty through dark teak trees or, in equally impressive contrast, the precise neatness of a tea estate. A halt anywhere along the way will enable you to take a closer look at the region's abundant flora, particularly the wild loveliness of orchids growing in casual abandon. Ponmudi is neat and contained in its smallness—perfect for a short respite from the heat of the lower altitudes or for long hikes into the beautiful surrounding hills. Set like a tiny jewel in a magical greenness, it is only one among a handful of such hill stations in the High Ranges.

Munnar, 137 kilometres (85 miles) east of Cochin, is the largest of the hill stations and, at 1,524 metres (5,000 feet), Kerala's highest town. Munnar is different, still preserving a way of life that has almost vanished elsewhere, the life of the tea planter. Their spacious sprawling bungalows conform to everyone's preconceptions of a planter's home. Central to the planter's existence is the club and here Munnar does not disappoint. The **High Range Club** is the hub of Munnar's social life, a comfortable building with all the traditional hallmarks of club life: billiard tables, a library and, of course, a Men Only bar. Although only members can stay here, visitors are welcome and can relax or enjoy a meal in the old-world atmosphere of the dining room.

Life in Munnar revolves around tea: much of India's tea is grown on the surrounding hills and the air is permeated with its aroma. Visitors are soon aware of the impact this delicate leaf has had on the region. Where a century or so ago there was nothing but forested hills, there are now tea estates. As they are all owned by the Tata industrial group, visit their central office to obtain permission to look around an estate and observe how tea is processed.

The world of tea estates seems to blend well with the magnificence of nature, for although it is easy to recognize the impact of tea on the High Ranges, much of the region's natural beauty remains untouched. A short drive to **Kundale,** one of the largest estates, takes you through some of the finest local scenery. At the **Eravikulam Wildlife Sanctuary,** hundreds of sure-footed Nilgiri tahr roam contentedly, grazing on rolling hills whose greenness stretches away across the valleys to merge into the misty blues of the distance. Just beyond this sanctuary is the **Rajmalai Park** and the mist-wrapped heights of South India's highest peak, **Anaimudi** (2,695 metres, or 8,840 feet).

Periyar Tiger Reserve and Wildlife Sanctuary

Between Trivandrum and Munnar is **Thekkady**, the home of one of India's oldest and best-known wildlife sanctuaries. The former princely state of Travancore began to develop the area as a sanctuary in 1934, using the artificial lake that had been formed by flooding in 1895 as its centre. By 1950 the sanctuary had reached its present size of 780 square kilometres (300 square miles) and was named the Periyar Wildlife Sanctuary. The sanctuary is in fact closer to Madurai

in Tamil Nadu, 145 kilometres (90 miles) to the east via an extremely attractive road, and Cochin, 192 kilometres (120 miles) to the west.

The vast calmness of the lake and the stark, skeletal remains of the trees that protrude from its waters give the area a primeval look. This impression is heightened by the mists that swirl ethereally over the water in the early morning. The wildlife remains largely undisturbed by visitors who must observe it from special boats which glide across the surface of the lake. Although the stars of the sanctuary are the families of wild elephants that often gather near the water's edge, other inhabitants include bears, sambhar, bison and spotted deer, as well as many screeching monkeys. The sanctuary was one of the first to come under the central government's successful Project Tiger. The birdlife is rich and varied and Periyar attracts dedicated bird-watching enthusiasts.

The Maharaja of Travancore's summer palace, set in the lake on a small promontory which can be reached only by boat, is now a hotel. Run by Kerala Tourism, it is a good enough reason for visiting the sanctuary.

The Andaman and Nicobar Islands

Just under 200 kilometres (120 miles) west of southern Burma and only 140
kilometres (88 miles) from Indonesia lies one of India's least-known but most
exciting destinations. The 293 islands that form the Andaman and Nicobar
Islands stretch 800 kilometres (500 miles) north to south and are over 900
kilometres (600 miles) east of India. They are in fact the remains of a now-
submerged hill range that extends from the Arakan to Sumatra.

The Andamans are made up of 274 islands, of which only 26 are inhabited;
12 of the 19 Nicobar Islands are inhabited, but all are unfortunately closed to
tourists. Only a few of the Andaman Islands are accessible, but the pleasures of
relaxing at **Corbyn's Cove**, exploring the colonial ruins on **Ross Island**,
visiting a lumber operation with working elephants, or bird-watching on
Chiriya Tapu, are only a few of the activities that are available.

Many of the islands have been challenged by the dual threats of the axe and
human migration from the mainland. At Independence, the islands' total population was only 50,000, made up of a mix of tribals, convicts, Burmese labour and
a small administration. The population is now close to two million, only a fifth
of whom are aboriginal. The tribal groups are of Mongoloid stock in the Nico-
bars, while the original Andamanese are Negreto and form four tribes: Onges,
Jharwas, Sentinelese and Andamanese. The Great Andamanese, once the most
prolific tribe, now number only 26 and live on Strait Island. The Onges, who
live on Little Andaman, now number only 98, while the Jharwas number 250.
'Civilization' has been, and still is, the greatest threat to the indigenous population.

Although remote, the islands have long been known. In the second century,
Ptolemy called them 'islands of good fortune'; in the seventh century, Buddhist
pilgrims travelling between India and Southeast Asia used to stop here; and in
the 15th century, Nicolo Conti referred to them as 'islands of gold'.

Modern records of the islands date from 1789 when Lieutenant Archibald
Blair was sent to survey the area and established the short-lived settlement at
Port Cornwallis. Development came only after the 1857 Mutiny, or the War of
Independence, when the British government established a new settlement at
Port Blair and developed a penal colony. 'Freedom Fighters' and convicts were
transported to the islands, and one of the few man-made sites was developed.
The **Cellular Gaol** was completed in 1906 and today part of it is a national
monument; remarkably it is still a functioning gaol. Incidentally, the food is re-
ported to have improved!

Port Blair is the entry point for both air and sea travellers. Indian Airlines
has thrice-weekly flights from Calcutta and Madras plus flights from New Delhi
via Bhubaneswar. While the tribal islands are strictly protected, the small but
interesting **Anthropological Museum** (closed on Saturdays) has a collection of

old photographs, models and tools which give some idea of their 'primitive' way of life. The population of the town includes migrants from all parts of India, with Burmese and Bengalis predominating.

Apart from the gaol and the museum, the natural beauty of the islands coupled with the extraordinary range of birds, flowers and marine life and the relics of colonial history make a visit rewarding.

Probably the best way to explore Port Blair is by bicycle, hired from a shop in **Aberdeen bazaar** for about Rs15 per day. Some of the roads are hilly but the effort is rewarded. Two kilometres (just over a mile) out of Port Blair, at **Haddo,** is a small **zoo** (closed on Mondays) where estuarine crocodiles are being bred for reintroduction to the island's small rivers and mangrove swamps where they were previously found. The avian collection is representative of the islands and includes such species as the Nicondam Hornbill which is otherwise restricted to a single island. Beyond Haddo, the **Chatham Saw Mill** is on an isthmus to the north. Both the Botanical Survey of India and the Zoological Survey have active units in Port Blair and their collections, especially the **herbarium**, are of interest.

While most of the islands are off-limits, local permission is available for **Redskin**, **Grub**, **Jolly Bay** and **Snob islands**. Permission is also occasionally given to visit **Ross** and **Viper islands**.

Wandoor Beach on the west coast, about an hour's drive from Port Blair, is ideal for snorkelling and diving. The Marine Department runs boats to the smaller outlying islands from here.

A visit to **Jolly Bay** takes most of the day (you cannot stay overnight) so food must be taken. The reefs around the island are best viewed from one of the glass-bottomed boats.

At the southernmost tip of South Andaman is **Chiriya Tapu** (Bird Island), with dense mangrove forest fringing an attractive beach noted for its butterflies. The guesthouse on the hill overlooking Chiriya Tapu also has a commanding view of the outlying islands and reefs.

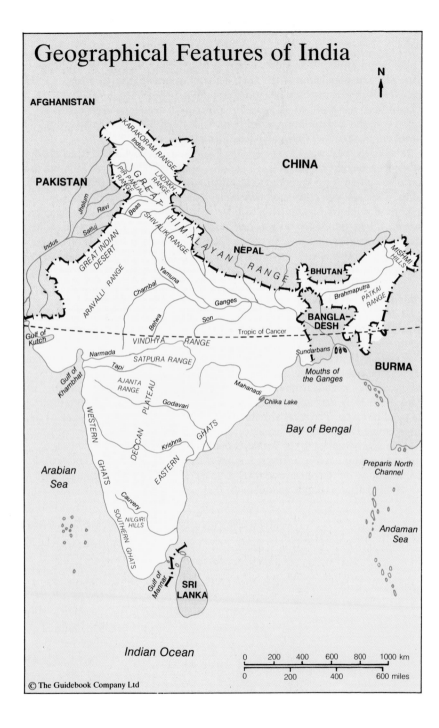

Geographical Features of India

N

AFGHANISTAN

CHINA

PAKISTAN

KARAKORAM RANGE

Indus

LADAKH RANGE

PIR PANJAL RANGE

GREAT

Jhelum

Ravi

Beas

Sattuj

SHIVALIK RANGE

HIMALAYAN

NEPAL

RANGE

BHUTAN

MISHMI HILLS

Indus

GREAT INDIAN DESERT

ARAVALLI RANGE

Yamuna

Chambal

Ganges

Brahmaputra

PATKAI RANGE

BANGLA-DESH

BURMA

Gulf of Kutch

Betwa

Son

Tropic of Cancer

VINDHYA RANGE

Narmada

SATPURA RANGE

Sundarbans

Gulf of Khambhat

Tapi

AJANTA RANGE

PLATEAU

Mahanadi

Mouths of the Ganges

Godavari

DECCAN

EASTERN

GHATS

Krishna

Chilka Lake

Bay of Bengal

Arabian Sea

WESTERN

GHATS

Cauvery

NILGIRI HILLS

SOUTHERN GHATS

Preparis North Channel

Andaman Sea

Gulf of Mannar

SRI LANKA

Indian Ocean

0   200   400   600   800   1000 km

0   200   400   600 miles

© The Guidebook Company Ltd

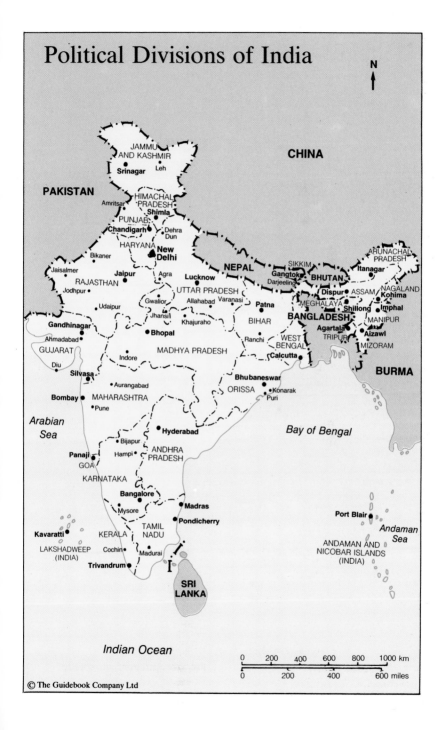

Political Divisions of India

N

CHINA

JAMMU
AND KASHMIR
Srinagar •Leh

PAKISTAN

HIMACHAL
PRADESH
Amritsar Shimla
PUNJAB•
Chandigarh •Dehra
Dun

HARYANA
Bikaner New
Delhi

Jaisalmer

Jaipur Agra Lucknow NEPAL SIKKIM
Gangtok ARUNACHAL
PRADESH
RAJASTHAN UTTAR PRADESH Darjeeling BHUTAN Itanagar
Jodhpur •Gwalior Allahabad Varanasi Dispur ASSAM NAGALAND
Udaipur •Jhansi •Patna MEGHALAYA Kohima
Khajuraho BIHAR Shillong Imphal
Gandhinagar •Bhopal BANGLADESH MANIPUR
Ahmadabad Ranchi Agartala Aizawl
GUJARAT MADHYA PRADESH WEST TRIPURA MIZORAM
Diu BENGAL
Silvasa Indore Calcutta BURMA
•Aurangabad Bhubaneswar
Bombay MAHARASHTRA ORISSA •Konarak
•Pune Puri

Arabian
Sea Hyderabad Bay of Bengal

•Bijapur
Panaji Hampi ANDHRA
GOA PRADESH

KARNATAKA

Bangalore Madras
•Mysore Pondicherry Port Blair Andaman
Sea
Kavaratti TAMIL ANDAMAN AND
NADU NICOBAR ISLANDS
LAKSHADWEEP KERALA Cochin• (INDIA)
(INDIA) •Madurai
Trivandrum

SRI
LANKA

Indian Ocean

0   200   400   600   800   1000 km

0   200   400   600 miles

© The Guidebook Company Ltd

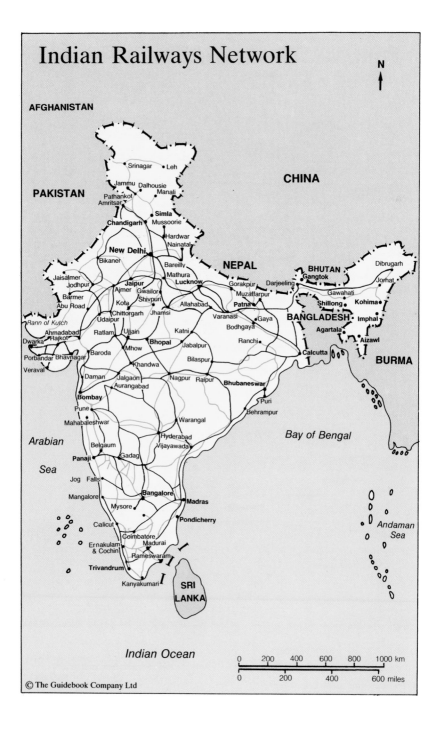

Indian Railways Network

N

AFGHANISTAN

CHINA

PAKISTAN

Srinagar • Leh
Jammu Dalhousie
Pathankot Manali
Amritsar
Simla
Chandigarh Mussoorie
Hardwar
Nainatal
New Delhi
Bikaner Bareilly
Mathura NEPAL
Jaisalmer Jaipur Lucknow BHUTAN
Jodhpur Ajmer Gwailor Gorakpur Darjeeling Gangtok Dibrugarh
Barmer Kota Shivpuri Muzaffarpur Jorhat
Abu Road Chittorgarh Jhamsi Allahabad Patna Gawahati
Udaipur Varanasi Gaya Shillong Kohima
Rann of Kutch Ratlam Ujjain Katni Bodhgaya BANGLADESH Imphal
Dwarka Ahmadabad Bhopal Jabalpur Ranchi Agartala
Rajkot Aizawl
Porbandar Bhavnagar Baroda Mhow Bilaspur Calcutta BURMA
Veraval Daman Khandwa
Jalgaon Nagpur Raipur
Aurangabad Bhubaneswar
Bombay Puri
Pune Behrampur
Mahabaleshwar Warangal Bay of Bengal
Arabian Hyderabad
Belgaum Vijayawada
Sea Panaji Gadag
Jog Falls
Mangalore Bangalore
Mysore Madras Andaman
Calicut Pondicherry Sea
Coimbatore
Ernakulam Madurai
& Cochin Rameswaram
Trivandrum
Kanyakumari SRI
LANKA

Indian Ocean

0   200   400   600   800   1000 km

0   200   400   600 miles

© The Guidebook Company Ltd

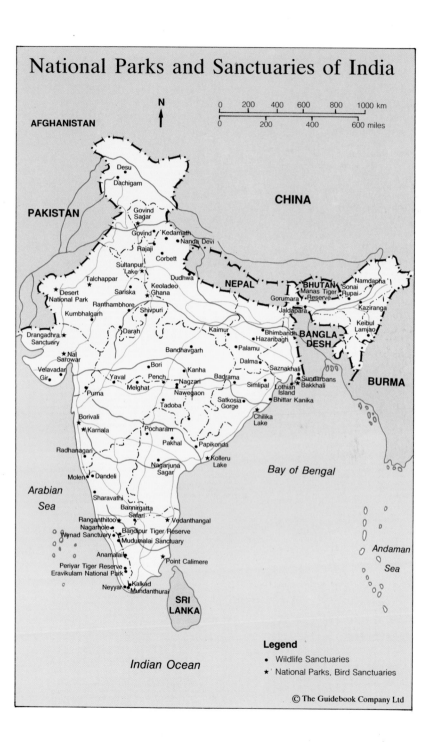

National Parks and Sanctuaries of India

N

| 0 | 200 | 400 | 600 | 800 | 1000 km |

| 0 | 200 | 400 | 600 miles |

AFGHANISTAN

CHINA

PAKISTAN

Desu

Dachigam

Govind Sagar

Govind • Kedarnath

Rajaji • Nanda Devi

Corbett

Sultanpur Lake ★ Dudhwa

Talchappar Sariska Keoladeo Ghana

★ Desert National Park Ranthambhore Shivpuri

Kumbhalgarh

Drangadhra Sanctuary Darah Kaimur

★ Nal Sarowar Bandhavgarh

Velavadar Bori Palamu

Gir Yaval Kanha Dalma

Purna Melghat Pench Nagzari Badrama

Nawegaon Simlipal

Tadoba Satkosia Gorge

Borivali Pocharam Chilika Lake

★ Karnala

Radhanagari Pakhal Papikonda

Dandeli Nagarjuna Sagar ★ Kolleru Lake

Molen •

Sharavathi

Bannirgatta Safari

Ranganthitoo ★ Vedanthangal

Nagarhole Bandipur Tiger Reserve

Wynad Sanctuary Mudumalai Sanctuary

Anamalai

Periyar Tiger Reserve ★ Point Calimere

Eravikulam National Park

Kalkad

Neyyar Mundanthurai

NEPAL

BHUTAN Namdapha

Manas Tiger Reserve Sonai

Gorumara Rupai

Jaldapara Kaziranga

Bhimbandh Keibul

Hazaribagh Lamjao

Saznakhali

Lothian Sundarbans

Island Bakkhali

Bhittar Kanika

BANGLA DESH

BURMA

Bay of Bengal

Arabian Sea

SRI LANKA

Andaman Sea

Indian Ocean

Legend
- Wildlife Sanctuaries
★ National Parks, Bird Sanctuaries

© The Guidebook Company Ltd

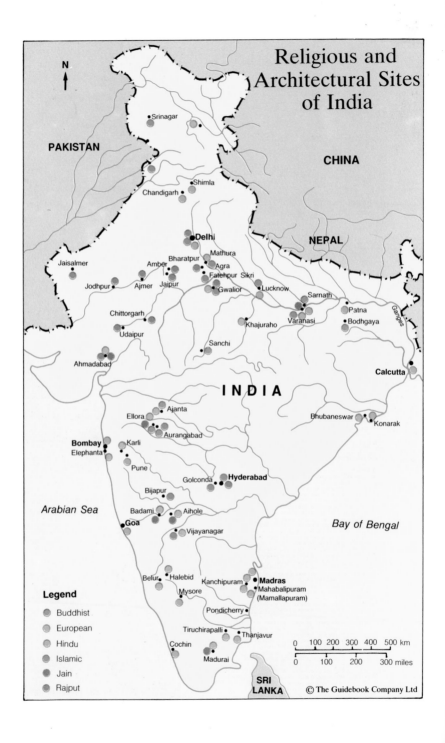

Religious and Architectural Sites of India

N

PAKISTAN

CHINA

NEPAL

INDIA

Arabian Sea

Bay of Bengal

SRI
LANKA

Ganges

• Srinagar
• Shimla
Chandigarh•
• Delhi
• Mathura
Bharatpur• •Agra
Amber• •Fatehpur Sikri
Jaisalmer• Jaipur• •Gwalior •Lucknow
Jodhpur• •Ajmer •Sarnath
•Patna
Chittorgarh• •Khajuraho •Bodhgaya
Udaipur• •Varanasi
•Sanchi
Ahmadabad• •Calcutta

Ellora• •Ajanta
•Aurangabad •Bhubaneswar •Konarak
Bombay• •Karli
Elephanta• •Pune
•Golconda •Hyderabad
Bijapur•
Badami• •Aihole
Goa• •Vijayanagar
Belur• •Halebid
•Kanchipuram •Madras
Mysore• Mahabalipuram
(Mamallapuram)
•Pondicherry
Tiruchirapalli• •Thanjavur
Cochin• •Madurai

Legend

- ● Buddhist
- ● European
- ● Hindu
- ● Islamic
- ● Jain
- ● Rajput

0 100 200 300 400 500 km
0   100   200   300 miles

© The Guidebook Company Ltd

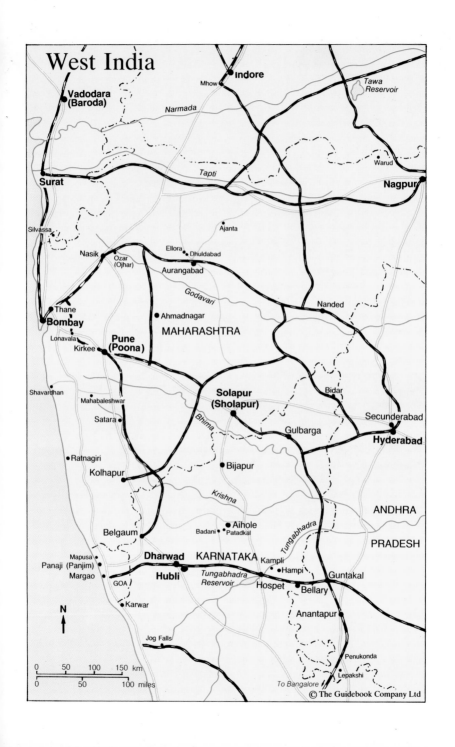

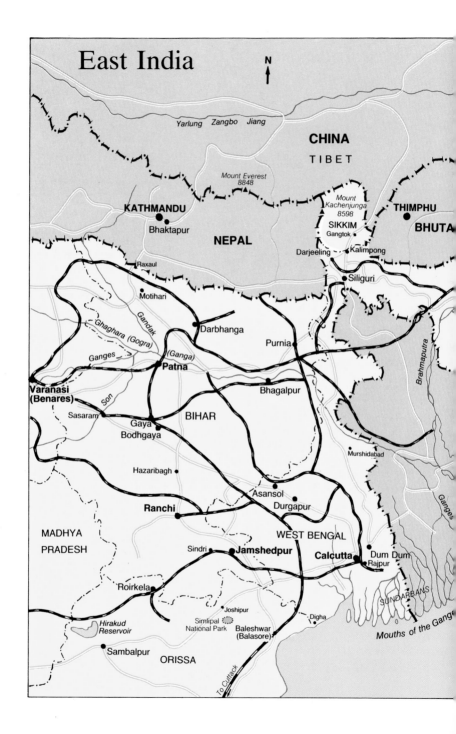

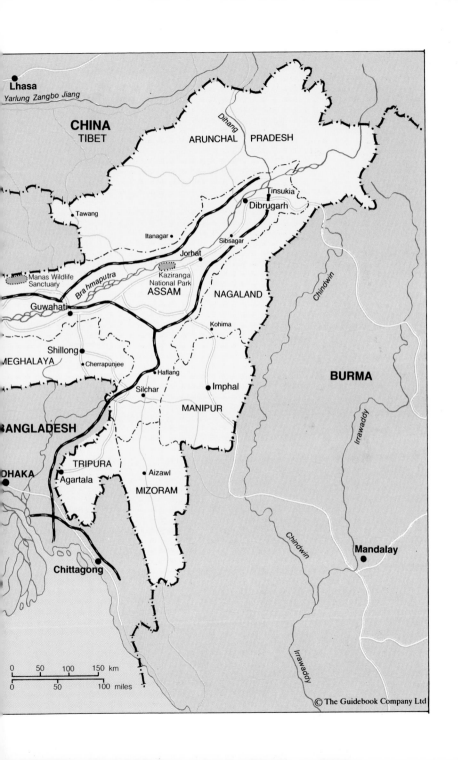

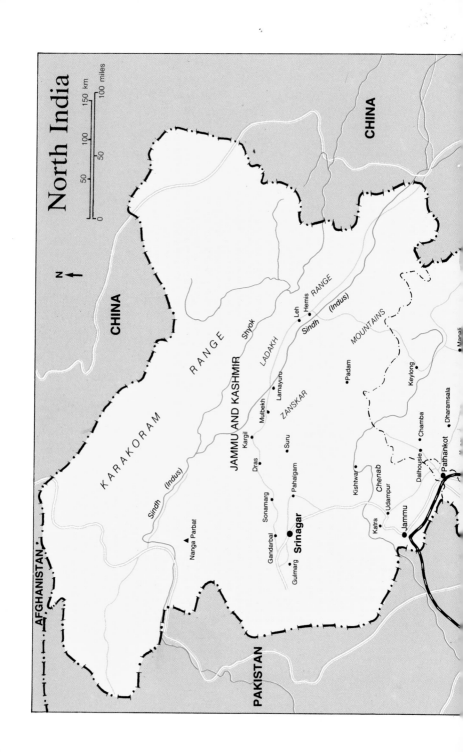

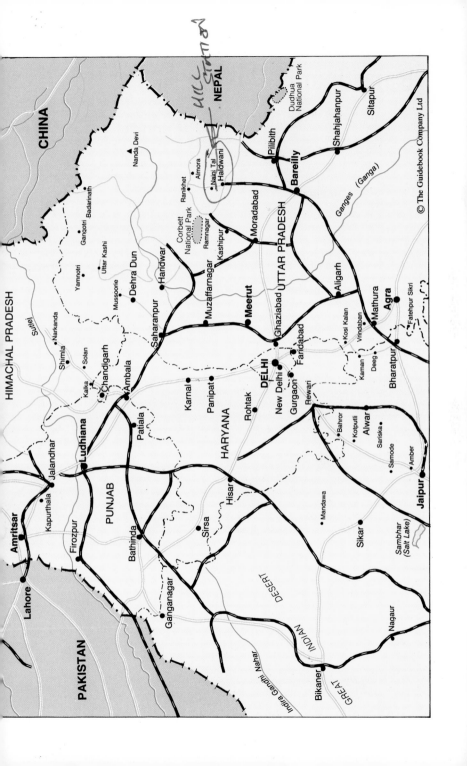

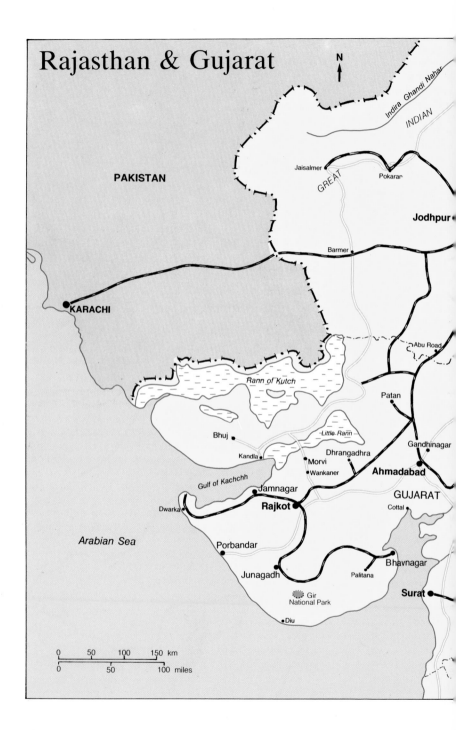

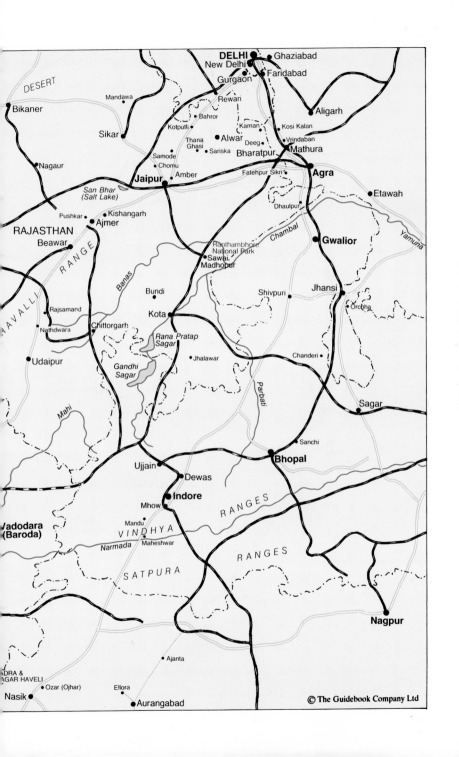

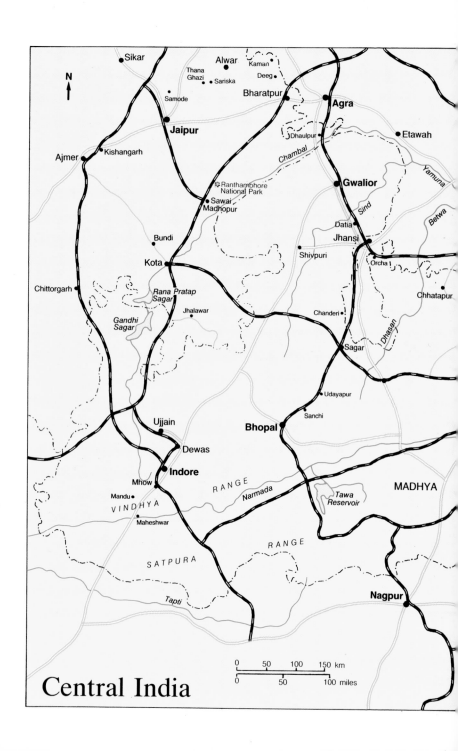

Central India

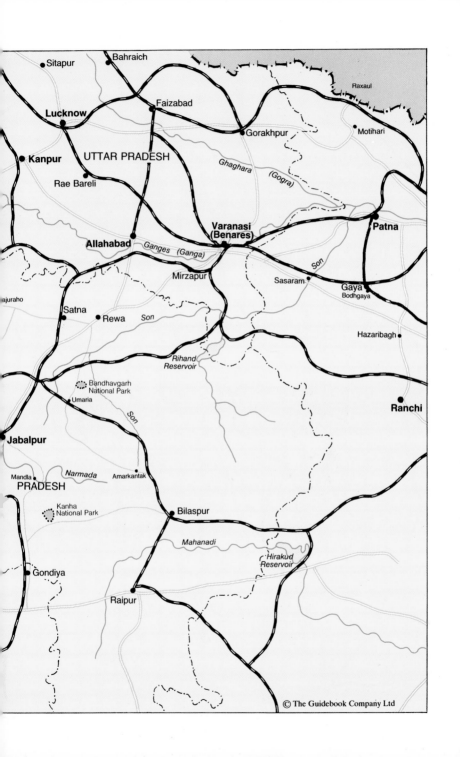

Sitapur
Bahraich
Raxaul

Lucknow
Faizabad
Gorakhpur
Motihari

Kanpur
UTTAR PRADESH

Rae Bareli
Ghaghara
(Gogra)

Patna

Varanasi
(Benares)
Allahabad
Ganges (Ganga)
Son

Mirzapur
Sasaram
Gaya
Bodhgaya

ajuraho
Satna
Rewa
Son

Hazaribagh

Rihand
Reservoir

Bandhavgarh
National Park

Umaria
Son

Ranchi

Jabalpur

Mandla
Narmada
Amarkantak
PRADESH

Kanha
National Park
Bilaspur

Mahanadi

Hirakud
Reservoir

Gondiya

Raipur

© The Guidebook Company Ltd

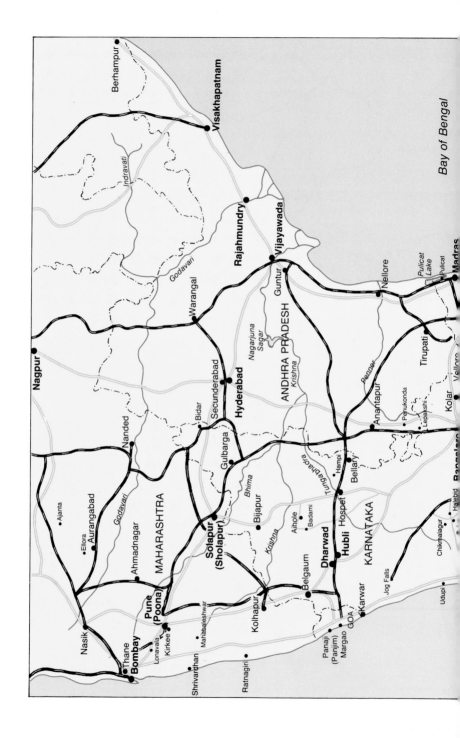

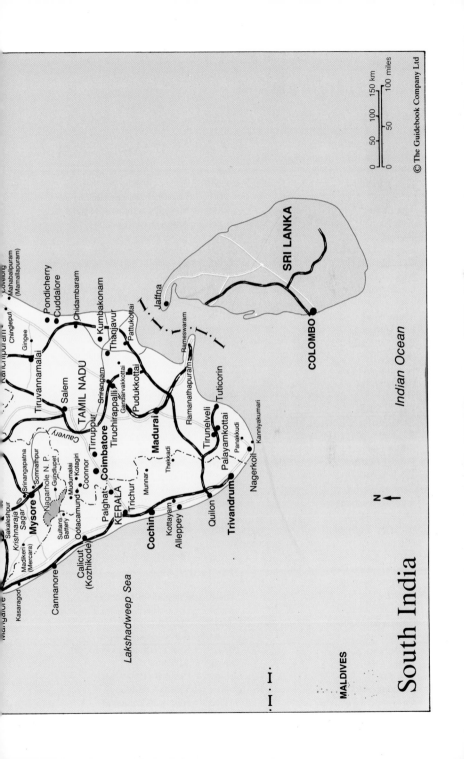

South India

MALDIVES

Indian Ocean

Lakshadweep Sea

SRI LANKA

COLOMBO

Jaffna

TAMIL NADU

KERALA

Mysore

Cochin

Madurai

Coimbatore

Trivandrum

Bangalore

Kasaragod

Madikeri (Mercara)

Cannanore

Calicut (Kozhikode)

Trichur

Palghat

Kottayam

Alleppey

Quilon

Nagerkoil

Panakkudi

Kanniyakumari

Tuticorin

Palayamkottai

Tirunelveli

Ramanathapuram

Rameswaram

Pattukkottai

Thanjavur

Kumbakonam

Chidambaram

Cuddalore

Pondicherry

Loveling

Mahabalipuram (Mamallapuram)

Kanchipuram

Chingleput

Gingee

Tiruvannamalai

Salem

Srirangam

Pudukkottai

Gandarvakkottai

Truchirappalli

Tiruppur

Munnar

Thekkadi

Sakaleshpur

Sagar

Srirangapatna

Somnathpur

Nagarhole N. P.

Gundlupet

Mudumalai

Kotagiri

Coonnor

Ootacamund

Sultans Battery

Krishnaraja Sagar

Cauvery

N

© The Guidebook Company Ltd

| 0 | 50 | 100 | 150 km |

| 0 | 50 | 100 miles |

Practical Information

Festivals

The Indian year is punctuated with a seemingly endless number of fairs and festivals. Many are religious in origin, some are secular, while others are recent institutions. The following is a list of festivals in 1991:

Desert Festival	28 Dec 1990 - Jan 1991	Jaisalmer (Rajasthan)
Magi Fair	13 - 14 Jan	Muksar Ludhiana (Punjab)
Kite Festival	13 - 15 Jan	Ahmadabad (Gujarat)
Pongal	13 - 17 Jan	Tamil Nadu
Elephant Marathon	16 - 20 Jan	Trivandrum (Kerala)
Republic Day	26 Jan	New Delhi and all state capitals
Nagaur Cattle Fair	2 - 5 Feb	Nagaur (Rajasthan)
Crafts Mela	1 -15 Feb	Suraj Kund (Haryana, 20 km from Delhi)
Yoga Week	2 - 7 Feb	Rishikesh (Uttar Pradesh)
Goa Carnival	9 - 12 Feb	Goa
Elephanta Music Festival	16 - 18 Feb	Elephanta (Bombay)
Heli-Skiing	7 - 21 Feb	Manali (Himachal Pradesh)
Konarak Festival	24 - 26 Feb	Konarak (Orissa)
Chapcharkut	26 Feb	Mizoram (NEF)
Holi	1 March	All India
Basant Utsav	March	Shantiniketan (West Bengal)
Bohag Bihu & Rangoli Bihu	14 - 15 March	Assam (NEF)
Khajuraho Dance Festival	12 - 18 March	Khajuraho (Madhya Pradesh)
Ellora Festival	23 - 25 March	Ellora (near Aurangabad)
Flower Festival	April	Gangtok (Sikkim)
Trichur Puram	April	Trichur (Kerala)
Hemis Festival	June	Hemis (Jammu and Kashmir)
Summer Festival	June	Mt Abu (Rajasthan)
Mango Festival	July	Saharanpur (Uttar Pradesh)
'Chariot' Festival	3 July	Puri (Orissa)
Alleppey	August (2nd week)	Alleppey (Kerala)
Ganesh Chaturhi	11 - 12 Aug	Bombay and Pune
Independence Day	15 August	All India
Tarnetar Festival	12 - 14 Sept	Surendra Nagar (Gujarat)
Onam	Sept	Trivandrum (Kerala)
Golconda Festival	Sept	Hyderabad (Andhra Pradesh)
Heikru Hitongba	Sept	Manipur
Navratri	8 Oct	Baroda (Gujarat)
Dussehra	17 - 18 Oct	Kullu (Himachal Pradesh)
Durga Puja	5 Nov	All India
Pushkar	18 - 21 Nov	Pushkar (Rajasthan)
Sonepur Mela	18 - 21 Nov	Vaishali (Bihar)
Vijayanagar Festival	Dec	Hampi (Karnataka)

Useful Addresses

Foreigners' Regional Registration Offices:

Annexe 2, Office of the Commissioner of Police, Dadabhoy Naroji Road, **Bombay**; tel: 268111

237 Acharya Jagdish Bose Road, **Calcutta**; tel: 443301

13 Victoria Crescent Road, Egmore, **Madras**; tel: 272790

or 9 Village Road, **Nugomb-akkam**; tel: 88210

Hans Bhawan, Tilak Bridge, Indraprastha, **New Delhi**; tel: 272790

For certification of antiques for export: Director, Antiquities, Archaeological Survey of India, Janpath, **New Delhi**

Superintending Archaeologist, Eastern Circle, Archaeological Survey of India, Narayani Building, Brabourne Road, **Calcutta**

Superintending Archaeologist, Southern Circle, Archaeological Survey of India, Fort St George, **Madras**

Superintending Archaeologist, Frontier Circle, Archaeological Survey of India, Minto Bridge, **Srinagar**

Airlines (apt = airport telephone)

Aeroflot (SU)

241–242 Nirmal Building, Nariman Point, **Bombay**; tel: 221682, 221743

58 Jawaharlal Nehru Road, **Calcutta**; tel: 443765, 447831, apt 572611

BMC House, N-1 Connaught Place, Middle Circle, **New Delhi**; tel: 3312843, 3310426, apt 5482331

19 Marshalls Road, Egmore, **Madras**; tel: 847799, 848899, apt 431656

Air Canada (AC)

Hotel Oberoi Towers, Nariman Point, **Bombay**; tel: 2027632/512

35-A Chowringhee Road, **Calcutta**; tel: 248371/4

341-D, Ashoka Hotel, Chanakyapuri, **New Delhi**; tel : 604755, 600121

733 Mount Road, **New Delhi**; tel: 867957

Air France (AF)

Maker Chamber VI, 220 Nariman Point, **Bombay**; tel: 2024818, 2025021, apt 6328070, 6323072

41 Chowringhee Road, **Calcutta**; tel: 296161/2

6 Scindia House, Connaught Circus, **New Delhi**; tel: 3310407, 3310424, apt 5452294, 5452099

Spencer's Building, 769 Anna Salai, **Madras**; tel: 868337, 862569

Air India (AI)

Air India Building, Nariman Point, **Bombay**; tel: 2024142, 2023747, apt 6329666, 6366767

50 Chowringhee Road, **Calcutta**; tel: 442356, apt 572031

Jeevan Bharti LIC Building, Connaught Circus, **New Delhi**; tel: 3311225, apt 5452050

19 Marshalls Road, Egmore, **Madras**; tel: 847799, 848899, apt 431656

Air Lanka (UL)

Mittal Towers, Nariman Point, **Bombay**; tel: 223299, 223599, apt 6322829

Hotel Imperial, Janpath, **New Delhi**; tel: 3324789

142 Nugambakkam High Road, **Madras**; tel: 471195, 475332, apt 433131

Geetabali Building, Ganpatti, **Trivandrum**; tel: 63261

Air Mauritius (MK)
Air India Building (ground floor),
Nariman Point, **Bombay** ; tel: 2028474,
2026430, apt 6329666

Air Tanzania (TC)
c/o Ethiopian Airlines, Taj Mahal Hotel,
Bombay; tel: 2024525

Alitalia (AZ)
Vir Nariman Road, Churchgate, **Bombay;**
tel: 222144, 222177, apt 6329082,
6328083, 2/3 Chitrakoot, 230A
Bose Rd, **Calcutta**; tel: 447394
Surya Kiran, 19 KG Marg, **New Delhi**;
tel: 3311019/20, apt 393140, 5483174
738 Anna Salai Road, **Madras**;
tel: 860836, 861406

Alyemda (DY)
Oberoi Towers, Nariman Point, **Bombay**;
tel: 2024229

Ariana Afghan Airlines (FG)
Surya Kiran, 19 K G Marg, **New Delhi**;
tel: 3311834, 3311432, apt 542173

Bangladesh Biman (BG)
199 J Tata Road, Churchgate, **Bombay**;
tel: 223342, 224580, apt 6320700
30/C Jawaharlal Nehru Road, **Calcutta**;
tel: 292832, 292843
c/o Jet Air, **New Delhi**; tel: 3312119,
3313221
Hardevi Chambers, 68 Pantheon Road,
Egmore, **Madras**; tel: 812775

British Airways (BA)
202 Vir Nariman Road, **Bombay**;
tel: 220888, apt 6329061
41 Chowringhee Road, **Calcutta**;
tel: 293430
1A Connaught Circus, **New Delhi**;
tel: 3327428 apt 5452077/8

Fagun Mansions, 26 C-in-C Road,
Madras; tel: 474272, 477388, apt 434921

Burma Airways (UB)
46C Chowringhee Road, **Calcutta**;
tel 231624, apt 572611 ext. 397

Cathay Pacific (CX)
Taj Mahal Hotel, **Bombay**; tel: 2029112/3,
2029561, apt 6321580, 6321965
Jeevan Deep, 1 Middleton Street,
Calcutta; tel: 293211
123 Tolstoy House, Tolstoy Marg, **New
Delhi**; tel 3323332, 3323919
Spencer Building, 769 Mount Road,
Madras; tel 869372, 867694

Czechoslovak Airlines (Ceskoslovenske Aeroline)
308 Raheja Chambers, 213 Nariman Point,
Bombay; tel: 220736, 220765
apt 6366767
104 Ansal Bhawan, K G Marg,
New Delhi; tel: 3311833

Druk Air (KB)
51 Tivoli Court, 1A Balygunge Circular
Road, **Calcutta**; tel: 434413, 444907,
apt 572611
Malbros Travels, 403 Nirmal Tower, 26
Barakhamba Road, **New Delhi**;
tel: 3322859, 3712031, apt 5452173

Egypt Air (MS)
7 J Tata Road, Churchgate, **Bombay**;
tel : 221415, 221562, apt 6326089
Hotel Ambassador, Sujan Singh Park,
New Delhi; tel: 697232

Emirates (EK)
Mittal Chambers, 228 Nariman Point,
Bombay; tel: 2871645/50, 2024142
Kunchenjunga, 18 Barakhamba Road,
New Delhi; tel: 3324665, 3324824,
apt 5482861, 5482851

Ethiopian Airlines (ET)
Taj Mahal Hotel, Apollo Bunder,
Bombay; tel: 2024525, apt 6328068
Hotel Janpath, **New Delhi**; tel: 3329235

Garuda Indonesian (GA)
Raheja Centre, Nariman Point, **Bombay**;
tel: 243075, 243725
703 Mount Road, **Madras**; tel: 867957,
869832

Gulf Air (GF)
Maker Chamber V, Nariman Point,
Bombay; tel: 2021626, 2024065,
apt 6327588, 6320925
5 Chitrakoot Building, 230A AJC Bose
Road, **Calcutta**; tel: 447783
G-12 Connaught Circus, **New Delhi**;
tel : 3327814, 3324293, apt 5452065
Haridevi Chambers, 68 Pantheon Road,
Egmore, **Madras**; tel: 867650, 867872

Indian Airlines (IC)
Air India Building, Nariman Point,
Bombay; tel: 2023031, 2023131
29 Chittranjan Avenue, **Calcutta**;
tel: 263390, 260731, apt 572567
Kanchenjunga, 18 Barakhamba Road,
New Delhi; tel: 3310071, 3310052
PTI Building, Parliament Street, **New
Delhi**; tel: 3719168, 3710369
Safdarjung Airport (open 24 hours), **New
Delhi**; tel: 615985, 3295433
19 Marshalls Road, Egmore, **Madras**;
tel: 478333, 477098, apt 433131
Indian Airlines Flight information:
Bangalore: 564433, **Calcutta**: 574433,
Hyderabad: 844433, **Madras**: 434433,
New Delhi: 3014433, 699555,
Bombay: 6144433

Iran Air (IR)
Sundar Mahal, Marine Drive, **Bombay**;
tel: 2047070, 2043524, apt 6329977
Ashok Hotel, Chanakyapuri, **New Delhi**;
tel: 606471

Iraqi Airways (IA)
Mayfair Building, 79 Vir Nariman Road,
Churchgate, **Bombay**; tel: 221217,
apt 6327530
Ansal Bhawan, K.G. Marg, **New Delhi**;
tel: 3318742, 3318632, apt 391429

Japan Airlines (JL)
Raheja Centre, Nariman Point, **Bombay**
tel: 2874941, 2333136
35A Chowringhee Road, **Calcutta**;
tel: 298370
Chandralok Building, 36 Janpath, **New
Delhi**; tel: 3327104, 3324922, apt 5452082
733 Mount Road, **Madras**; tel: 867957

Kenya Airways (KQ)
199 J Tata Road, Churchgate, **Bombay**;
tel: 220064, apt 6322577
10-B Scindia House, Connaught Place,
New Delhi; tel: 3318502, 3314796

KLM (KL)
198 J Tata Road, Churchgate, **Bombay;** tel
221013, 221185
1 Middleton Street, **Calcutta;**
tel: 292451, 297466
Prakash Deep, 7 Tolstoy Marg, **New
Delhi**; tel: 3315841, 3311747,
apt 5452874, 5482852
Connemara Hotel, Binny Road, **Madras**;
tel: 869752

Korean Air (KE)
40/2 Pearelal Building, Janpath,
New Delhi; tel: 3324042, 3329561

Kuwait Airways (KU)
Chateau Windsor, 86 Vir Nariman Road,
Bombay; tel: 2041612, 2045351,
apt 6327269
Hansalaya, Barakhamba Road,
New Delhi; tel: 3314221/3, apt 5452295
Embassy Towers, 55 Montieth Road,
Egmore, **Madras**; tel: 811810

LOT (LO)

6 Maker Arcade, Cuffe Parade, **Bombay**;
tel: 221431, 211440
G-55 Connaught Circus, **New Delhi**;
tel: 3324482, 3326958, 3326523

Lufthansa (LH)

Express Tower, Nariman Point, **Bombay**;
tel 2023430, 2020887, apt 6321485
44/2 Dickenson Road, **Bangalore**;
tel: 570740, 564791
30 A/B Jawaharlal Nehru Road, **Calcutta**;
tel: 299365

56 Janpath, **New Delhi**; tel: 3327609,
3327268, apt 5452063/4
167, Mount Road, **Madras**; tel: 869197,
869095

Maldives Airways

7 Brabourne Stadium, Churchgate,
Bombay; tel: 2029020

Malaysian Airlines (MH)

6 Maker Arcade, Cuffe Parade, **Bombay**;
tel: 211431, 211440

Hotel Imperial, Janpath, **New Delhi**;
tel: 3324787/9, 3324308, apt 5452011
189 Mount Road, **Madras**; tel: 868985,
868970, apt 431656

PIA (PK)
Hotel Oberoi Towers, Nariman Point,
Bombay; tel: 2021455, 2021373,
apt 6320700
26 Kasturba Gandhi Marg, **New Delhi**;
tel : 3313161/2, apt 5484246

Pan Am (PA)
Taj Mahal Hotel, **Bombay;** tel: 2029221,
2029048 apt 6323660
42 Chowringhee Road, **Calcutta**;
tel: 295001
Chandralok Building, 36 Janpath, **New
Delhi;** tel: 3325222 apt 5452093/4
Wellington Estate, C-in-C Road, **Madras**;
tel: 422611, 869985

Qantas (QF)
Hotel Oberoi Towers, Nariman Point,
Bombay; tel: 2026373, 2020410,
apt 6327864, 6329865
Mohan Dev, Tolstoy Marg,
New Delhi; tel: 3321424

Royal Jordanian (RJ)
Chitrakoot Building, 230A A J C Bose
Road, **Calcutta**; tel: 447783,
G-56 Connaught Circus, **New Delhi**;
tel: 3323710, 3327667, apt 5452011

Royal Nepal Airlines (RA)
41 Chowringhee, **Calcutta**; tel 298534 apt
572611
44 Janpath, **New Delhi**; tel: 3321572,
3320817 apt 5453876

Sabena (SN)
Nirmal Building, Nariman Point, **Bombay**;
tel: 2023817, apt 6329922

Himalaya House, KG Marg, **New Delhi**;
tel: 3312701, 3312928
Regency House, 250 Mount Road,
Madras; tel: 451786

Saudia (SV)
Express Towers, Nariman Point, **Bombay**;
tel: 2020049, apt 6329991
Hansalaya, 15 Barakhamba Rd,
New Delhi; tel: 3310466, apt 5481279

Singapore Airlines (SQ)
Air India Building, Nariman Point,
Bombay; tel: 2023365, 2023316,
apt 6327024, 6327861
18-D Park Street, **Calcutta**; tel: 291525,
290740, apt 569611 ext 318
G-11 Connaught Circus, **New Delhi;**
tel: 3326373, apt 5452011 ext 2398/9
167 Anna Salai, **Madras**; tel: 862871,
861872, apt 433860

Swiss Air (SR)
Maker Chamber VI, 220 Nariman Point,
Bombay; tel: 2870121, 2872210,
apt 6326082
Everest, 46-C, Chowringhee Road,
Calcutta; tel: 444643
56 Janpath, **New Delhi**; tel: 3325511,
3327892
40 Mount Road, **Madras;** tel: 861583,
862692

Syrian Arab Airlines (RB)
7 Brabourne Stadium, Churchgate,
Bombay; tel: 226143, 232996, apt
6322028
13/90 Connaught Place, **New Delhi;**
tel : 344977, 343218

Thai (TG)
15 World Trade Centre, Cuffe Parade,
Colaba, **Bombay**; tel: 214180, 215207
18G Park Street, **Calcutta**; tel: 249696,
apt 573937

12A Connaught Place, **New Delhi**;
tel: 3323608, 3323638, apt 5482526

Turkish Airlines (TK)

Maker Chambers V, Nariman Point,
Bombay; tel: 2046491, 2043605,
apt 6322220
56 Janpath, **New Delhi**; tel: 3326661,
3326613, apt 5452021

Vayudoot (PF)

Air India Building, Nariman Point,
Bombay; tel: 2048585, apt 6121397
28B Shakespeare Sarani, **Calcutta**;
tel : 447062, apt 576582
Samrat Complex, Saifabad, **Hyderabad**;
tel: 234717, apt 823200
Malhotra Build, Connaught Place, **New
Delhi**; tel: 3312587 apt 3295313

Safdarjung Airport, **New Delhi**; tel 693851
24 Wellington Estate, C-in-C Road,
Madras; tel: 4342783

Yemen Airways (IY)

7 Brabourne Stadium, Churchgate,
Bombay; tel: 226043, 226143 ,
apt 6320700 ext 584

Yugoslav Airlines

Grosvenor House, 21 Cama Street,
Calcutta; tel :292323

Zambia Airways

2/207 Maker Chambers V, Nariman Point,
Bombay; tel: 241251, 222944,
apt 6366700
Mohan Dev, Tolstoy Marg, **New Delhi**;
tel: 3328129, 3325521

Car Hire

Most hotels and travel agencies will arrange car hire. For reasons of language, safety and
insurance most car hire includes a driver. However, in 1990 drive-it-yourself hire
operations began. There are some international franchises.

Budget Rent-a-car, G-3 Arunachal,
Barakhamba Road, New Delhi 110001
tel: 3715657/8, 3318600
Agra tel: 64771/2;

Hertz—Wheels Rent-a-car, Nirmal, 16th
floor, Nariman Point, Bombay 400021;
tel: 2023734, 2023764, 4948168, 4948157;
tlx: 011-5092 KITL IN and 011-71091
ABCP IN
Bangalore tel: 215874, 211102;
tlx: 0845-2336 TCI IN
Hyderabad tel: 242457, 241697;
tlx: 0425-6251 TCI IN
Madras tel : 865491, 860626;
tlx: 041-7059 TCI IN
New Delhi tel: 3318695, 3310190;
tlx 031-61153 TCI IN
Pune tel: 56033, 54291;
tlx: 0145-208 TCI IN

A Reluctant Bride

*J*ayanthi Mandel, only sister of the three Mandel brothers, came home from her art college on the day the family was to meet and decide whom she was to marry, and found two pairs of slippers left, as was the courteous custom, on the floor outside her sister-in-law's grand drawing-room. At first Jayanthi thought the slippers must belong to friends of her sister-in-law, though she had never seen these two pairs before. But when she opened the door and saw, sitting on the sofa, the wife of Superintendent Babu and another lady, she felt astonished, feeling sure these two were not friends of Lala.

"You know Mrs Babu, Jayanthi, and this lady is the wife of the Calcutta police chief," said Lala, smiling.

The two visiting ladies turned a gaze upon Jayanthi that was both appraising and critical and Jayanthi suddenly understood that they were considering her as a wife for the police chief's son. Jayanthi stood poised in the doorway, her hand still grasping the knob, and became filled with an intense desire to shout 'No!' However she said nothing and neither did the ladies. They continued to stare at her, looking her up and down as though she was a piece of merchandise they were considering buying.

Lala said, "Come in, Jayanthi, and let these ladies have a good look at you!"

Jayanthi entered the room, and swivelled slowly round in front of her scrutinisers, filled with a savage delight that, instead of wearing a sari as her sister had instructed her in the morning, she had on a pair of paint-dabbed jeans, and a T-shirt upon which was printed the name of Kapoor, her favourite film star. She thrust out her bosom until the a and the o were higher than the other letters, and said, "I don't think I will do for your son. I'm sure you will agree!"

The wife of the police chief shuddered, and said to Lala, "Please ask her to put on a sari. I would like to see her properly dressed."

"She is a pretty girl," Mrs Babu said faintly. "I have known her since she was a baby. She was a pretty baby too."

The wife of the police chief turned upon Mrs Babu fiercely.

"We have not come here to find prettiness!" she announced sternly. Mrs Babu let out a moan, and sank back into her chair.

Sara Banerji, The Wedding of Jayanthi Mandel

Accommodation

All hotels are listed alphabetically by town.

Agra, Uttar Pradesh

Deluxe and 5 star
Welcomgroup Mughal Sheraton, Taj Ganj, Fatehabad Road, Agra 282001
tel: 64701 tlx: 0565-210 ITCO IN
Taj View (Taj), Taj Ganj, Fatehabad Road, Agra 282001
tel: 64171, 74071; tlx: 0565-202, 348 TAJV IN

4 star
Agra Ashok (ITDC), 6-B The Mall, Agra 282001
tel: 76223, 73271; tlx: 0565-313
Clarks Shiraz, 54 Taj Road, Agra 282001
tel: 72421, 68654 tlx: 0565-211 SHRZ IN
Mumtaz, Fatehabad Road, Agra 282001
tel: 64771 tlx: 0565-222 MMTZ IN

Others
Amar, Fatehabad Road, Agra 282001
tel: 65696-8 tlx: 0656-341 AMAR IN
Grand Hotel *(2 star)*, 137 Station Road, Agra Cant, Agra; tel. 74014
Lauries Hotel, M G Road, Agra 282001
tel.: 72536

Ahmadabad, Gujarat

Cama Hotel *(4 star)*, Khanpur, Ahmadabad 380001
tel: 25281; tlx: 0121-6377 CAMA IN
Hotel Karnavati, Cinema Premises, Ashram Road, Ahmadabad 380019
tel: 402161, 402170; tlx: 0121-6519 CSCO IN
Hotel Natraj *(4 star)*, Near ITO, Ashram Road, Ahmadabad 380009 tel: 448747; tlx: 0121-6685 SHIV IN

Ajmer, Rajasthan

Hotel Mansingh Palace, Vaishali Nagar, Ajmer 305001
tel: 30855, 30856

Allahabad, Uttar Pradesh

Presidency Hotel *(2 star)*, 19-D Sarojini Naidu Marg, Allahabad 211001
tel: 4460, 4097

Alleppey, Kerala

Alleppey Prince Hotel *(3 star)*, A S Road, N H 47, Alleppey, 68800
tel: 3752–58; tlx:0883-202 JONS IN

Amritsar, Punjab

Airlines *(3 star)*, Cooper Road, Amritsar
tel: 44545
Amritsar International Hotel *(3 star)*, City Centre, Amritsar 143001
tel: 34146, 52864/5
Mohan International Hotel, Albert Road, Amritsar
tel.:66484/7; tlx.:0384-300 MOHN IN
Ritz Hotel *(3 star)*, 45 The Mall, Amritsar 143001
tel: 66641, 65150; tlx: 0384-242 RITZ IN

Aurangabad, Maharashtra

Ajanta Ambassador *(5 star)*, Chikalthana, Aurangabad 431210
tel: 82211, 82451 tlx: 0745-211 AMBA IN
Ashok Travellers Lodge (ITDC), Ajanta Caves, Dist. Aurangabad 431117
tel: 26 (situated at Ajanta, 106 kilometres from Aurangabad airport)
Welcomgroup Rama International, R-3 Chikalthana, Aurangabad 431210
tel: 82455/7, 82241; tlx: 0745-212 RAMA

Bangalore, Karnataka *(5 star)*

Ashok (IDTC), Kumara Krupa, High
Grounds, Bangalore 560001
tel: 79411; tlx: 0845-2433
Holiday Inn-Bangalore, 28 Sankey Road,
Bangalore 560052
tel: 79451, 77931; tlx: 0845-2354
Taj Residency (Taj), 14 Mahatma Gandhi
Road, Bangalore 560001
tel: 568888; tlx: 0845-8367 TBLR IN;
fax: 0812-563548, 575009
**Welcomgroup Windsor Manor Shera-
ton**, 25 Sankey Road, Bangalore 860052,
tel.: 79431/28031 tlx: 0845-8209 WIND
IN; fax: 0812-74941
West End Hotel (Taj), Race Cource Road,
Bangalore 560001
tel: 292281, 74191; tlx: 0845-2337
WEND IN fax: 0812-27610

Others
Aurangabad Ashok(ITDC *2 star*),Dr.
Rajendra Prasad Marg, Aurangabad
431001, tel: 24520-29 tlx: 0745-229
Hotel Bangalore International *(3 star)*,
2A/B Crescent Road, High Grounds,
Bangalore 560001
tel: 258011-7; tlx: 0845-2340 HOBI IN
Gateway Hotel (Taj), 66 Residency Road,
Bangalore 560025
tel: 573265-9 tlx: 0845-2567
fax: 0812-573382
Nilgiris Nest *(2 star)*, 171 Brigade Road,
Bangalore 560001, tel 577501

Baroda (Vadodara), Gujarat

Express Hotel *(4 star)*, R.C. Dutt Road,
Vadodara 390005
tel: 323131, 321960 tlx: 0175-311;
fax: 0265-325980
Hotel Utsav *(2 star)*, Navrang Cinema
Compound, Prof Manekrao Road,
Vadodara 390001
tel: 551415; tlx: 0175-274 UTSA IN
Welcomgroup Vadodara *(4 star)*, R.C.
Dutta Road, Baroda 390005
tel: 323232; tlx:0175-525 GHL IN

Bharatpur, Rajasthan

Bharatpur Forest Lodge (ITDC),
Koladeo National Park, Bharatpur 321001
tel: :2322, 2864, 2260
Golbagh Palace Hotel, Agra Road,
Bharatpur 321001; tel: 3349
Saras Tourist Bungalow, Fatehpur Sikri
Road, Bharatpur 321001, tel:.2169

Bhavnagar, Gujarat

Welcomgroup Nilambag Palace,
Bhavnagar, 364002, tel: 24340, 24422;
tlx: 0162-253 WGNP IN

Bhopal, Madhya Pradesh

Hotel Ramsons International *(2 star)*,
Hamidia Road, Bhopal 462001
tel: 72298, 72299, 73331; tlx: 0705-354
Hotel Lake View Ashok (ITDC), Shamla
Hills, Bhopal 462002
tel: 540452, 541075; tlx: 0705-303
Jehan Numa Palace Hotel *(3 star)*,
Shamla Hill, Bhopal 452013
tel: 540100 ; tlx: 0705-343 JNPH IN

Bhubaneswar, Orissa

Kalinga Ashok (ITDC) *(2 star)*, Gautam
Nagar, Bhubaneswar 751014
tel: 53318; tlx: 0675-282
Oberoi Bhubaneswar *(5 star)*, Nagapalli,
Bhubaneswar 751013
tel: 56116; tlx: 0675-348 HOB IN
The Kenilworth *(5 Star)*, 86/A-1 Gautam
Nagar, Bhubaneswar 751014
tel: 54330/1, 56543; tlx: 0675-343

Bijapur, Karnataka

Ashok Travellers Lodge (ITDC), Station
Road, Bijapur 586101
Hotel Mayura Adil Shahi, Anand Mahal
Road, Bijapur 556101, tel: 634 401

Bikaner, Rajasthan

Hotel Lallgarh Palace, Bikaner, 334001
tel: 3263, 5963

Bodhgaya, Bihar

Ashok Travellers Lodge (ITDC),
Bodhgaya, Dist Gaya 824231
tel: 22708/9; cable: TOURISM

Bombay, Maharastra

Deluxe

Hotel President (Taj), 90 Cuffe Parade,
Colaba, Bombay 400005
tel: 4950808; tlx: 011-4135, 5769, 3124,
PRES IN; fax: 91-22-4951201
The Leela Kempinski, Bombay International Airport, Bombay 400059
tel: 6363636; tlx: 011-79236, 79241
KEMP IN; fax: 91-22-6360606
Oberoi Towers, Nariman Point, Bombay
400021, tel: 2024343; tlx: 022-4153, 4154
OBBY IN fax: 204-3282
The Oberoi, Nariman Point, Bombay
40021 tel: 2025757: tlx: 022-2337, 2335
**The Taj Mahal Hotel & The Taj Mahal
Inter-Continental**, Apollo Bunder,
Bombay 400039 tel: 2023366 tlx: 011-
2442,3837, 6175 TAJB IN; fax: 91-22-
2872711

5 star

Centaur Hotel, Santa Cruz Airport,
Bombay 400099
tel: 6126660; tlx: 011-71171 CHTL IN
Centaur Hotel Juhu Beach, Juhu Tara
Road, Juhu Beach, Bombay 400049
tel: 6143040; tlx: 011-78181
Holiday Inn, Balraj Sahani Marg, Juhu,
Bombay 400049
tel: 6204444 tlx: 011-71266 HINN IN,
011-71432 HOLI IN; fax: 91-22-6204452
Ramada Inn Palm Grove, Juhu Beach,
Juhu, Bombay 400049
tel: 6149361, 6149343; tlx 011-71419
PALM IN: fax:91-22-6142105
Welcomgroup Sea Rock Sheraton,
Land's End, Bandra, Bombay 400050
tel: 6425454; tlx: 011-71230, 71140
ROCK IN; fax: 91-22-6408046

4 star

The Ambassador, Veer Nariman Road,
Churchgate Extn, Bombay 400020
tel: 2041131; tlx: 011-2918 AMBA IN
Fariyas Hotel, 25 Arthur Bundar Road,
Colaba, Bombay 400005
tel: 2042911; tlx: 011-3272 ABAN
Hotel Natraj, 135 Netaji Subhash Road
(Marine Drive), Bombay 400020
tel: 2044164; tlx: 011-2302
Ritz Hotel, 5 Jamshedji Tata Road,
Churchgate, Bombay 400020
tel: 220141, 220116; tlx: 011-2520

Calcutta, West Bengal

Deluxe

Oberoi Grand, 15 Jawaharlal Nehru
Marg, Calcutta 700013
tel: 292323 ; tlx: 021-5919, 5971, OBCL
IN: fax: 91-33-291217
Taj Bengal (Taj), 34 B Belvedor Road,
Alipore, Calcutta 700027
tel: 2883939 ; tlx: 021-4776, 5998 TAJC
IN fax:033-281766, 288805

5 star

Airport Ashok (ITDC), Calcutta Airport,
Calcutta 700052
tel: 569111; tlx: 021-2271
Hindustan International, 235/1A, JC
Bose Road, Calcutta 700020
tel: 442394; tlx: 021-7164, 2321
Park Hotel, 17 Park St. Calcutta 700016
tel: 297941, 297336; tlx: 021-7159, 3177
New Kenilworth Hotel, 1 & 2 Little
Russel Street, Calcutta 700071
tel: 448394; tlx: 021-3395 NKAY IN

Others

Great Eastern Hotel, 1, 2 & 3 Old Court
Home St. Calcutta 700069
tel: 282311, 282331 tlx: 021-7571
Fairlawn Hotel *(2 star)*, 13/4 Sudder St.
Calcutta 700016
tel: 244460, 241835; cable: FAIROTEL

Chandigarh

Hotel Chandigarh Mountview *(2 star)*,
Sector-10, Chandigarh 160010
tel: 21257, 41773, 21738; tlx: 0395-337
Hotel Kapil, SCO 303-304, Sector 35B,
Chandigarh, tel: 33366

Chiplun, Maharastra

Gateway Riverview Lodge (Taj), Village
Dhamandivi, Taluka Khed, Chiplun, Dist
Ratnagiri 415707
tel: 58/7, 67, 69 Chiplun (via Lote)
(six hours drive from Bombay on the Goa
road).
Chingleput, Tamil Nadu (32 kilometres
south of Madras)
Fisherman's Cove *(Taj, 4 star)*, Covelong
Beach, Chingleput Dist, 603112
tel: 04114-6268; tlx: 041-7194 TAJM IN;
fax: c/o 91-44-470070

Chorwad, Gujarat

Palace Beach Resort, Chorwad, 362250
tel: 56/8, (40 kilometres from Keshod
Airport)

Cochin, Kerala

Casino Hotel *(3 star)*, Willingdon Island,
Cochin 682003
tel: 6821; tlx: 0885-6314 SAFE IN
Grand Hotel *(2 star)* MG Road, Ernakulam, Cochin 682001
tel: 33211
Malabar Hotel *(Taj, 5 star)*, Willingdon
Island, Cochin 682009
tel: 6811; tlx: 0885-6661 MLBR IN;
fax: 91-484-69497

Cuttack, Orissa

Hotel Akbari Continental, Dolmundai,
Haripur Road, Cuttack 753001
tel: 25242, 25204, 33243; tlx:0676-272
AKBR IN
Hotel Ashoka, Ice Factory Road, College
Sq. Cuttack 753003
tlx: 25708, 025709 cable: HOTASH

Coonoor, Nilgiris, Tamil Nadu

Hampton Manor, Church Road, Coonoor,
Nilgiris 643101; tel: 244, 961

Darjeeling, West Bengal

Bellevue Hotel *(2 star)*, The Mall,
Darjeeling 734101
tel: 2129, 2221,272
Hotel Sinclairs Darjeeling, 18/1 Gandhi
Road, Darjeeling 734101; tel: 3431/2
Windamere Hotel *(3 star)*, Observatory
Hill, Darjeeling 734101 tel: 2397, 2841;
tlx: 02601-201/2 WNDO IN

Dehra Dun, Uttar Pradesh

Hotel Madhuban *(3 star)*, 97 Rajpur
Road, Dehra Dun, tel: 24094/7
tlx: 0585-268 HMB IN
Hotel Ajanta Continental, Rajpur Road,
Dehra Dun 248001
tel: 29595/8; tlx: 0585-330 AC IN
Hotel Meedo's Grand, 28 Rajpur Road,
Dehra Dun 248001, tel: 27171/2, 26878/9;
tlx: 0585-288 HMG IN

New Delhi/Delhi

Deluxe

Ashok Hotel (ITDC) 50-B Chanakyapuri,
New Delhi 110021; tel: 600121, 600412
tlx: 031-65207, 65647.
Holiday Inn, Barakhamba Avenue,
Connaught Place, New Delhi 110001
tel: 3320101; tlx: 031-61186 HIND IN;
fax: 91-11-3325335
Hyatt Regency, Bhikaji Cama Place, Ring
Road, New Delhi 110066
tel: 609911; tlx: 031-61512 HTY IN;
fax: 91-11-678833
Le Meridien, Windsor Place, Janpath,
New Delhi 110001 tel: 383960, 389379
tlx: 031-63076 HOME IN; fax: 91-11-
384220

The Oberoi Dr Zakir Hussain Marg,
New Delhi 110003, tel: 363030;
tlx: 031-74019, 63222, 63222. OBDL IN;
fax: 91-11-360484
The Taj Mahal Hotel,
1 Mansingh Road, New Delhi 110011
tel: 3016162; tlx 031-66874, 61898 TAJD
IN; fax: 91-11-3017299
The Taj Palace Inter-Continental Hotel,
2 Sadar Patel Marg, New Delhi 110021
tel: 3010404; tlx: 031-61673, 62761 TAJS
IN; fax: 91-11-3011252
Welcomgroup Maurya Sheraton,
Diplomatic Enclave, New Delhi 110021.
tel: 3010101 tlx: 031-61447 WELC IN;
fax: 91-11-3010908

4 and 5 star
Centaur Hotel, Delhi Airport,
New Delhi 110037 tel: 5452223, 5481411;
tlx: 031-62744 CHDA IN
The Connaught Palace, 37 Shaheed
Bhagat Singh Marg, New Delhi 110001
tel: 344225, tlx: 031-61508, 61516 PROM
IN
Claridges Hotel,12 Aurangzeb Road, New
Delhi 110011 tel: 3010211, tlx: 031-65526
CLAR IN; fax: 91-11-3010625
Hans Plaza, 15 Barakhamba Road, New
Delhi 110001 tel: 3316868; tlx: 031-63126
HANS IN
Hotel Imperial, Janpath, New Delhi
110001 tel: 3325332; tlx: 031-62603;
fax: 91-11-3314542
Hotel Kanishka (ITDC), 19 Ashok Road,
New Delhi 110001, tel: 3324422,
tlx: 031-62788, 62736
Hotel Samrat (ITDC), Chanakyapuri, New
Delhi 110021
tel: 603030; tlx: 031-72122, 72126
Janpath Hotel (ITDC), Janpath, New
Delhi 110001, tel 3320070; tlx 031-61546
Qutab Hotel (ITDC), Off Sri Aurobindo
Marg, New Delhi 110016,
tel: 660060; tlx: 031-62537

Hotel Siddharth, 3 Rajindra Place, New
Delhi 110008 tel: 5712501; tlx 031-77125
Hotel Sofitel Turya, Friends Colony,
New Delhi 110065, tel: 6835070;
tlx: 031-66700, 75192 SURA IN
Vasant Continental, Vasant Vihar,
New Delhi 110057, tel: 678800;
tlx: 031-72386; fax: 91-11-678899

Medium and Budget Hotels
Ashok Yashri Niwas (ITDC Budget), 19
Ashok Road, New Delhi 110001
tel: 3324511
Ambassador Hotel, Sujan Singh Park,
New Delhi 110003, tel: 690391;
tlx: 031-3277
Diplomat, 9 Sadar Patel Marg,
New Delhi 110021, tel: 301-1070;
tlx: 031-2532
Jakaso Inn, 50 Sundar Nagar,
New Delhi, tel: 690308
Lodhi Hotel (ITDC), Lala Lajpat Rai
Marg, New Delhi 110003
tel: 362422; tlx: 031-74068
Marina, G-59, Connaught Circus,
New Delhi 110001, tel: 3324658;
tlx: 031-62969
Nirulas, L Block, Connaught Circus,
New Delhi 110001, tel: 3322419
tlx: 031-66224 NCHS IN
Sartaj Hotel, A-3 Green Park, New Delhi
tel: 663277,667759, 667831;
tlx: 031-73009 SRTJ IN
YWCA International Guest House
Parliament Street, New Delhi 110001
tel: 311561
YMCA Tourist Hostel, Jai Singh Road,
New Delhi 110001, tel: 311915,
tlx: 031-62547 YMCA IN

Gangtok, Sikkim
Hotel Nor-Khill *(3 star)*, Stadium Road,
Gangtok 737101, tel: 3186, 3187
Hotel Tashi Delek (3 star), Mahatma
Gandhi Marg, Gangtok 737101
tel: 2991, 2038, 2362

'Indglish'

First you have to get used to the accent, and contrary to rumour it is no closer to Welsh than Bombay Duck is to quacking. Then you realize that Indians have adapted English in other ways to suit the needs of a country with 15 official languages, in which Indglish is still the most common form of communication between people from different regions.

At its literary best, the English used by Indians can be exquisite, with writers like R K Narayan adding an extra dimension to the language. But while well-educated, middle-aged people talk like British characters out of Paul Scott's *Raj Quartet*, Indian English at street level can be almost incomprehensible to the foreigner. The vocabulary is lurid and the grammar a riot of prepositions, participles and plurals. Verbs lurk at the end of sentences; one word is seldom used when two will do. But don't be worrying, if you study about it, you will soon be understanding.

Start by practising on newspaper headlines:
DACOITS ABSCOND WITH Rs 4 LAKHS means that bandits got away with 400,000 rupees, or bucks. A hundred lakhs make a crore (ten million).

Eve-teasing, pestering young women, which can reach epidemic proportions around college campuses, features regularly in the media. Meanwhile, potential brides are being described in the 'Matrimonials' columns as homely, wheat-complexioned girls (which makes them desirably domesticated), with smooth olive skin.

Before sniggering, the pukka (proper) English sahib should remember that his forebears borrowed kedgeree from the Hindi khicari and turned the Tamil mi-lakutanni (pepper-water) into mulligatawny soup. How the British came up with an insipid insult like curry powder is another story. . .

Today's kitchen Indglish could almost have been scrambled, rumble-tumble, in revenge. Breakfast eggs come half-fried (sunny side up), double-fried, half-boiled or full-boiled, accompanied by toast made from double-roti (Western-style bread). Before breakfast you can have bed tea brought to your room. This is usually served in a pot, with the milk and sugar separate, an arrangement which is known as tray tea at other times of day. Tea minus milk is black, literally. In ready-made tea, as sold by chai-wallahs, everything is boiled up together, both physically and linguistically. Chai, like the tea shrub itself, is Chinese in origin.

Indians enjoy snacks, and menus often list finger-chips, alias French fries, among the pakooras and samosas. The word 'chips' on its own means either potato crisps or rupees.

Lunch is still tiffin and like all meals may be veg or non-veg; desk-bound babus will be bringing it to office in tiffin-carrier, or sending peon to fetch khana from hotel.

Not all self-styled hotels are offering boarding and lodging; they may be mere restaurants, or roadside cafés where truck drivers can stretch out on cots or charpoys outside. If there is a WC in such establishments it is usually located backside.

When you are up-country, or not staying at a five-isstar* hotel, you may need to ask for a second bedsheet and to lock your belongings in the almirah, a cupboard or wardrobe filched from Portuguese.

Indians love to reduce things and people to initials or acronyms. Hypothetical headlines after the 1989 elections might have read: Cong-I MPS Unseated in UP (Congress-Indira Party Members of Parliament lost their seats in Uttar Pradesh), or VP Heads JD-BJP Coalition as PM (Mr Vishwanath Pratap Singh heads a Janata Dal-Bhartiya Janata Party coalition as Prime Minister).

VIPS, or worse, VVIPs, are notorious for taking over Dak bungalows or government rest houses wholesale, giving the push to ordinary Indian travellers as well as the faranghi, or foreigner. Officials, especially those belonging to the ICS (Indian Civil Service), certainly do move around a lot. When you ask to speak to someone in authority, you will often be told, 'Sorry Sahib/Memsahib. Nothing doing. The incharge is out of station'.

Station here doesn't mean railway station, though he may have left from one, travelling first AC, as airconditioning helps to keep out the dust. The best trains sound like newspapers: Frontier Mail, or Dehra Dun Express. The booking clerk will politely ask your goodname, then usually garble it on the Reservations List stuck up on the car you are assigned to. What to do? While you are consulting the conductor, small boys will be competing to give you a shoeshine, even if you are wearing keds or fleetfoots (trainers or sneakers).

Buses also have conductors, complete with Complaint Books, but they leave from stands not stations. On deluxe buses there may be videos of ear-splitting Hindi movies, and they sometimes charge extra—as do taxi-wallahs—for putting your baggages in the dickey or on the carrier (boot or roof-rack). Fellow travellers often open a conversation with 'Where are you coming from?', to which the correct response is UK, USA or wherever it is you stay (live), not the most recent stop on your journey.

If you are taking an internal flight and it is overbooked, upgrade yourself to J Class rather than risk the Chance List, unless they tell you 'Chances are good seat will be there.'

By the time you are reaching back to your native place you will be too much understanding Indian English. No problem.

Above all, you will have discovered that Shakespeare, Kipling and Paul Scott are all flourishing, combined with the redoubtable Hobson-Jobson in what must be one of the most exciting, entertaining, frustrating and above all living versions of the English language extant today.

Sue Earle

---

* It's not uncommon for an 'is' sound to precede words which begin with 's' followed by a hard consonant. For example, 'Chowkidar (watchman) should be sitting on this isspot'.

Goa

Deluxe and 5 star
Aguada Hermitage (Taj), Sinquerim,
Bardez, 403515,
tel: 7501/7; tlx: 0194-291 TAJ IN
Fort Aguada Beach Resort (Taj),
Sinquerim, Bardez 403515
tel: 7501/7; tlx: 0194-291 TAJ IN
Majorda Beach Resort, Majorda, Salcette
403713, tel: 20751, 20303
tlx: 0196-234 MBR IN
Oberoi Bogmalo Beach, Bogmalo,
Nr Dabolim Airport, 403806, tel: 2191,
3311/5; tlx: 0191-297 OBGA IN
Cidade de Goa, Vainguinim Beach, Dona
Paula 403004,
tel: 3301/8; tlx: 0194-257 DONA IN

3 and 2 star
Hotel Baia Do Sol *(2 star)*, Baga Beach,
Calangute
tel: Baga 84/6, Panjim 5207, 3345;
tlx: 0194-303 SOL IN
Hotel Fidalgo *(3 star)*, 18th June Road,
Panjim 403001
tel: 6291/9 ; tlx: 0194-213 REST IN
Hotel Mandovi *(3 star)*, D B Bandodkar
Marg, Panjim 403001
tel: 6270/9 tlx: 0194-226 SHOME IN
Taj Holiday Village (Taj), Sinquerim,
Bardez 403515,
tel: 7515/7; tlx: 0194-291 TAJ IN

Gopalpur on Sea, Orissa
Oberoi Palm Beach, Gopalpur-on-Sea,
Dist. Ganjam 761026,
tel: 23; tlx: 0673-261

Gulmarg, Kashmir
Hotel Highland Park *(3 star)*,
Gulmarg 193403,
tel: 207, 230; tlx: 0375-320 HHPF IN

Gwalior, Madhya Pradesh
Motel Tansen, 6-A Gandhi Marg, Gwalior
470002, tel: 21568, 26742
Welcomgroup Usha Kiran Palace,
Jagendraganj, Lashkar, Gwalior 474009
tel: 23453, 22049

Guwahati, Assam
Hotel Bellevue, MG Road (Nr Raj
Bhawan), Guwahati 780001
tel: 28291/2; tlx: 0235-2322
Hotel Brahmaputra Ashok (ITDC), M G
Road, Guwahati 781001
tel: 32538, 32615, 32632/3; tlx: 0235-2422

Hassan, Karnataka
Hotel Hassan Ashok (ITDC), Bangalore-
Mangalore Road, Hassan 573201
tel: 8731/7; tlx: 8306-201

Hyderabad, Andhra Pradesh
5 star
Gateway Hotel (Taj), Road No 1, Banjara
Hills, Hyderabad 500034
tel: 222222 ; tlx: 0425-6947 GATE IN
fax: 0842-222218
Krishna Oberoi, Road No 1, Banjara
Hills, Hyderabad, 500034
tel: 222121; tlx: 0425-6931 OBH IN

3 star
Hotel Ashoka, 6-1-70 Lakadikapool,
Hyderabad 500004, tel: 230105

Others
Rock Castle Hotel *(2 star)*, Road No 6,
Banjara Hills, Hyderabad 500034
tel: 33541/3

Indore, Madhya Pradesh
Hotel Kanchen, Kanchen Baugh, Indore
452001, tel: 33394/7
Lantern Hotel *(3 star)*, 28 Yashwant
Niwas Road, Indore, tel: 35327, 39426

Jabalpur, Madhya Pradesh
Jackson's Hotel *(2 star)*, Civil Lines,
Jabalpur, tel: 21320; tlx: 0765-207

Jaipur, Rajasthan

Deluxe
Rambagh Palace Hotel (Taj), Bhawani
Singh Road, Jaipur 302005
tel: 75141; tlx: 0365-2254   RBAG IN;
fax: 91-141-73798

5 and 4 star
Clarks Amer *(4 star)*, Jawaharlal Nehru
Marg, Jaipur 302017
tel: 822616/9; tlx: 0365-2276
The Jai Mahal Palace Taj *(5 star)*, Jacob
Road, Civil Lines, Jaipur 302006
tel: 68381; tlx: 0365-2250 JMPH IN;
fax: 91-141-68337
Hotel Mansingh *(4 star)*, Sansar Chandra
Road, Jaipur 302001,
tel: 78771; tlx: 0365-2344 WLCO IN

Others
Bissau Palace, Chandpole Gate, Jaipur
302016, tel: 74191, 67728
Meru Palace *(3 star)*, Ramsingh Road,
Jaipur 302004,
tel: 61212; tlx: 0365-2259 KEPL IN
Narain Niwas Palace Hotel, Kanota
Bagh, Narain Singh Road, Jaipur 302004
tel: 65448

Jaisalmer, Rajasthan
Narayan Niwas Palace, Near Malka Prol,
Jaisalmer 345001, tel: 2408, 2397

Jammu
Asia Jammu Tawi *(4 star)*, Nehru
Market, Jammu 180001, tel: 43930,
43932; tlx: 0377-224 ASIA IN
Hotel Jammu Ashok (ITDC), opp Amar
Mahal, Jammu Tawi 180001
tel: 43127, 43864; tlx: 0377-227

Jodhpur, Rajasthan
Ajit Bhawan, Near Circuit House,
Jodhpur 342006; tel: 20409
Hotel Ratanda Ashok (ITDC), Residency
Road, Jodhpur 342001,
tel: 25910; tlx: 25910
Welcomgroup Umaid Bhawan Palace,
Jodhpur 342006,
tel: 22516, 22316; tlx: 0552-202 UBP IN

Kargil, Jammu & Kashmir (Ladakh)
Highlands, Baroo, Kargil, Ladakh
194105; tel: 41

Khajuraho, Madhya Pradesh
Chandela *(Taj 5 star)*, Khajuraho, Dist.
Chhatrapur 471606, tel: 523, 55
Jass Oberoi *(5 star)*, Khajuraho, Dist.
Chhatrapur, 471606, tel: 85/8
Khajuraho Ashok *(ITDC 3 star)*,
Khajuraho 417606, tel: 24

Khimsar, Rajasthan
Welcomgroup Royal Castle, P O
Khimsar, Dist. Nagaur, tel: 28

Kodaikanal, Tamil Nadu
Carlton Hotel *(3 star)*, Lake Road,
Kodaikanal 624101
tel: 560 to 576; tlx: 0445-285 CARL IN

Kota, Rajasthan
Brijraj Bhawan Palace Hotel, Civil
Lines, Kota 324001; tel: 23071
Chambal Tourist Bungalow, Nayapura,
Kota; tel: 26527

Kottayam, Kerala
Anjali Hotel *(2 star)*
K.K. Road, Kottayam 686001
tel: 3661; tlx: 0888-212

Kovalam, Kerala
Kovalam Ashok Beach Resort (ITDC),
Kovalam, Vizhinjam, Trivandrum 695522
tel: 68010, 65232; tlx: 0435-216

Kulu, Himachal Pradesh
Ambassador's Resorts, Chandhiri,
Manali, Dist Kulu, tel: 173 (Manali)
Span Resorts *(3 star)*, Kulu-Manali Road,
P O Katrain, Dist. Kulu,
tel: Katrain 38, 40

Lakshadweep Islands
Bangaram Island Resort, Bangaram
Island, Lakshadweep,
c/o Casino Hotel, Willingdon Island,
Cochin 682003, Kerala
tel: 6821 (Cochin); tlx; 0885-6314

Leh, Ladakh, Jammu & Kashmir
The Ladakh Sarai, Stok, Ladakh
(Book through Mountain Travel India,
New Delhi tel: 771055/523057

Lonavla, Maharastra
Fariyas Resort *(4 star)*, Frichley Hills,
Tungarli, Lonavla 410401
tel: 2701-5 ; tlx: 011-3272 ABAN IN

Lucknow, Uttar Pradesh
Clarks Avad *(4 star)*, 8 Mahatma Gandhi
Marg, Lucknow 226001
tel: 40130; tlx: 0535-243 HTLC IN
Carlton Hotel *(3 star)*, Shahnajaf Road,
Lucknow 226001, tel: 44201/4;
tlx: 0535-217

Madras, Tamil Nadu

Deluxe and 5 star
Taj Coromandel Hotel (Taj), 17
Nungambakkam High Road, Madras
600034; tel: 474849; tlx: 041-7194
TAJM IN fax: 044-470070

Welcomgroup Park Sheraton, 132 TTK
Road, Madras 600018,
tel: 452525; tlx: 041-6868 WELC IN;
fax: 91-44-455913
Welcomgoup Chola Sheraton, 10
Cathedral Road, Madras 600086
tel: 473347; tlx: 041-7200 WELC IN;
fax: 91-44-478779

4 star
Connemara Hotel (Taj), Binny Road,
Madras 600002
tel: 860123; tlx: 041-8197/488 CH IN
fax: 91-44-860193
Hotel President, Edward Elliots Road,
Mylapore, Madras 600004
tel: 842211; tlx:041-6699 ARIF IN;
fax: 91-44-832299; cable: GAYTIME
The Trident (Oberoi), 1/24 G S T Road,
Madras 600027
tel: 434747, 434751; tlx: 041-26055,
26069; fax: 91-44-434743

3 and 2 star
Hotel Ashoka *(3 star)*, 33 Pantheon Road,
Egmore, Madras 600008
tel: 568977; tlx: 041-7510 ASHOK IN
Hotel Dasaprakash (Vegetarian), 100
Poonamalle High Road, Madras 600084
tel: 661111; tlx: 041-7837

Madurai, Tamil Nadu
Hotel Madurai Ashok (ITDC), Ala-
garkoil Road, Madurai 625002
tel: 42531; tlx: 0445-297
Pandyan Hotel *(3 star)*, Race Course,
Tallakulam, Madurai 625002
tel: 42471; tlx: 0445-214 COSY IN

Mahabalipuram, Tamil Nadu
Silversands Beach Resort *(3 star)*,
Kovelong Road, Mahabalipuram 603104
tel: 04113, 228 tlx: 041-8082 SANDS IN
Temple Bay Ashok Beach Resort
(ITDC), Mamallapuram 603104,
tel: 251/7

Mandawa, Rajasthan
Hotel Castle Mandawa, Mandawa,
Dist. Jhunjhunu, Shekhavati 337004
tel: 24 (Jaipur Tel:75358);
cable: CASTLEMANDAWA;
tlx: 0365-2342 CMDW IN

Mangalore, Karnataka
Hotel Srinavas *(3 star)*, Ganapatti High
School Road, Mangalore 575001
tel: 22381; tlx: 0832-328 SIRI IN
Moti Mahal *(3 star)*, Falnir Road,
Mangalore 575001
tel: 22211; tlx: 0832-314 MOTI IN
Welcomgroup Manjarunm *(4 star)*, Old
Port Road, Mangalore 575001
tel: 31791; tlx: 0832-316 WELH IN

Mussoorie, Uttar Pradesh
Savoy Hotel, Library, Mussoorie 248179
tel: 2510, 2628; tlx: 0585-302 SAVY IN

Mysore, Karnataka
Lalitha Mahal Palace Hotel (ITDC),
Mysore 570011
tel: 27650; tlx: 0846-217
Hotel Metropole *(3 star)*, 5 Jhansila-
kshmibai Road, Mysore 570005
tel: 20681; tlx: 0846-214 RITZ IN
Hotel Rajendra Vilas Palace, Chamundi
Hills, Mysore 570018
tel: 20690; tlx: 0846-230
Quality Inn Southern Star, Vinobha
Road, Mysore 570005
tel: 27217/9; tlx: 0846-256 QSSM IN

Nanital, Uttar Pradesh
Shervani Hilltop Inn, Shervani Lodge,
Mallittal, Nanital 263001
tel: 2504, 2498, 2128
Grand Hotel, The Mall, Nanital 263001
tel: 2406
Hotel Arif Castles, Nanital
tel: 2232, 2801/3

Ootacamund (Ooty), Nilgiris, Tamil Nadu
Hotel Dassaprakash (Vegetarian), Oota-
camund, Nilgiris 643001
tel: 2434/5, 3613
Savoy Hotel *(Taj 3 star)* Ootacamund,
Nilgiris 643001
tel: 4142/4; tlx: 08504-207 SAHO IN
Quality Inn Southern Star, 22 Havelock
Road, Ootacamund 643001
tel: 3601/9; tlx: 08504-249 QSSO IN

Pahalgam, Kashmir
Hotel Woodstock, Pahalgam 192126
tel: 27 Cable: WOODSTOCK
Pahalgam Hotel *(3 star)*, Pahalgam,
192126, tel: 26,52,78;
tlx: Srinagar 0375-345 PGMH IN
Senator Pine-N-Peak, Pahalgam 192126
tel: 11; tlx: Srinagar 0375-343 SHPL IN

Patna, Bihar
Hotel Chanakya *(3 star)*, Birchand Patel
Marg, Patna 800001, tel: 23141
Hotel Pataliputra Ashok *(ITDC,3 star)*,
Birchand Patel Marg, Patna 800001
tel: 26270, 23487; tlx: 022-311
Welcomgroup Maurya-Patna *(5 star)*,
South Gandhi Maidan, Patna 800001
tel: 22061; tlx: 022-214 MAUR IN,
022-352 WELC IN

Port Blair, Andaman Islands
Andaman Beach Resort, Corbyn's Cove,
Port Blair 744101, tel: 2599, 2781
Welcomgroup Bay Island, Marine Hill,
Port Blair 744101
tel: 20881, 21389 ; tlx: 069-5207 BAY IN

Pune (Poona), Maharashtra
Hotel Blue Diamond *(4 star)*, 11 Kore-
gaon Road, Pune 411001
tel: 663775; tlx: 0145-369;
fax:91-212-666101

Hotel Amir *(3 star)*, 15 Connaught Road, Pune 411001
tel: 661840 ttx: 0145-292 AMIR IN

Puri, Orissa
Hotel Nilachal Ashok, Adjoining Raj Bhavan, VIP Road, Puri 752001
tel: 2968/80; tlx: 0675-335

Rajgir, Bihar
Centaur Hokke Hotel, Rajgir, Dist. Nalanda, Bihar 803116; tel 32, 45

Rajkot, Gujarat
Hotel Tulsi, Kanta Shree Vikas Gruth Road, Rajkot 360002
tel: 31791; tlx: 0169-339 YOGI IN

Ranchi, Bihar
Hotel Arya *(3 star)*, H.B. Road, Lalpur, Ranchi 834001
tel: 20477; tlx: 0625-253
Hotel Yuuraj *(2 star)*, Doranda, Ranchi 834002
tel: 300403, 300514, 300358; tlx: 0625-229 HYRE IN

Rishikesh, Uttar Pradesh
Hotel Natraj, Dehra Dun Road, Rishikesh
tel: 1099, 1272; tlx: 0585-303 NTRJ IN

Sariska, Rajasthan
Hotel Sariska Palace, Sariska, Dist Alwar 301022, tel: Sariska 22

Shillong, Meghalaya
Hotel Pinewood Ashok (ITDC), Shilong 793001, tel: 23116, 23765; tlx: 0237-222

Shimla, Himachal Pradesh
Oberoi Clarkes *(3 star)*, The Mall, Shimla 171001, tel: 6091/5;
tlx: 0391-206 OBCL IN

Asia The Dawn *(4 star)*, Mahavir Ghati, Shimla 171001
tel: 5858, 6464; tlx: 0391-205 ASIA IN

Siliguri, West Bengal
Hotel Sinclairs *(3 star)*, Pradhan Nagar, Siliguri 734403, tel: 22674

Srinagar, Kashmir

4 star
Hotel Broadway, Maulana Azad Road, Srinagar
tel: 75621/3; tlx: 0375-212 BWAY IN
Oberoi Palace, Gupkar Road, Srinagar 190001
tel: 71241/2, 75651/2; tlx: 0375-201 LXSR IN
The Centaur Lake View Hotel, Dal Lake, P O BOX 221, Srinagar 190001
tel: 75631/3; tlx: 0375-205 CLVH IN

Houseboats
Welcomgroup Gurkha Houseboats , P O Box 57, Srinagar 190001
tel: 75229, 73848; tlx: 0375-286

Thanjavur, Tamil Nadu
Hotel Parisutham, 55 G A Canal Road, Thanjavur 613001
tel: 21466, 21844; tlx: 0468-220 PTS IN

Trichur, Kerala
Hotel Elite International, Chembottil Lane, Trichur 680001
tel: 21033 tlx: 0087-202 ELITE IN

Tiruchirapalli (Trichy), Tamil Nadu
Hotel Sangam *(3 star)*, Collector's Office Road, Tiruchirapalli 620001
tel: 41514 ; tlx: 0455-221

Converting the Heathen

*I*f Christian salvation came out of suffering, here was one who must
have attained it. A European missionary with a long beard, escorted
by a group of Indian converts carrying violins and harmoniums,
would station himself modestly at the junction between Vellala Street
and Purasawalkam High Road. A gentle concert would begin
unobtrusively. A few onlookers stopped by, the priest nodded to
everyone in a friendly manner, casting a genial look around, while
the musicians rendered a full-throated Biblical hymn over the babble
of the street, with its hawkers' cries and the jutka-drivers' urging of
their lean horses. Urchins sat down in the front row on the ground,
and all sorts of men and women assembled. When the preacher was
satisfied that he had gathered a good audience, he made a sign to the
musicians to stop. His speech, breaking into the abrupt silence that
ensued, was delivered in an absolutely literary Tamil, stiff and
formal, culled out of a dictionary, as far away from normal speech as
it could be. It was obvious that he had taken a lot of trouble to learn
the local language so that he could communicate his message to the
heathen masses successfully. But Tamil is a tongue-twister and a
demanding language even for Indians from other provinces, the
difficulty being that the phonetic value and the orthography are
different, and it cannot be successfully uttered by mere learning; it
has to be inherited by the ear. I am saying this to explain why the
preacher was at first listened to with apparent attention, without any
mishap to him. This seemed to encourage him to go on with greater
fervour, flourishing his arms and raising his tone to a delirious pitch,
his phrases punctuated with 'Amen' from his followers.

Suddenly, the audience woke up to the fact that the preacher was addressing them as 'sinners' (Pavigal in Tamil) and that he was calling our gods names. He was suggesting that they fling all the stone gods into the moss-covered green tanks in our temples, repent their sins, and seek baptism. For God would forgive all sinners and the Son of God would take on the load of their sins. When the public realized what he was saying, pandemonium broke out. People shouted, commanded him to shut up, moved in on his followers—who fled to save their limbs and instruments. The audience now rained mud and stone on the preacher and smothered him under bundles of wet green grass. Actually, every evening a temporary grass market sprang upon this piece of ground for the benefit of jutka-drivers, and all through the evening hot exchanges went on over the price of each bundle, the grass-selling women shrieking at their customers and trying to match their ribaldry while transacting business. It was impolitic of the preacher to have chosen this spot, but he had his own reasons, apparently. Now people snatched up handfuls of grass and flung them on him, but his voice went on unceasingly through all the travail; lamps lit up by his assistants earlier were snatched away and smashed. The preacher, bedraggled and almost camouflaged with damp grass and water, went through his programme to the last minute as scheduled. Then he suddenly disappeared into the night. One would have thought that the man would never come again. But he did, exactly on the same day a week hence, at the next street corner.

R K Narayan, My Days: A Memoir

Hotel Aristo, 2 Dindigul Road, Tiruchirapalli 620001
tel: 41818; tlx: 0455-265 ARIS IN

Trivandrum, Kerala

Hotel Horizon *(3 star)*, Aristo Road,
Thampanoor, Trivandrum 695014
tel: 66888; tlx: 0435-346 HRZN IN
Mascot Hotel *(3 star)*, Palayan, Trivandrum 695033
tel: 68990; tlx: 0435-229 KTDC IN

Udaipur, Rajasthan

5 star

Lake Palace Hotel (Taj), Pichola Lake,
Udaipur 313001
tel: 23241; tlx: 033-203 LPAL IN
Shivnivas Palace, City Palace, Udaipur
313001, tel: 28239; tlx: 033-226 IPAL
IN; fax: 91-294-23823

Others

Hotel Shikarbadi, *(4 star)*, Goverdhan
Vilas, Udaipur 313001
tel: 83200/4; tlx: 033-227 BADI IN
Hotel Anand Bhawan, Fatehsagar Road,
Udaipur 313001; tel: 23256/7,

Udipi, Karnataka

Summer Sands Beach Resort, Chota-
mangalore, Ullal 574159; tel: 6400/7

Varanasi (Banares), Uttar Pradesh

5 star

Hotel Clarks Varanasi, The Mall,
Varanasi Cantt., 221002
tel: 42401/6; tlx: 0545-204 CLAK IN
Taj Ganges (Taj), Nadesar Palace
Grounds, Varanasi 221002
tel: 42485, 42495;
tlx: 0545-219 TAGA IN

Others

Hotel Varanasi Ashok (ITDC), The Mall,
Varanasi 221002 tel: 42550; tlx: 0545-
205
Pallavi International *(3 star)*, Hathwa
Market, Chetganj, Varanasi 221001
tel: 54894, 66483

The four main hotel chains each have a
central reservations system, as do many of
the newer smaller groups. Bookings can be
made either through another member of
the same chain or through a travel agency.

THE ASHOK GROUP- Many ITDC
hotels can be booked through Golden
Tulip World-Wide Hotels (KLM). ITDC
Central Reservations are c/o Hotel Samrat,
Chanakyapuri, New Delhi 110021. tel.
603030; tlx: 031-72122 SMRT IN, 031-
72126 SMRT IN; fax: 91-11-6873216.

OBEROI HOTELS – Bookings
worldwide through LOEWS Reservation
or The Oberoi, Dr. Zakir Hussain Marg,
New Delhi 110003. tel: 363030; tlx: 031-
74019, 031-63222 OBDL IN; fax.91-11-
360484

THE TAJ GROUP OF HOTELS -
Booking through UTEL International
worldwide, The Leading Hotels of the
World and Supereps International, London
for selected properties. Sales headquarters
at The Taj Mahal Hotel, Apollo Bunder,
Bombay 40039, tel: 2023366, 2022524;
tlx: 11-2442/3791/6176/6175 TAJB IN;
fax: 91-22-2872771

THE WELCOMGROUP—Some
properties are booked through Sheraton
Hotels or through Welcomgroup Headquarters c/o Maurya Sheraton, Diplomatic
Enclave, New Delhi 110021 tel: 3010101,
3010136; tlx: 031-65217 WELC IN
fax: 91-11-3010908.

Restaurants

The statement that the best food is prepared and served in local homes is especially true in India. Not only is the most interesting food usually prepared by family cooks but in many cities decent restaurants are rare and most of those are restricted to the better hotels. There is, however, a popular tradition of 'street food' prepared and served at roadside restaurants or stalls known as *dhabas*. As with all generalities, there are exceptions and the selection of restaurants that follows is an indication of what is available. The greatest range of food types is inevitably to be found in the major cities.

Ahmadabad

Vishala Village, Sarkhej
Situated 12 kilometres from Ahmadabad on the Airport Road, this extraordinary and popular 'village' restaurant serves a wide range of local vegetarian dishes. It has an interesting Utensils Museum in the compound.

Bangalore

Indian Cuisine

Coconut Grove, Church Street (tel: 579132)
Excellent Malabar seafood and meat dishes, located at the back of Spencer's Building.

Mezban, Gupta Towers, 50/1 Residency Road (tel: 575021)
Good Northwest Frontier food.

Mavalli Tiffin Room, Lalbagh Gate
Very popular for its South Indian breakfasts.

Amaravathi, 45/3 Residency Cross Road
Popular for its spicy Andhra Pradesh dishes.

Others

The Farmhouse, 45 Agrahara, Mt Joseph P O, Bannerghatta Road; (tel: 644201)
Delightful outdoor setting and a wide range of good food. Open Friday evening

and for Saturday and Sunday lunch and dinner. Advance booking required.

Paradise Island, West End Hotel, Race Course Road (tel: 269281)
A new restaurant with smart decor and a mixed menu. Good steaks.

Bombay

Indian Cuisine

Chetana Vegetarian Restaurant, 34 Rampart Row, Fort (tel: 244968)
Gujarati and Rajasthani food with good lunchtime thalis.

City Kitchen, 310 Shaheed Bagat Singh Marg, Fort (tel: 260002)
A popular Goan restaurant with a daily change of menu. Many dishes have a liberal amount of spices and chillies! Closed on Sundays.

Copper Chimney, Rampart Row, Fort (tel 2041661)
Good food and service specializing in tandori dishes. Has a branch at Worli (tel: 4924488/4924499).

Khyber, Kala Ghoda, Fort (tel: 273227, 273939).
Worth visiting for its collection of works by some of India's foremost artists. Spicy and tasty food.

Chinese

China Garden, Om Chambers, Kemp's
Corner (tel: 8280841)
One of Bombay's best and most popular
(with the glitzarati) restaurants. Reservations are a must.

Golden Dragon, The Taj Mahal Hotel,
Apollo Bunder (tel: 2023366)
The Taj's first Sichuan restaurant and still
excellent.

The Great Wall, Leela Kempinski Hotel,
Sahar (tel: 6363636)
Excellent food at the best airport hotel in
India.

Others

Menage à Trois, The Taj Mahal Hotel,
Apollo Bunder (tel: 2023366)
Wonderful lunchtime views of downtown
Bombay. French nouvelle cuisine lunches
only.

Rangoli, NCPA, Nariman Point
(tel: 233211, 2023366)
Taj-run restaurant in the heart of the
business district. Buffet lunch.

La Rotisserie, The Oberoi, Nariman Point
(tel: 2025757)
Luxurious French restaurant with an
expensive menu but very reasonable
business lunches.

Trattoria, Hotel President, Cuffe Parade
(tel: 4950808)
Perhaps the best Italian food in Bombay,
open 24 hours a day.

Calcutta

Indian Cuisine

Mogul Room, Oberoi Grand Hotel, 15 J L
Nehru Road (tel: 290181)

Has buffet lunches and à la carte dinners
accompanied by ghazal singers.

Sonargaon, Taj Bengal Hotel, 34B
Belvedere Road, Alipore (tel 283939)
The Taj's latest contribution to Calcutta's
range of Indian restaurants.

Banyan Tree, Astor Hotel, 15
Shakespeare Sarani
Serving Bengali and Mughalai menus
amidst trees and village huts.

Suruchi, 89 Eliot Road (tel: 293292)
Bengali food prepared with the finest ingredients by the All Bengal Women's
Union. Unpretentious, with moderate
prices.

Chinese

Chinoiserie, Taj Bengal Hotel, 34B
Belvedere Road, Alipore
The Taj's usual high standard of Sichuan
food has become extremely popular and
needs advance booking.

Ming Court, Oberoi Grand Hotel, 15 J L
Nehru Road
A small and attractive restaurant serving
Sichuan cuisine.

Others

La Rotisserie, Hotel Oberoi Grand, 15 J L
Nehru Road
An excellent, but expensive, French
restaurant.

Esplanade, Taj Bengal Hotel, 34B
Belvedere Road, Alipore
The Taj's 24-hour coffee shop has
interesting Bengali dishes in addition to
European and Indian fare.

The Skyroom, Park Mansions, 57 Park
Street (tel: 294362)
Popular and prior bookings advisable.

Flury's, 18 Park Street (tel: 297664)
Originally Swiss-managed, Calcutta's
famous tearoom has been a popular
rendezvous since 1928. Open from early
morning to 8 pm.

Trinca's, 17B Park Street (tel: 298947)
Originally a tearoom like Flury's, Trinca's
is now a group of restaurants serving
Chinese, Indian and Continental food.

Hyderabad

Indian Cuisine
Dakhni, Gateway Hotel, Banjara Hills
(tel: 222222)
Perhaps the best Andhra food outside a
private home.

Kabab-a-Bahar, Gateway Hotel, Banjara
Hills (tel: 222222)
Barbecue, kababs and a Hyderabadi buffet
every evening.

Daawat, Hotel Basera (tel: 840200)
South Indian vegetarian cuisine.

Others
Gardenia, Krishna Oberoi, Banjara Hills
(tel: 222121)
24-hour coffee shop in the luxurious
Oberoi Hotel.

Golden Gate, Three Aces compound,
Abid Road (tel: 230019)
Multi-cuisine and with attached bar.

Madras

Indian Cuisine
Dasaprakash, 100 Poonmallee High Road
(tel: 661111)
Inexpensive vegetarian food.

Matsya, Udipii House, 1 Halls Road,
Egmore (tel: 567191)
Vegetarian food.

Rain Tree, Connemara Hotel, Binny Road
(tel: 860123)
Open-air restaurant serving Chettinad
food.

Woodlands, Cathedral Road
The flagship of a successful chain of
vegetarian restaurants.

Chinese
Golden Dragon, Taj Coromandel Hotel,
17 Nungambakkam High Road
(tel: 474849)
Sichuan food, Taj style.

New Delhi

Indian Cuisine
Dum Pukht, Maurya Sheraton, Sadar
Patel Marg (tel: 3010101)
The Welcomgroup's spectacular tribute to
Lucknow cuisine.

Buhkhara, Maurya Sheraton, Sadar Patel
Marg (tel: 3010101)
A successful and popular restaurant
serving excellent Northwest Frontier food.

Andhra Pradesh Bhavan, near India Gate
Cheap, hot and generous thalis at lunch,
both meat and vegetarian.

Coconut Grove, Ashok Yatri Niwas,
Ashok Road (tel: 3324511)
Branch of the successful Bangalore
restaurant.

Dasaprakash, Hotel Ambassador, near
Khan Market (te:l 690391)
Popular branch of the South Indian chain
of vegetarian restaurants.

Corbetts, Claridges Hotel, 12 Aurangzeb
Road (tel: 3010211)

Outdoor tandoori restaurant with a 'rustic'
atmosphere.

Chinese
The House of Ming, Taj Mahal Hotel,
1 Mansingh Road (tel: 3016162)
Recently renovated and serving ever-
popular Sichuan food.

The Tea House of the August Moon, Taj
Palace Intercontinental, 2 Sadar Patel
Marg (tel: 3010404)
Good atmosphere and menu. Ask for the
daily special .

Taipan, The Oberoi, Zakir Hussain Marg
(tel: 363030)
Smart, expensive, good food and an
excellent view over the golf course
towards India Gate.

Pearls, Hyatt Regency, Bhiaiji Cama
Place (tel: 609911)
Cantonese and Sichuan menus.

Others
Orient Express, Taj Palace Intercontinental, 2 Sadar Patel Marg (tel: 3010404)
A gourmet menu in a replica of a
carriage from the famous train.

Casa Medici, The Taj Mahal Hotel, 1
Mansingh Road (tel: 3016162)
Italian food and wonderful views of the
full length of Rajpath.

Nirula's L-block, Connaught Place
(tel: 332419)
Main branch of local chain of salad bars
and pizza restaurants.

La Rochelle, The Oberoi, Zakir Hussain
Marg (tel: 363030)
Perhaps Delhi's smartest restaurant.

El Arab, Regal Building, Connaught Place
(tel: 3321444)
Delhi's only Lebanese restaurant.

Garden Party, Hotel Imperial, Janpath
(tel: 3325332)
Mixed menu and worth eating on the
lawns during the winter months.

Embassies, Consulates and High Commissions

Afghanistan
115 Walkeshwar Road, Bombay;
tel: 8128577, 8126067
5/50 Shanti Path, Chanakyapuri, New
Delhi; tel: 603331, 603328

Algeria
15 Anand Lok, New Delhi; tel: 6445216,
6441805

Argentina
B-8/9 Vasant Vihar, New Delhi;
tel : 671345, 671348

Australia
Maker Towers 'E', 16th floor, Cuffe
Parade, Bombay; tel: 211071
1/50 Shanti Path, Chanakyapuri, New
Delhi; tel: 601336, 601406

Austria
Taj Building, 210 D N Road, Bombay;
tel: 2042044
96/1 Sarat Bose Road, Calcutta;
tel: 472795
13 Chandragupta Marg,: Chanakyapuri,
New Delhi; tel: 601112, 601555

Bahrain
Maker Towers 'F', Cuffe Parade, Bombay;
tel: 216114/217900

Bangladesh
HC-9 Circus Avenue, Calcutta;
tel: 445208, 445524
56 Ring Road, Lajput Nagar III, New
Delhi; tel: 6834668, 6839209

Belgium
11 M L Dahanukar Marg, Bombay;
tel : 4929261, 4929402
50N Shantipath, Chanakyapuri,
New Delhi; tel: 608295, 608067

Benin
B-22 Mayfair Garden, New Delhi;
tel: 660455

Bhutan
Chandragupta Marg, Chanakyapuri, New
Delhi; tel: 609213, 609217

Bolivia
Cooks Building, 342 D N Road, Bombay;
tel: 317343

Brazil
8 Aurangzeb Road, New Delhi;
tel: 3017301

Bulgaria
16/17 Chandragupta Marg, Chanakyapuri,
New Delhi; tel: 607411, 607413

Burma (Myanmar)
3/50-F Naya Marg, Chanakyapuri, New
Delhi; tel: 600251, 600252

Canada
Hotel Oberoi Tower, Suite 2401, Nariman
Point, Bombay; tel: 2024343
7/8 Shantipath, Chanakyapuri, New Delhi;
tel: 6876500

Chile
1/13 Shantiniketan, New Delhi;
tel: 671363, 671718

China (PRC)
50-D Shantipath, Chanakyapuri, New
Delhi; tel: 600328, 600329

Colombia
82-D Malcha Marg, New Delhi;
tel: 3012771

Costa Rica
Standard Building, D N Road, Bombay;
tel: 2040351

Cuba
D-5 South Extension, Pt II, New Delhi;
tel: 6449162, 6442897

Cyprus
52 Jor Bagh, New Delhi;
tel : 697503, 697508

Czechoslovakia
Marcopolo, 5 G Deshmukh Marg,
Bombay; tel: 4928629
50-M Niti Marg, Chanakyapuri, New
Delhi; tel: 608215, 609205

Denmark
L & T House, N Morajee Marg, Ballard
Estate, Bombay; tel: 268181
2 Golf Links, New Delhi; tel: 616273

Egypt
1/50-M Niti Marg, Chanakyapuri, New
Delhi; tel: 602074, 608904

Ethiopia
7/50-G Satya Marg, Chanakyapuri, New
Delhi; tel: 604411, 604407

European Community
YMCA, Jai Singh Road, New Delhi;
tel: 344222, 350430

Finland
E-3 Nyaya Marg, Chanakyapuri, New
Delhi; tel: 605409

France
Tata Prasas N Gamadia Road, off Peddar
Road, Bombay; tel: 4949808
23 Park Street, Calcutta; tel: 290978
26 Cathedral Road, Madras
2/50 E Shantipath, Chanakyapuri, New
Delhi; tel: 604004, 604037
2 Rue de la Marine, Pondicherry;
tel: 24174

Germany
2 Nyaya Marg, Chanakyapuri, New Delhi;
tel: 3014204, 3014205
Hoechst House, 10th floor, Nariman Point,
Bombay; tel : 232422
1 Hastings Park Road, Alipore, Calcutta;
tel 459141
22 Commnder-in-Chief Road, Madras;
tel: 471747
6/50 G Shantipath, Chanakyapuri, New
Delhi; tel: 604861

Ghana
A-42 Vasant Marg, Vasant Vihar, New
Delhi; tel: 670788

Greece
16 Sunder Nagar, New Delhi;
tel: 617800, 617854

Guyana
85 Poorvi Marg, Vasant Vihar, New
Delhi; tel: 674194, 674195

Holy See (Vatican)
50-C Niti Marg, Chanakyapuri, New
Delhi; tel: 606921, 606520

Hungary
2/50-M Niti Marg, Chanakyapuri, New Delhi; tel: 608414, 608152

Iceland
38 Western India House, Sir P M Road, Bombay; tel: 251931, 251642

Indonesia
50-A Chanakyapuri, New Delhi; tel: 602358, 602348

Iran
5 Barakhamba Road, New Delhi; tel: 3329600

Iraq
169 Jor Bagh, New Delhi; tel: 618011, 618012

Ireland
13 Jor Bagh, New Delhi; tel: 617435, 615485

Israel
Kailash, 50 G Deshmukh Marg, Bombay; tel: 362793

Italy
Vaswani Mansion, D Vacha Road, Bombay; tel: 222192, 222178
3 Raja Santosh Road, Alipore, Calcutta; tel: 281426
Sudarsan Building, 86 Chamiers Road, Madras; tel: 452329
50-E Chandragupta Marg, Chanakyapuri, New Delhi; tel: 6873840, 6873841

Japan
1 B, Dahanukar Marg, Bombay; tel: 4923847
12 Pretoria Street, Calcutta; tel 442241
60 Spur Tank Road, Madras; tel: 865594

4 & 5/50-G Shantipath, Chanakyapuri, New Delhi; tel: 604071, 606265

Jordan
35 Malcha Marg, Chanakyapuri, New Delhi; tel: 3013495, 3015516

Kampuchea (Cambodia)
E23 Defence Colony, New Delhi; tel: 693417, 623157

Kenya
E-66 Vasant Marg, Vasant Vihar, New Delhi; tel: 672303, 672312

Korea - Democratic Peoples' Republic
42-44 Sunder Nagar, New Delhi; tel: 617140, 616889

Korea (South)
9 Chandragupta Marg, Chanakyapuri, New Delhi; tel: 601601, 601602

Kuwait
5-A Shantipath, Chanakyapuri, New Delhi; tel: 600791

Laos
20 Jor Bagh, New Delhi; tel: 616187, 615865

Lebanon
10 Sadar Patel Marg, New Delhi; tel: 3013174

Liberia
74 Poorvi Marg, Vasant Vihar, New Delhi; tel: 602800, 607717

Libya
22 Golf Links, New Delhi; tel: 698027, 697717

Luxemburg
2 Panchsheel Marg, New Delhi;
tel: 3015855

Madagascar
Ismail Building, Flora Fountain, Bombay;
tel: 2046735, 2044598

Malaysia
23 Khadar Nawaz Khan Road, Madras;
tel: 453580, 453599
50-M Satya Marg, Chanakypuri,
New Delhi; tel: 601291, 601297

Mauritius
5 Kautilya Marg, New Delhi;
tel: 3011112, 3011113

Mexico
10 Jor Bagh, New Delhi;
tel: 697991, 697992

Monaco
114 Sunder Nagar, New Delhi;
tel: 623193

Mongolia
34 Golf Links, New Delhi;
tel: 618921, 617989

Morocco
33 Golf Links, New Delhi;
tel: 611038, 611588

Nauru
C-5/4 Safdarjung Dev Area, New Delhi;
tel: 651274, 667977

Nepal
19 Woodlands, Alipore, Calcutta;
tel: 452024, 4459027
Barakhamba Road, New Delhi;
tel: 3328191, 3329969

Netherlands
6/50-F Shantipath, Chanakyapuri,
New Delhi; tel: 609571

New Zealand
25 Golf Links, New Delhi;
tel: 697296, 697977

Nicaragua
E-514 Greater Kailash II, New Delhi;
tel: 6442083, 6442022

Nigeria
21 Palam Marg, Vasant Vihar, New Delhi;
tel: 670446, 670405

Norway
50-C Shantipath, Chanakyapuri,
New Delhi; tel: 605982, 605003

Oman
16 Palam Marg, Vasant Vihar, New Delhi;
tel: 671575, 670215

Pakistan
2/50-G Shantipath, Chanakyapuri,
New Delhi; tel: 600603, 600604

Palestine Liberation Organisation (PLO)
D1/27 Vasant Vihar, New Delhi;
tel: 676605, 672859

Panama
B-129 Panchsheel Enclave, New Delhi;
tel: 6438620

Peru
D-1/39 Vasant Vihar, New Delhi;
tel: 674085, 673937

Head of the Household

*T*he most vicious fight I witnessed between my parents was when they had to decide on a bride for my second brother. My father was screaming and shouting in his usually bellowing voice and my mother was soft and steely, holding her ground. They threw pillows at each other, the female throw as fierce as the male one. All of a sudden they subsided, and I remember my father saying, "There is a child in the room, woman." "All right," my mother replied, "it is decided then. I choose." Imperiously, she walked out of the room. It was the only time in my young-adult life that my father had come and hugged me close. "Don't take any notice of these women, my son," he had whispered as he held me in his arms. "They are different from us." Then he paused, laughed a big laugh to himself, patted me on the cheek, and declared, "But you will learn soon enough."

For years I did not know what he meant. But now I think I have a vague idea.

My mother was as severe and ruthless a dictator in her own domain as my father was in his. But she had wholly different methods of enforcing her diktat. The strange and sad thing is that her regime still holds good today, while his has crumbled to dust. On her daughters-in-law, she imposed the most punishing routine. They were made to cook, not allowed to go out to the cinema more than about twice a month, and intimate verbal dialogue during the day between husband and wife (we all lived in a large communal house where the concept of privacy was totally alien and doors were never either shut or locked) was strictly forbidden. The wives of her sons chafed at the leash. But there was nothing they could do about it. Both my elder brothers obeyed my mother as if she were the goddess Durga incarnate. They would never have dreamt of defying her.

Mother was the quintessential Indian, more than any man from that subcontinent can ever be. She was not torn by doubts. She had no intellect; she was, I think, simply fiercely intelligent. As the youngest daughter-in-law in the house when my father married her, she had been subjected to ferocious indignities. She had put up with it, and decided that in her time she would do the same. She did not question the system. Emotionally, she accepted male over-lordship, but she also believed very firmly that men were basically babies. There was no need to challenge them in their own territory; there were other ways of exercising one's sovereign will.

Sasthi Brata, India: Labyrinths in the Lotus Land

Philippines
50-N Nyaya Marg, Chanakyapuri,
New Delhi; tel: 608842, 601120

Poland
50-M Shantipath, Chanakyapuri,
New Delhi; tel: 608762, 608321

Portugal
B-76 Greater Kailash-I, New Delhi;
tel: 6441263, 6449648

Qatar
A-3 West End, New Delhi;
tel: 673745, 674447

Romania
A-52 Vasant Vihar, New Delhi;
tel: 670700, 674447

Sahrawi Arab Democratic Republic
E-16 East of Kailash, New Delhi;
tel: 6435804

San Marino
15 Aurangzeb Road, New Delhi;
tel: 3015850

Saudi Arabia
S-347 Panchshila Park, New Delhi;
tel: 6445419

Singapore
E-6 Chandragupta Marg, Chanakyapuri,
New Delhi; tel: 604162, 608149

Somalia
12-A Golf Links, New Delhi;
tel: 619559, 619277

Spain
12 Prithviraj Road, New Delhi;
tel: 3015892, 3013834

Sri Lanka
9D Nawab Hanbibullah Road (off
Anderson Road), Madras
27 Kautilya Marg, Chanakyapuri,
New Delhi; tel: 3010201, 3010202

Sudan
M-14 South Extension Pt II, New Delhi;
tel: 6440434

Swapo of Namibia
351 Asian Games Village, New Delhi;
tel: 6442513

Sweden
Nyaya Marg, Chanakyapuri, New Delhi;
tel: 604961, 604963

Switzerland
Nyaya Marg, Chanakyapuri, New Delhi;
tel: 604225, 604323

Syria
28 Vasant Marg, Vasant Vihar,
New Delhi; tel: 670233, 670285

Tanzania
27 Golf Links, New Delhi;
tel: 694351, 694352

Thailand
19B Mandeville Gardens, Ballygunj,
Calcutta; tel: 460836
56-N Nyaya Marg, Chanakyapuri,
New Delhi; tel: 605985, 605679

Trinadad & Tobago
131 Jor Bagh, New Delhi;
tel: 618186, 618187

Tunisia
23 Palam Marg, Vasant Vihar, New Delhi;
tel: 676204, 672812

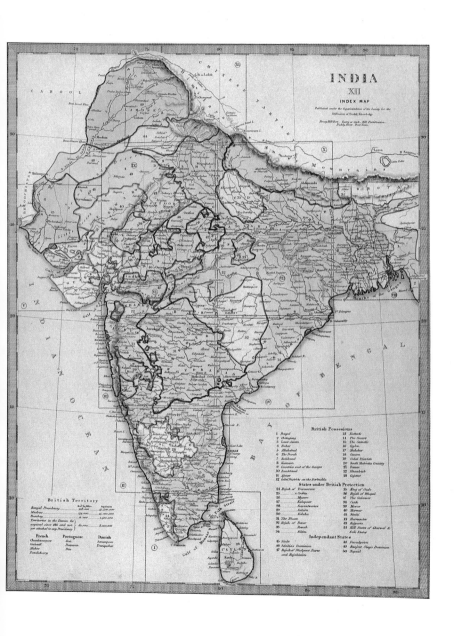

Turkey
N-50 Nyaya Marg, Chanakyapuri,
New Delhi; tel: 601921, 601701

Uganda
61 Golf Links, New Delhi;
tel: 693584, 693585

United Arab Emirates
A-7 West End, New Delhi;
tel: 670830, 670945

United Kingdom
Hongkong Bank Building, 2nd Floor,
M G Road, Bombay; tel 274874
1 Ho Chi Minh Sarani, Calcutta;
tel: 445171
24 Anderson Road, Madras
Shantipath, Chanakyapuri, New Delhi;
tel: 601371

USA
Lincoln House, Bhulabhai Desai Road,
Bombay; tel: 8223611
5/1 Ho Chi Minh Sarani, Calcutta;
tel: 443611
220 Anna Salai (Mount Road), Madras;
tel: 473040
Shantipath, Chanakyapuri, New Delhi;
tel: 600651

USSR
51 Bhulabhai Desai Road, Bombay;
 tel : 8223611
31 Shakespeare Sarani, Calcutta;
tel: 442006, 444982
14 San Thome High Road, Madras;
tel: 71112
Shantipath, Chanakyapuri, New Delhi;
tel: 606026, 606558

Venezuela
N-114 Panchshila Park, New Delhi;
tel: 6436913, 6436783

Vietnam
17 Kautilya Marg, Chanakyapuri,
New Delhi; tel: 3018059, 3010532

Yemen— Arab Republic
B-55 Vasant Vihar, New Delhi;
tel: 674472, 674064

Yemen - People's Democratic Republic
B-70 Greater Kailash I, New Delhi;
tel: 6414623, 6414731

Yugoslavia
3/50-G Niti Marg, Chanakyapuri, New
Delhi; tel: 6873661, 6872073

Zaire
160 Jor Bagh, New Delhi;
tel: 619455, 619456

Zambia
14 Jor Bagh, New Delhi;
tel: 619328, 619294

Zimbabwe
B-8 Anand Niketan, New Delhi;
tel: 677460, 677436

Selected Travel Agencies

Agra
Taj Travels, Kaushalya Sadan, D L
Agarwal Marg, Taj Gunj, Agra 282001
tel: 75128, 68363; tlx: 0565-223 TTAG IN
Travel Bureau, Near Hotel Taj View,
Agra 282001
tel: 66118, 73719, 75945;
tlx: 0565-284 BURO IN
(Branches at Gwalior, Khajuraho, Jhansi,
Varanasi.)

Ahmadabad (Gujarat)
Travel Guide Services, 106 Sampawn
Complex, Navrangpura, Ahmadabad
380009
tel: 46541, 25474

Aurangabad (Maharastra)
Aurangabad Transport Syndicate, June
Bazar, Aurangabad 431101
tel: 4872, 5108; tlx: 0745-234 ATS IN

Bangalore
Cox & Kings, 4111 High Point IV, 45/1
Palace Road, Bangalore 560001
tel: 70509; tlx: 0845-8499 COXS IN
Marco Polo Travels, Janardhan Tower, 2
Residency Road, Bangalore 560025
tel: 211485, 214441/5;
tlx: 0845-2967 POLO IN

Belgaum (Karnataka)
M G Chougule & Sons, 96 Bandhar Gali,
Belgaum 590001
tel: 21388, 21919

Bhopal (Madhya Pradesh)
Radiant Travels, 24 Ahmadabad Road,
Bhopal 462001
tel: 73074, 75660

Bhubaneswar (Orissa)
Travel Link, Hotel Swosti, 103 Janpath,
Bhubaneswar 751001
tel: 54178/9, 56617;
tlx: 0675-321 HSPL IN

Bikaner (Rajasthan)
Rajasthan Tours, Daudsar House,
Bikaner 334001
tel: 4834, 3235

Bombay
Asiatic Travel Service, 12 Murzban
Road, Fort, Bombay 400001
tel: 2048151; tlx: 011-3151 AIRA IN
Cox & Kings, 270/2 Dr D N Road,
Bombay 400001
tel: 2043065/8, 2048724;
tlx: 011-2865 COXS IN
Indtravels, Neville House, Currimbhoy
Road, Ballard Estate, Bombay 400038
tel: 265761/6; tlx: 011-73534 AFT IN
Travel Corporation (India), Chander
Mukhi Bldg, Nariman Point, Bombay
40 0027
tel: 2021881

Calcutta
Delta Travel, 'Kanchana', 7/1 Russel
Street, Calcutta 700072
tel: 291714; tlx: 021-7252
SITA World Travel, 3-B Camac Street,
Calcutta 700016
tel: 291025/9; tlx: 021-5790 SITA IN

Chandigarh
Cosy Tours, S C F 22, Sector 10,
Chandigarh 160010
tel: 28638, 26238

Cochin (Kerala)
Chanakya Group Travels, 4th Main
Road, Willingdon Island, Cochin 683003
tel: 6518, 69561

Darjeeling (West Bengal)

Clubside Tours, Robertson Road,
Darjeeling 734101
tel: 2122, 2123

Delhi

Abercrombie & Kent, Chiranjiv Tower,
43 Nehru Place, New Delhi 110019
tel: 6436207, 6434417; tlx: 031-66956/
66381 AKAS IN; fax: 91-11-6444966
American Express, A Block, Connaught
Place, New Delhi 110001
tel: 3325221; tlx: 031-66211
Cox & Kings, Indra Palace, Connaught
Place, New Delhi 110001
tel: 3320067; tlx: 031-62609 COXS IN;
fax: 91-11-3317373
Indica Travels, 103 Akash Deep, 26A
Barakhamba Road, New Delhi 110001
tel: 3315702, 3315709;
tlx: 031-61193 INDI IN
Mountain Travel India, 1/1 Rani Jhansi
Road, New Delhi 110057
tel: 771055, 523057;
tlx: 031-36016 TREK IN; fax: 777483
SITA Word Travel, F-12 Connaught
Place, New Delhi 110001
tel: 3311133; tlx: 031-66663
Thomas Cook, Rishya Mook Bldg, 85-A
Panchkuin Road, New Delhi 110001
tel: 350404; tlx: 031-62026
Trade-Wings, 60 Janpath, New Delhi
110001
tel: 3321822; tlx: 031-66086 TWND IN;
fax: 91-11-3324005
TCI (Travel Corporation of India),
Metro Hotel, N-49 Connaught Circus,
New Delhi 110001
tel: 3312570, 3315834; tlx: 031-65656

Goa

Goa Tours, 2 Mayfair, Dada Vaidya
Road, Panjim, Goa 403001
tel: 3277, 3278; tlx: 194-326 CALL IN

Guwahati

Sheeba Travels, G N Bordoloi Road,
Ambari, Guwahati 781001
tel: 22135

Hyderabad

Ashok Travels, IV 0-43 Lal Bahadur
Stadium, Hyderabad 500001
tel: 42971, 230766

Jaipur

Rajasthan Tours, Rambagh Palace,
Jaipur 302005
tel: 76041, 69885; tlx: 036-2288 RAJI IN

Khajuraho

Khajuraho Tours, Khajuraho 471606
tel: 33

Lucknow

Travel Bureau, 15 Prem Nagar, Sapru
Marg, Lucknow 226001
tel: 31019

Madras

Cox & Kings, A-15 Parsn Complex, 121
Mount Road 1, Madras 600006
tel 470162, 471927;
tlx: 041-6009 COXS IN
Mercury Travels, 191 Mount Road,
Madras 600006
tel: 869993, 868995; tlx: 041-7899

Madurai

South India Travel Agency, 32-A West
Veli Street, Madurai 625001
tel: 22345, 33456; tlx: 0445-235 SIT IN
Trade-Wings, 184-A/1 North Veli Street,
Madurai 625001
tel: 37271, 30272;
tlx: 0445-202 TWMU IN

Patna (Bihar)

Travel Bureau, A/6 People Coop Colony,
Kankarbagh, Patna 800020, tel: 53712

Pune (Maharashtra)

Girikand Travels, 759/908 Deccan Gymkhana, Bhandarkar Institute Road, Pune 411004
tel: 55547; tlx: 0145-302 GIRI IN

Srinagar

Johansons, Nawa-i-Subh Complex, Zero Bridge, Srinagar 190001
tel: 74000, 78181

Razdan Travel, Polo View, Srinagar 190001
tel: 73259, 76340; tlx: 0375-227 RAZD IN

Trivandrum (Kerala)

Chanakya Group Travels, St Joseph's Building, Cotton Hill, Trivandrum
tel: 65498; tlx: 0435-224 CGT IN

Government of India Tourist Offices

In some towns the Government of India tourist office provides better local information than the state government tourist office. In other places the situation is reversed. Every state has a tourist and information office in New Delhi, and the larger states have information offices in Bombay, Calcutta, Madras and other major cities. In some towns the state and Government of India tourist offices organize regular local tours with a guide. In most towns the tourist office maintains a list of recommended budget accommodation. They can also recommend guides who speak English, French, German, Italian, Russian, Japanese and Spanish.

In India:

191 The Mall, Agra; tel: 72377
Krishna Vilas, Station Road, Aurangabad; tel: 4817
FC Building, 48 Church Street, Bangalore; tel: 579517
B-21 Area, Bhubaneswar; tel: 54203
123 M Karve Road, Churchgate, Bombay; tel: 293144
4 Shakespeare Sarani, Calcutta; tel: 441402, 441475
Willingdon Island, Cochin; tel: 6045
88 Janpath, New Delhi; tel: 320005
B K Kakati Road, Ulubari, Guwahati; tel: 31381
3-6-369/A-30+31 Sandozi Building, 2nd

floor, Himayat Nagar, Hyderabad; tel: 66877
Jail Road, Imphal; tel: 21131
Khasa Kothi Hotel, Jaipur; tel: 72200
Near Western Group of Temples, Khajuraho; tel: 47
154 Mount Road, Madras; tel: 869685
Communidade Building, Church Square, Panaji, Goa; tel: 3412
Tourist Bhawan, Bir Chand Patel Marg, Patna; tel: 26721
VIP Road, Jungli Ghat, Port Blair; tel: 3006
Directorate of Tourism, GS Road, Police Bazaar, Shillong; tel: 25632
15B The Mall, Varanasi; tel: 43189

Overseas:

The overseas offices of the Government of India Tourist Offices vary in quality of service but all have a good stock of informative and well-produced brochures. Hardest to find is information on accommodation 'off the beaten track', such as private camps near national parks.

Australia
Carlton Centre, 55 Elizabeth Street, Sydney, NSW 2000; tel: 02-232 1600
8 Parliament Court, 1076 Hay Street, West Perth, WA 6005; tel: 06-321 6932

Austria
Opernring 1/E/II, 1010 Vienna; tel: 587 1462

Belgium
60 Rue Ravenstein, Boite 15, 1000 Brussels; tel: 02-511 1796

Canada
60 Bloor Street, West Suite 1003, Toronto, Ontario M4W 3B8; tel: 416-962 3787

France
8 Boulevard de la Madeleine, 75009 Paris; tel: 4265 83 86

Germany
Kaiserstrasse 77-III, 6000 Frankfurt Main-1; tel: 235423

Italy
Via Albricci 9, 20122 Milan; tel: 804952

Japan
Pearl Building, 9-18 Ginza, 7 Chome, Chuo ku, Tokyo 104; tel: 571 5062

Malaysia
Wisma HLA, Lot 203 Jalan Raja Chulan, 50200 Kuala Lumpur; tel: 242 5301

Singapore
Podium Block, 4th floor, Ming Court Hotel, Tanglin Road, Singapore 1024; tel: 235 5737, 235 3804

Spain
31-32 Pio XII, Madrid; tel: 457 0209

Sweden
Sveavagen 9-11 (Box 40016), S-III-57, Stockholm; tel: 08-215081

Switzerland
1–3 Rue Chantepoulet, 1201 Geneva; tel: 022-321813, 315660

Thailand
Singapore Airlines Building, 3rd floor, 62/5 Thaniya Road, Bangkok; tel: 235 2585

United Arab Emirates
P O Box 12856, DNATA, Dubai; tel: 236870

United Kingdom
7 Cork Street, London W1X QAB; tel: 071-437 3677/8

USA
30 Rockefeller Plaza, 15 North Mezzanine, New York 10020; tel (212) 586 4901
230 North Michigan Ave, Chicago IL 60601; tel: (312) 236 6899
3550 Wilshire Boulevard, Suite 204, Los Angeles, CA 90010; tel: (213) 380 8855

Recommended Reading

Akbar, M J
The Siege Within Penguin Books, Harmondsworth, 1984
Nehru: The Making of India Viking, London, 1988

Ali, Salim
The Book of Indian Birds Natural History Society, Bombay, 1979
Pictorial Guide to Birds in the Indian Sub-continent
Bombay Natural History Society/Oxford University Press, 1983

Ali, Tariq
The Nehrus and the Gandhis Chatto & Windus, London, 1985

Allen, Charles
Lives of the Indian Princes Century, London, 1984

Basham, A L
The Wonder That Was India Sidgwick & Jackson, London, 1954
Cultural History of India Oxford University Press, London, 1975

Brown, Judith M
Modern India Oxford University Press, London, 1984
Gandhi–a biography Oxford University Press, New Delhi, 1990

Chaudhri, N C
Hinduism Chatto & Windus, London, 1979

Craven, Roy C
Indian Art: A Short History Thames and Hudson, London, 1976

Crowther, Geoff
India: a travel survival kit 4th edition Melbourne, Lonely Planet, 1990

Dawood, N J
The Koran: Penguin Books, Harmondsworth

Davies, Philip
The Splendours of the Raj John Murray, London, 1984
Monuments of India, Vol II: Islamic, Rajput and European Viking, London, 1989

Durrans, Brian
India—Past into Present BMP, London, 1982

Gandhi, M K
My Experiments with Truth Penguin Books, Harmondsworth, 1982

Harle, J C
The Art and Architecture of the Indian Subcontinent Penguin Books, London, 1986

Humphries, C
Buddhism Penguin Books, Harmondsworth, 1951

Hutt, Antony
Goa—A Historical and Architectural Guide Scorpion, London, 1988

Israel, Samuel and Sinclair, Toby, eds.
Indian Wildlife APA Productions, Hong Kong, 1987

Jayakar, Pupul
The Earthern Drum National Museum, New Delhi, 1980

Kaye, Myriam
An Illustrated Guide to Bombay and Goa, The Guidebook Company, Hong Kong, 1990

Keay, John,
India Discovered Windward, London, 1981

Kramrisch, Stella
Art of India Phaidon, London, 1965
The Hindu Temple Motilal Banarsidas, New Delhi
The Presence of Shiva Oxford University Press, New Delhi, 1980

Kusy, Frank
India Cadogan Guides, London, 1987

Lannoy, Richard
The Speaking Tree: A Study of Indian Culture and Society Oxford University Press, London, 1971

Michell, George
Monuments of India, Vol I: Buddhist, Jain, Hindu, Viking, London, 1989

Mookerjee, Ajit
Arts of India Oxford University Press, London, 1966

Nehru, Jawaharlal
The Discovery of India ICCR, London, 1946, Oxford University Press, 1980
An Autobiography Oxford University Press, New Delhi, 1980

Nicholson, Louise	*An Illustrated Guide to Delhi, Agra and Jaipur*, The Guidebook Company, Hong Kong, 1990
O'Flaherty, W	*Hindu Myths* Penguin Books, Harmondsworth, 1975
Prater, S H	*The Book of Indian Animals* Natural History Society, Bombay, 1948
Punja, Shobita	*Museums of India* The Guidebook Company, Hong Kong, 1990
Radhakrishnan, S	*Indian Religions* Vision Books, New Delhi
Randhava, M S	*Indian Painting* Vakils, Bombay, 1968
Sen, K M	*Hinduism* Penguin Books, Harmondsworth, 1961
Sarkar, Sumit	*Modern India 1885-1947* Macmillan, New Delhi
Sen, Geeti T	*The Paintings of the Akbar Nama* Lustre Press, New Delhi, 1984
Sivaramamurti, C	*Approach to Nature in Indian Art and Thought* Kanale Publications, New Delhi, 1980
	Art of India Harry N Abrams, New York, 1977
	5000 Years of Art of India Tulsi Shah, Bombay
Spear, Percival	*A History of India, Vol II* Pelican, Harmondsworth, 1966
Stutley, M and J	*A Dictionary of Hinduism* Routledge & Kegan Paul, London,1977
Thapar, Romila	*A History of India, Vol I* Pelican, Harmondsworth, 1965
Tillotson, G H R	*The Rajput Palaces* Oxford University Press, London, 1987
	Mughal India (Architectural Guides for Travellers) Viking, London, 1990
Watson, Francis	*A Concise History of India* Thames and Hudson, London, 1974
Woodcock, Martin	*Guide to the Birds of the Indian Sub-continent* Collins, London, 1980
Zimmer, H	*Myths and Symbols in Indian Art and Civilization* Boston, 1962
	The Art of Indian Asia Princeton, 1955

Glossary

Atcha - OK, yes
Arrack - drink made from coconut sap or rice wine
Ashram - religious school and retreat
Avalokitesvara - important disciple of the Buddha
Ayah - children's nurse or nanny
Ayurvedic - Indian natural and herbal medicine

Baba - religious master, father; a term of respect
Babu - lower-level clerical worker
Bagh - garden
Baksheesh - tip, bribe or donation
Bearer - a butler
Begum - Muslim woman of high rank
Bidis (Beedis) - cigarettes—rolled up tobacco leaf
Black money - undeclared income
Brahma - Creator of the universe; head of the Trimurti (the Hindu trinity) of Brahma, Vishnu and Shiva. Saraswati is his daughter or consort; Hamsa the goose is his vehicle. The lotus that sprang from Vishnu's navel to give birth to Brahma is a popular symbol in Hindu art and architecture
Bund - embankment or dyke

Cantonment - administrative and military area
Chaitya - Buddhist temple
Chance list - the waiting list on Indian Airline flights
Chappals - sandals
Chappati - unleavened bread
Chatri - tomb or mausoleum
Chaukidar - doorman, watchman
Choli - sari blouse
Chowk - courtyard or marketplace
Crore - ten million
Curd - yoghurt

Dacoit - robber, particularly armed robber
Dhobi - clothes washer
Dhoti - like a *lunghi* but pulled up between the legs
Diwan-i-Am - hall of public audience
Diwan-i-Khas - hall of private audience
Durbar - court audience or government meeting
Durrie - rug

Feni - spirit drink made from cashews, especially found in Goa

Ganesh - elephant-headed god of learning and good fortune, son of Shiva and Parvati; also called Ganapati
Ganga - Ganges River
Ghat - steps on a river where corpses are cremated
Ghee - clarified butter
Godown - warehouse
Gopuram - gate tower of a South Indian temple
Gurdwara - Sikh temple

Hanuman - the monkey god; Rama's ally in defeating Ravana in the epic *Ramayana*
Haveli - courtyard town house
Howdah - elaborate seat on top of an elephant

Imam - Muslim religious leader
Indra - god of rain and thunder

Jali - carved and pierced stone or marble screens

Kathak - classical dance of northern India
Krishna - the blue-skinned god in human form, worshipped in his own right or as an incarnation of Vishnu; consort and love of the milkmaid Radha
Kurta - shirt

Lakh - 100,000
Laxmi (or Lakshmi) - Vishnu's consort, goddess of wealth
Lenga - baggy cotton pants
Lingam - phallic symbol, symbol of Shiva
Lunghi - sarong-like garment

Mahal - house or palace
Maidan - open place or square
Mali - gardener
Mandapa - pillared pavilion in front of a temple
Mandir - Hindu temple, composed of a *mandapa* (entrance), a *vimana* (sanctuary) with the *garbhagriha* (unlit shrine), and a *sikhara* (spire) topped by a *kalasa* (finial)
Masjid - mosque
Mela - a fair
Memsahib - term of respect for married European women
Moghul - see **Mughal**
Monsoon - rainy season from June to October when it rains every day
Mughal - the Muslim dynasty of Indian emperors from Babur to Aurangzeb

Namaste - respectful greeting when people meet or depart, accompanied by putting hands together, fingers upwards
Nautch girls - dancing girls; nautch means dance
Nawab - Muslim ruling prince or land-owner

Pan or Paan - betel nut plus other spices, chewed after a meal
Parvati - Daughter of the Mountains, goddess of peace and beauty. The female energy of the gods, she is the consort of Shiva. As Devi, her destructive powers are manifest in various forms including Kali (goddess of death and destruction) and Durga
Puja - offering or prayer

Purdah - isolation of Muslim women
Pyjama - baggy trousers, usually worn with a *kurta* (long shirt)

Raj - rule or sovereignty. Specifically British rule in India
Raja - king
Rajput - Hindu warrior caste, royal rulers of Rajasthan
Rama - Vishnu's seventh incarnation, the human god-hero of the epic

Sadhu - ascetic, holy person
Sahib - 'lord', title applied to any gentle-man and most Europeans
Shiva or Siva - The Auspicious; third member of the Hindu Trinity (see **Brahma**) and the symbol of both destruction and creative energy manifested in such forms as Nataraja (Lord of the Dance) and the lingam. Parvati is his consort; Ganesh and Kartikeya (god of war) are his sons; Nandi the bull is his vehicle; the *lingam* is his emblem
Sikhara - Hindu temple spire or temple

Tank - artificial lake for storing water
Tempo - three-wheeler public transport vehicle
Thali - traditional south Indian vegetarian meal
Tiffin - snack, particularly around lunchtime
Tikka - dot of paste, often red, worn by Hindus; the dot worn by married Hindu women is called a *suhag*
Toddy - alcoholic drink, tapped from the palm tree
Tonga - two-wheeled horse-drawn carriage
Torana - architrave over temple entrance

Urs - death-anniversary of a Muslim saint, when he was united with God

Vihar - monastery

Vishnu - The Preserver; second member of the Hindu Trinity (see **Brahma**). He symbolizes the creation and preservation that maintain the balance of the forces which sustain the universe. His ten principal avatars (incarnations) include Matsya (first, fish), Kurma (second, turtle), Varaha (third, boar), Narsimha (fourth, man-lion), Rama (seventh, hero-king), and blue-skinned Krishna or his brother Balaram (eighth, both human; opinions differ as to which is the avatar). Lakshmi is his consort; Garuda the eagle or mythical sunbird is his vehicle; the disc-like *chakra* is his weapon; Shesha is the snake on which he reclines on the Cosmic Ocean.

Wallah - person skilled in a specific occupation: thus dhobi-wallah (clothes washer), taxi-wallah (taxi driver)

Zenana - women's quarters

Hindi Survival Vocabulary

Basics

hello, goodbye, good-day (spoken hands together, fingers up)	*namaste*
yes/no	*han/nahin*
please	*meharbani se, kripaya*
thank you	*shukriya, dhanyawad*
OK, good	*atcha*
correct, genuine	*pucka*
bad	*kharab*
hot/cold	*garam/thanda*

Numbers

1 *ek*; 2 *do*; 3 *tin*; 4 *char*; 5 *panch*; 6 *chhe*; 7 *sat*; 8 *ath*; 9 *nau*; 10 *das*; 100 *sau*; 1,000 *hazar*; 100,000 *lakh* (written 1,00,000); 10,000,000 *crore* (written 1,00,00,000).

Getting Around

where is (the tourist office)?	*(turist afis) kahan hia?*
how far is?	*kitne dur hai?*
how much?/too much	*kitne paise?/bahut zyada hai*
what is this?/what is that?	*yeh kya hai?/who kya hai?*
what is your name?	*apka shubh nam?*
what is the time?	*kya baja hai?*
today	*aaj*
let's go, hurry up/stop	*chalo/ruko*
left/right	*baya/dhaina*
straight ahead	*seedha*
big/small	*bara/chota*

Drink and Food

food	*khana*
water	*pani*
ice	*baraf*
tea	*chai*
coffee	*kafi*
sugar	*chini*
milk	*dudh*
yoghurt drink	*lassi*
yoghurt	*dahi, curd*
egg	*anda*
fruit (banana, lime)	*phal (kela, nimbu)*
vegetable	*sabzi*
rice	*chawal*
pulse (lentil, split pea, etc.)	*dhal*

Love's Question

nd is this all true,
   My ever-loving friend?
That the lightning-flash of the light in my eyes
Makes the clouds in your heart explode and blaze,
    Is this true?
That my sweet lips are red as a blushing new bride,
   My ever-loving friend,
     Is this true?

That a tree of paradise flowers within me,
That my footsteps ring like vinas beneath me,
    Is this true?
That the night sheds drops of dew at the sight of me,
That the dawn surrounds me with light from delight in me,
    Is this true?
That the touch of my hot cheek intoxicates the breeze,
   My ever-loving friend,
     Is this true?

That daylight hides in the dark of my hair,
That my arms hold life and death in their power,
    Is this true?
That the earth can be wrapped in the end of my sari,
That my voice makes the world fall silent to hear me,
    Is this true?
That the universe is nothing but me and what loves me,
   My ever-loving friend,
     Is this true?

That for me alone your love has been waiting
Through worlds and ages awake and wandering,
    Is this true?
That my voice, eyes, lips have brought you relief,
In a trice, from the cycle of life after life,
    Is this true?
That you read on my soft forehead infinite Truth,
   My ever-loving friend,
     Is this true?

           Rabindranath Tagore
         translated by William Radice

INDEX

Holy Monkey Business

Along with elephants, bulls, cows, snakes and birds, monkeys are among the most popularly worshipped animals in India. The origins of this practice are difficult to trace, but it is easy to imagine how early man developed an attitude of reverence for a creature so similar to himself in both appearance and behaviour.

Hanuman the monkey god is portrayed as a hero in the Hindu epic, the *Ramayana*, wherein he liberates the goddess Sita on behalf of the great Rama. To accomplish this Hanuman leads a band of monkey soldiers to Lankah (present-day Sri Lanka), where he builds a dam of mountains and rocks between the mainland and the island; on each trip he carries as many stones as there are hairs on his body. Finally he bursts into the palace where the demon giant Ravana is holding Sita captive. By setting her free and killing Ravana he obtains immortality.

As the son of the wind god, Hanuman could fly at birth. His first naughty deed was to fly in the direction of the sun, which he imagined was a piece of fruit. At Hanuman's approach, the sun fled to Indra's heaven, and just as the monkey was about to overtake it, Indra struck Hanuman in the jaw with his thunderbolt. . . It is an Indian belief that people who steal fruit are destined to become monkeys in their next reincarnation.

Hanuman's wisdom and prowess as a general accounts for his being the patron deity of Hindu wrestlers, who worship him every Tuesday and rub their bodies with smoke from the incense burnt at his shrine to give them strength and courage. In old texts Hanuman's simian band have been described as 'heroes of boundless energy, in size equal to elephants or mountains incarnate; in haughtiness and might equalling the tiger and lion; able to wield in combat rocks and mountains. . . skilled in every kind of weapon, they would remove the greatest mountains, pierce the stoutest trees. . . they could seize inebriated elephants, and with their shout cause the feathered songsters to fall to the ground.'

You will run into Hanuman in temples and shrines all over India, where devotees and wish-makers smear his usually crudely-hewn image with red ochre, or more likely today, fire-engine red paint. It is believed that Hanuman is a giver of children. In Bombay, women visit his temple in the early morning, remove all their clothing, and embrace the monkey's image. Elsewhere, farmers will crucify a monkey on the edge of their village to ward off crop-destroying monkeys, a practice they may have begun as a fertility rite. A place where a monkey has been killed is regarded as highly inauspicious, and monkey bones can pollute a home if they are discovered on the building site. At the other extreme, certain wealthy Rajas held elaborate wedding ceremonies for the dominant monkey in the troop.

There are over 30 species of monkey in India, from the nocturnal slow loris to the Hanuman langur. Large numbers of monkeys congregate at temples and depend on the faithful for their meals. Feeding them rice or vegetables is considered a holy act.

As monkey business knows no national boundaries, it is probably best to keep your distance from living, breathing Hanumans. One frequent visitor to India tells of sitting one evening beneath the vast canopy of a banyan tree that was the favourite resting place of a large troop of monkeys. Most monkey species detest tigers, and will panic en masse at the sound of a tiger's approach. That evening a tiger happened to be prowling in the vicinity, and suddenly there was a heavy 'downpour' and 'hailstorm' under the tree. But there wasn't a single cloud in the sky.

Don J Cohn